THE LITTLE FLOWERS OF
ST. FRANCIS OF ASSISI

SAINT FRANCIS

THE LITTLE FLOWERS OF SAINT FRANCIS OF ASSISI

TRANSLATED FROM THE ITALIAN AND EDITED BY THE RIGHT REVEREND H. E. MANNING D.D.

THE ASCENT OF MOUNT ALVERNIA

THE LITTLE FLOWERS OF SAINT FRAN- CIS OF ASSISI

TRANSLATED FROM THE ITALIAN, AND EDITED BY CARDINAL MANNING

KONECKY&KONECKY

Konecky & Konecky
72 Ayers Pt. Road
Old Saybrook, CT 06475

ISBN: 1-56852-559-1

Printed and bound in the United States of America

PREFACE

As the author of the *Imitation of Christ* is unknown, so is the writer of the *Little Flowers of
St Francis*. These admirable poems in prose
may justly be compared to flowers which give
evidence of the season which has brought them
forth, but do not reveal the name of the garden-
er who planted them. Every page of this little
book breathes of the faith and the simplicity of
the Middle Ages. It is generally supposed to
have been written during the first half of the
fourteenth century, and to be partly the work
of John of San Lorenzo, of the noble family of
Marignalle, who was raised to the bishopric of
Bisignano in 1354. Indeed, no one author could
have composed this book. Compiled from a variety of sources, it is as it were the work of a whole
century.

Each of the little flowers is in itself a sacred
poem. A divine ideal forms their principal feat-
ure from beginning to end, and throws a halo
round the personages they describe. This ideal
is Christ, whose saints are all, in a certain sense
and measure, reproductions of Himself. St
Francis owes all his greatness to his conformity
with his divine Lord; and the purport of the
Little Flowers is to draw out and exhibit this
resemblance.

They begin by showing us the wonderful
penitent of Assisi at the moment of his conversion. Further on, we find him fasting in the
desert, evangelising Tuscany and Umbria, and
then preaching in the East to the Sultan of
Babylon. It would be difficult to draw with

greater purity, precision, and effect the ascetic figure of the Saint, or with greater force and grace the almost unearthly life of one who seemed to have broken every tie which bound him to the world, and yet who understood, far better than the greatest statesmen, the sorrows, the dangers, the wants, and the necessities of his times.

Around him are grouped his saintly disciples, each in a distinct attitude and a distinct character. We read of Brother Leo, his favourite companion, to whom he gave the name of the "little lamb of God" (pecorella di Dio). Of Brother Bernard, whose intelligence soared, like the eagle, far above the things of this world. Of St Anthony of Padua, drawing the multitude after him by the strength of his eloquence; and on one occasion, when men refused to listen to him, going down to the seashore to preach to the fishes. Then we behold the gentle figure of St Clare, softening, by its mild light, the sterner features of these monastic portraits.

Do not let us for a moment imagine that the *Little Flowers* are superficial trivial sketches, only intended to familiarise the public mind with the austere virtues of the cloister. Notwithstanding their great simplicity they are full of strong doctrine, and fitted for men deeply versed in theology. In the story of St. Louis, going in his pilgrim's garb to visit Brother Giles at Perugia, where the two saints clasped each other in a long embrace, and separated without having uttered a single word, because

PREFACE

their hearts had been mutually revealed to each other in that silent interview, we recognise a type of the Communion of Saints, which breaks down every barrier, and unites the soul of a king with that of a mendicant. When St. Francis received St. Clare at the convent of Santa Maria degli Angioli, and, making her sit down by his side, broke bread with her in the presence of his disciples, did he not intend to give an example of the respect due to women in a country where the tyranny of the Roman laws had so long held them in bondage? When, in conversing with Brother Leo, he asked him in what perfect joy consists, and then showed him that neither in learning, nor in preaching, nor in working of miracles, is it to be found, but only in the pardon of injuries, did he not lay his finger on the festering wound of the Italian nation—one so richly endowed with all the gifts of nature and of art, but even then about to fall a prey to internal discord, the fruit of rancorous hatred and unforgivingness of spirit?

And if the description of the peace concluded by the Saint between the inhabitants of Gubbio and the savage wolf of the mountain, provoke a smile, is it not because we do not at once discern in the animal who feeds on the spoils and takes away the lives of men, but, docile to the voice of St Francis, places his paw in his hand as a pledge that he will never again harm his neighbour, the representative of the people of the Middle Ages, fierce and terrible when their passions were excited, but never despaired of by the Church, who took their blood-stained hands into her divine ones, and gently led them on till she succeeded in inspiring them with a horror of rapine and violence?*

These *Little Flowers of St Francis* are now for the first time published in English. They are translated with the literal simplicity which such a work requires; for if it is difficult to give in our language an idea of the exquisite beauty and the artless charm of the original Italian, it would be preposterous to relate them in a different manner, and to add any foreign ornaments of style to their peculiar phraseology, and, if one may venture so to speak, their sublime triviality.

If we cannot enjoy to the full, in a translation, the enchanting poetry of the unknown chronicler of the fourteenth century, we can at least study in these pages the heavenly spirit of the Saint of Assisi, and feed our souls with the spiritual instruction contained in these records of lives as nearly angelic as the world has ever witnessed.

*These comments on the *Little Flowers of St Francis* are extracted from the writings of the celebrated and pious French professor, Frederick Ozanam.

CONTENTS

CHAP.   PAGE

I. In the name of our Saviour Jesus Christ
crucified, and of His Mother the Virgin
Mary, the miracles and pious examples
of the glorious servant of Christ St Francis, and of some of his very holy companions, have been put together in this
book; all to the glory and praise of Jesus
Christ   3

II. Of Brother Bernard of Quintavalle, first
companion of St Francis   .   .   .   4

III. How St Francis, having allowed an unkind thought to arise in his mind against
Brother Bernard, ordered him to place
his foot on his neck and on his mouth
three times   9

IV. How the angel of God put a question to
Brother Elias in the Convent of Val di
Spoleto, and how Brother Elias having
answered proudly, the angel departed
from him, and took the road to San Giacomo, where he met Brother Bernard
and told him what follows .   .   .   12

V. How the holy Brother Bernard of Assisi
was sent to Bologna by St Francis, and
how he founded a convent there   .   17

VI. How St Francis, when about to die, blessed the holy brother Bernard, and named
him Vicar of the Order   .   .   .   20

VII. How St Francis passed the time of Lent
in an island, on the Lake of Perugia,
where he fasted forty days and forty
nights, eating only one half of a small
loaf   24

VIII. How St Francis, walking one day with
Brother Leo, explained to him what
things cause perfect joy   .   .   .   26

IX. How St Francis would teach Brother Leo
what to answer, and how the latter could
never say aught but the contrary to what
St Francis wished   29

X. How Brother Masseo asked St Francis,
in a mocking tone, why the world went

FLOWERS OF SAINT FRANCIS

CHAP.   PAGE

after him; and how St Francis answered that it was so, to the confusion of
the world and through the grace of
God   32

XI. How St Francis made Brother Masseo
turn round and round like a child, and
then went to Sienna   .   .   .   33

XII. How St Francis gave to Brother Masseo
the office of porter, of almoner, and of
cook; and how, at the request of the
other brothers, he afterwards took
these functions from him .   .   .   36

XIII. How St Francis and Brother Masseo
placed the bread they had collected on
a stone near a fountain; and how St
Francis praised the virtue of holy poverty, and prayed St Peter and St Paul
to make him greatly love holy poverty.
How St Peter and St Paul appeared to
him   38

XIV. How the Lord appeared to St Francis
and to his brothers as he was speaking
with them   42

XV. How St Clare ate with St Francis and
his companions at Santa Maria degli
Angioli   43

XVI. How St Francis, having been told by
St Clare and the holy Brother Silvester that he should preach and convert
many to the faith, founded the Third
Order, preached to the birds, and reduced to silence the swallows .   .   46

XVII. How a little child who had entered the
Order saw St Francis in prayer one
night, and saw our Lord, the Blessed
Virgin Mary, and many other saints
talking with him   50

XVIII. Of the wonderful chapter held by St
Francis at St Mary of the Angels, at
which more than 5000 friars were present   52

XIX. How the vine of the priest of Rieti,

CONTENTS

CHAP.   PAGE

          in whose house St Francis entered
          to pray, was trampled under foot by
          the great numbers who came to see
          him, and how it produced a greater
          quantity of wine than usual, as St
          Francis had promised; and how the
          Lord revealed to the saint that heav-
          en would be his portion when he
          left this world   57

   XX. Of a beautiful vision which appeared
          to a young man who so hated the
          habit of St Francis, that he was on
          the point of leaving the Order   60

  XXI. Of the most holy miracle of St Francis
          in taming the fierce wolf of Gubbio   62

 XXII. How St Francis tamed the wild doves   66

XXIII. How St Francis delivered the broth-
          er who, being in sin, had fallen into
          the power of the devil .   .   .   68

XXIV. How St Francis converted to the faith
          the Sultan of Babylon .   .   .   69

  XXV. How St Francis miraculously healed
          a leper both in his body and in his
          soul, and what the soul said to him
          on going up to heaven   .   .   .   71

XXVI. How St Francis converted certain
          robbers and assassins, who became
          monks; and of the wonderful vision
          which appeared to one of them who
          was a most holy brother   .   .   75

XXVII. How St Francis converted at Bologna
          two scholars who became brothers,
          and how he delivered one of them
          from a great temptation   .   .   85

XXVIII. Of an ecstasy which came to Brother
          Bernard, and how he remained from
          morning till night in a state of rav-
          ishment   88

XXIX. How the devil often appeared to Bro-
          ther Ruffino in the form of a cruci-
          fix, telling him that all the good he
          did was of no use, as he was not of

CHAP.   PAGE

the number of the elect of God;
which having been revealed to St
Francis, he made known to Brother Ruffino the error into which he
had fallen   90

XXX. Of the beautiful sermon which St
Francis and Brother Ruffino preached at Assisi   94

XXXI. How St Francis was acquainted
with the secrets of the consciences
of all his brothers . . .   96

XXXII. How Brother Masseo obtained from
Christ the grace of humility .   98

XXXIII. How St Clare, by order of the Pope,
blessed the bread which was on the
table, and how on each loaf appeared the sign of the holy cross .   100

XXXIV. How St Louis, king of France, went
in person in a pilgrim's garb to visit
the holy Brother Giles . .   101

XXXV. How St Clare, being ill, was miraculously carried, on Christmas-
night, to the church of St Francis,
where she assisted at the Office .   103

XXXVI. How St Francis explained to Brother Leo a beautiful vision he had
seen   104

XXXVII. How Jesus Christ the Blessed, at
the prayer of St Francis, converted
a rich nobleman who had made
great offers to St Francis, and inspired him with a wish to become a
religious   105

XXXVIII. How it was revealed to St Francis
that Brother Elias was damned,
and was to die out of the Order;
and how at the desire of the said
brother he prayed to Christ for him,
and how his prayer was granted .   108

XXXIX. Of the wonderful discourse which St
Anthony of Padua, a Friar Minor,
made in the Consistory . .   111

CONTENTS

CHAP.   PAGE

XL. Of the miracle which God performed when St Anthony, being at Ri-
mini, preached to the fish of the sea   112

XLI. How the venerable Brother Simon
delivered a brother from a great
temptation, on account of which he
was on the point of leaving the
Order   115

XLII. Of several wonderful miracles which
the Lord performed through the
means of the holy brothers, Brother Peter of Monticello, and Brother Conrad of Offida, and how Brother Bentivoglio carried a leper
fifteen miles in a very short time;
how St Michael spoke to another
brother, and how the Blessed Virgin Mary appeared to Brother
Conrad and placed her Divine Son
in his arms   118

XLIII. How Brother Conrad of Offida converted a young brother, who was a
stumbling-block to the other brothers; and how after death his soul
appeared to Brother Conrad, begging him to pray for him; and how
through his prayers he was delivered from the great pains of
Purgatory   122

XLIV. How the Mother of Christ and St
John the Evangelist appeared to
Brother Conrad, and told him who
had suffered the greatest sorrow at
the Passion of Christ .   .   .   124

XLV. Of the conversion, life, miracles, and
death of the holy Brother John della
Pinna   126

XLVI. How Brother Pacifico, being in prayer, saw the soul of Brother Umile, his
brother in the flesh, go up to Heaven   131

XLVII. Of a holy brother to whom the Mother
of Christ appeared when he was ill,

and brought him three vases of healing ointment 133

XLVIII. How Brother James della Massa saw
in a vision all the Friars Minor in
the world in the form of a tree; and
how the virtues, the merits, and the
vices of all were made known to him 135

XLIX. How Christ appeared to Brother John
of Alvernia 139

L. How Brother John of Alvernia, as he
was saying Mass on the day of All
Souls, saw many souls liberated
from Purgatory 145

LI. Of the holy Brother James of Fallarone, and how, after his death, he appeared to Brother John of Alvernia 145

LII. Of the vision of Brother John of Alvernia, by which he became acquainted with all the order of the
Holy Trinity 149

LIII. How, as he was saying Mass, Brother
John of Alvernia fell down as if he
had been dead 150

OF THE SACRED AND HOLY STIGMATA
OF ST FRANCIS, AND CERTAIN CON-
SIDERATIONS THEREUPON . . 153

LIV. How a holy friar, having read in the
legend of St Francis of the secret
words spoken to him by the seraph,
prayed so earnestly to God that St
Francis revealed them to him . 201

LV. How St Francis appeared, after his
death, on Mount Alvernia, to Brother John, while he was in prayer . 204

LVI. Of a holy friar who saw a wonderful
vision of a companion who was dead 206

LVII. How a noble knight who was devout to
St Francis was assured of his death
and of the sacred stigmata . . 209

LVIII. How Pope Gregory IX., who had
doubted of the stigmata of St Francis, was assured of their truth . 211

CONTENTS

LIFE OF BROTHER JUNIPER

CHAP.   PAGE
I. How Brother Juniper cut off the foot of a pig to give it to a sick brother . . 215
II. Instance of Brother Juniper's great power against the devil 218
III. How, by the contrivance of the devil, Brother Juniper was condemned to the gallows 219
IV. How Brother Juniper gave all that he had to the poor for the love of God . 224
V. How Brother Juniper took certain little bells from the altar, and gave them away for the love of God 225
VI. How Brother Juniper kept silence for six months together 228
VII. Remedy for temptations of the flesh . 228
VIII. How Brother Juniper made himself contemptible for the love of God . . 230
IX. How Brother Juniper, in order to be despised, played at see-saw . . . 231
X. How Brother Juniper once cooked for the brethren enough to last for a fortnight . 232
XI. How Brother Juniper went one day to Assisi for his own confusion . . 234
XII. How Brother Juniper fell into an ecstasy during the celebration of Mass . . 235
XIII. Of the sorrow which Brother Juniper felt at the loss of his companion Brother Amazialbene 235
XIV. Of the hand which Brother Juniper saw in the air 236
XV. How St Francis commanded Brother Leo to wash the stone 237

LIFE OF THE BLESSED BROTHER GILES OR EGIDIUS,

THE COMPANION OF ST FRANCIS.

I. How Brother Giles, with three companions, was received into the Order of Friars Minor 241

FLOWERS OF SAINT FRANCIS

CHAP.   PAGE

II. How Brother Giles went to St James's,
in Galicia 244

III. Of Brother Giles's manner of life when he
went to the Holy Sepulchre . . 245

IV. How Brother Giles praised obedience
more than prayer 246

V. How Brother Giles lived by the labour of
his hands 247

VI. How Brother Giles was miraculously assisted in a great necessity when, by reason of a heavy fall of snow, he was hindered from going out to quest . . 249

VII. Of the day of the holy Brother Giles's
death 252

VIII. How a holy man, being in prayer, beheld the soul of Brother Giles pass to
eternal life 252

IX. How, by the merits of Brother Giles, the
soul of the friend of a Friar Preacher
was delivered from the pains of Purgatory 252

X. How God gave especial graces to Brother
Giles; and of the year of his death . 254

CHAPTERS CONTAINING CERTAIN INSTRUCTIONS AND NOTABLE SAYINGS OF BROTHER GILES

CHAP.   PAGE

		PAGE
I.	On vices and virtues	257
II.	On faith	259
III.	On holy humility	261
IV.	On the holy fear of God	264
V.	On holy patience	265
VI.	On sloth	270
VII.	On the contempt of temporal things	275
VIII.	On holy chastity	276
IX.	On temptations	278
X.	On holy penance	283
XI.	On holy prayer	285
XII.	On holy spiritual prudence	290
XIII.	On useful and useless knowledge	292
XIV.	On speaking well and speaking ill	294
XV.	On holy perseverance	296
XVI.	On true religion	297
XVII.	On holy obedience	300
XVIII.	On the remembrance of death	302

THE LITTLE FLOWERS OF
ST FRANCIS OF ASSISI

THE LITTLE FLOWERS OF ST FRANCIS OF ASSISI BY CARDINAL MANNING

CHAPTER ONE

IN THE NAME OF OUR SAVIOUR JESUS CHRIST CRUCI-
FIED, AND OF HIS MOTHER THE VIRGIN MARY, THE
MIRACLES AND PIOUS EXAMPLES OF THE GLORIOUS
SERVANT OF CHRIST ST FRANCIS, AND OF SOME OF
HIS VERY HOLY COMPANIONS, HAVE BEEN PUT TO-
GETHER IN THIS BOOK; ALL TO THE GLORY AND
PRAISE OF JESUS CHRIST

FIRST LET US CONSIDER HOW every action of the life of the glorious St Francis was in conformity with that of our Blessed Lord. As Christ, before He began to preach, called twelve Apostles, teaching them to despise all the things of this world, to follow Him in poverty, and in the practice of every other virtue, so St Francis, on the first founding of his Order, chose twelve companions, all lovers of poverty. As one of the twelve Apostles, called Judas Iscariot, betrayed Christ, and hung himself by the neck, so among the twelve companions of St Francis was one, called Brother John della Capella, who apostatised, and finally hung himself by the neck. This should be for the elect a great example, and a great cause of humility and fear, when they consider how no one is certain of persevering in the grace of God to the end. As the holy Apostles shone forth before the world in holiness and humility, being filled with the Spirit of God, such were also the companions of St Francis; for from the time of the Apostles till the present day the world had never witnessed

3

FLOWERS OF SAINT FRANCIS

men so wonderful and so holy. One of them, Brother Egidio, was raised to the third heaven, like St Paul; another, Brother Felippo Lungo, like the prophet Isaias, was touched by an angel with a burning coal. Brother Silvester held converse with God, like a friend with a friend, as did Moses of old. Another, the very humble Brother Bernardo, through the penetration of his intellect, reached the light of divine science, like the eagle,—the emblem of St John the evangelist,—and explained all the deepest mysteries of the Holy Scriptures. One there was who was sanctified and canonised in heaven, whilst still living on earth; this was Brother Ruffino, a nobleman of Assisi. These all bore singular marks of sanctity, as we shall see hereafter.

CHAPTER   TWO
OF BROTHER BERNARDO OF QUINTAVALLE, FIRST
COMPANION OF ST FRANCIS

The first companion of St Francis was Brother Bernardo of Assisi, who was converted in the following way. St Francis had not yet taken the religious habit, though he had renounced the world, and was so given to penance and mortification that many looked upon him as on one out of his mind. He was scoffed at as a madman; and was rejected and despised by his relations and by strangers, who threw stones and mud at him when he passed. He went on nis way, and accepted these insults as patiently as if he had been deaf and dumb. Bernardo

4

of Assisi, one of the richest and most learned noblemen of the city, began to consider deeply the conduct of St Francis; how he despised the world, how patiently he suffered injuries, and how his faith remained firm, though he had been for two years an object of contempt, and rejected by all. He began to think and say within himself, "It is evident that this brother must have received great graces from God." He resolved to invite him to supper and to sleep in his house. St Francis accepted the invitation. Bernardo, who was resolved to contemplate the sanctity of his guest, ordered a bed to be prepared for him in his own room, where a lamp burnt all night. St Francis, in order to conceal his sanctity, as soon as he entered the room, threw himself on the bed, and pretended to fall asleep. Bernardo likewise shortly after went to bed, and soon appeared to be sleeping soundly. St Francis, thinking Bernardo was really fast asleep, got up, and began to pray. Raising his hands and eyes to heaven, he exclaimed, with great devotion and fervour, "My God! My God!" at the same time he wept bitterly, and remained on his knees all night, repeating the words, "My God! my God!" and none others. He did so because, enlightened by the Holy Spirit, he contemplated and admired the divine majesty of God, who condescended to take pity on the perishing world, and not only save the soul of poor Francis, but those of many others through his means. He foresaw the great things which

5

FLOWERS OF SAINT FRANCIS

God intended to accomplish through him and through his order; and considering his insufficiency and unworthiness, he prayed and implored the Lord, through His power and wisdom, to supply, help, and accomplish that which he could not do of himself. Bernardo, seeing by the light of the lamp the attitude of St Francis, the expression of his countenance, and having heard the words he uttered with such devotion, was touched by the Holy Spirit, and resolved to change his life. The next morning he called St Francis, and thus addressed him: "Brother Francis, I am disposed in my heart to leave the world, and to obey thee in all thou shalt command me." St Francis rejoiced in spirit at these words, and said, "Bernardo, a resolution such as the one thou speakest of is so difficult and so great an action, that we must take counsel of the Lord Jesus Christ, and pray to Him that He may point out to us what is His will, and teach us to follow it. Let us go together to the Bishop's palace, where we shall find a good priest who will say Mass for us. We will then remain in prayer till the third hour, imploring the Lord to point out to us the way He wishes us to select, and for this object we will open the Missal three times." Bernardo answered that he was well pleased with this proposal, and they set out together, heard Mass, and after they had remained in prayer till the time fixed, the priest, at the request of St Francis, took the Missal, and having made the holy sign of the cross, he opened

6

it three times, in the name of our Saviour Jesus Christ. The first place which he opened upon was at the answer of Christ to the young man who inquired the way to perfection: "If thou wilt be perfect, go and sell all that thou hast, and give to the poor, and come, follow Me." The second time he opened at the words which the Saviour addressed to the Apostles when He sent them forth to preach the Word of Truth: "Take nothing with you for your journey; neither staff, nor scrip, nor bread, nor money"; wishing to teach them thereby to commit the care of their lives to Him, and give all their thoughts to the preaching of the Holy Scriptures. The third time the Missal was opened they found these words: "If any one will come after Me, let him deny himself, and take up his cross, and follow Me." St Francis, turning to Bernardo, said, "This is the advice the Lord has given us; go and do as thou hast heard; and blessed be the Lord Jesus Christ for having pointed out to thee the way of His angelic life." Upon this, Bernardo went and sold all that he had. He was very rich, and with great joy he distributed his wealth to widows, to orphans, to prisoners, to monasteries, to hospitals, and to pilgrims. In all this St Francis assisted him with prudence and fidelity. Now it happened that a man of the name of Silvester, seeing that St Francis gave so much money to the poor, urged on by avarice, went to him and said, "Thou hast not paid me enough for the stones I sold thee to

7

repair the church; now thou hast money, pay me that thou owest." St Francis, much surprised at such a demand, but, according to the precepts of the Scriptures, not wishing to dispute with him, put his hands into Bernardo's lap, filled them with money, which he gave to Silvester, saying that if he wanted more, he would give it to him. Silvester was satisfied, and returned home. In the evening of the same day he reflected on his avarice, and on the holiness and fervour of St Francis. In the night he saw in a vision St Francis, and it seemed to him as if a golden cross came out of his mouth, which reached up to heaven, and extended to the extreme east and west. After this vision he gave all he possessed to the poor, out of love to God, and made himself a Brother Minor. He became so holy, and was favoured with such especial graces, that he conversed with the Lord as a friend converses with a friend, of which St Francis was often a witness, as we shall see further on. Bernardo likewise received many graces from God,—he was ravished in contemplation, and St Francis said he was worthy of the greatest respect, and that he had founded the Order, because he was the first who had abandoned the world, giving all he possessed to the poor of Christ, without keeping back any thing for himself; thus putting into practice the poverty taught in the Gospel, and placing himself naked in the arms of the Crucified, whom may we all eternally bless!

CHAPTER THREE

St Francis, the devoted servant of the crucified
Jesus, through severe penance and constant
weeping, had become nearly blind, so that he
could scarcely see at all. Wishing one day to
speak with Brother Bernardo on divine things,
he left the place where he was and went to join
him. Being told, on arriving, that he was in
the forest praying, St Francis proceeded thither, and, calling out, said, " Brother Bernardo,
come and speak with the blind Francis." Brother Bernardo did not answer ; his soul being
rapt in divine contemplation, he did not hear
him call; one of the especial graces of Brother
Bernardo being that of holding converse with
the Lord Almighty, of which St Francis had
often been a witness. The saint, wishing especially to speak with him at that hour, called
him again a second and a third time. Brother
Bernardo, not having heard him, neither answered nor went to him; at which St Francis
went away rather sorrowful, and wondering in
himself how it was that, having called him three
times, Brother Bernardo had not come to him.
With this thought on his mind, when he had
proceeded a little way, he told his companion
to wait for him, and, retiring to a solitary spot,
he fell on his knees, and prayed God to reveal
to him why Brother Bernardo had not answered his call. As he prayed, a voice came from
heaven, which said, "O short-sighted man, why

9

art thou troubled? Is it meet for man to leave God for the creature? When thou didst call Brother Bernardo he was with Me, and could neither hear thee, nor go to thee; be not then surprised if he did not answer thee, for he was rapt in contemplation." St Francis, having received this answer from God, went back in a great hurry to Brother Bernardo, to accuse himself humbly of the unkind thought he had allowed to enter his mind against him. Brother Bernardo, seeing St Francis coming towards him, went to meet him, and threw himself at his feet. The saint, telling him to get up, confessed most humbly what had been his thoughts about him and the answer God had made him; and he concluded with these words: "I command thee, out of holy obedience, to do whatsoever I shall order thee." Brother Bernardo, fearing St Francis would oblige him to inflict upon him some great punishment, as was his custom, would most willingly have avoided obeying him. " I am ready," he answered, "to obey thee, father, if thou wilt also promise me to do whatsoever I shall command thee." St Francis consented; and Brother Bernardo then asked him what he wished him to do. "I command thee," said St Francis, "out of holy obedience, in order to punish my presumption and the evil thoughts of my heart, when I lie down on the ground to place one of thy feet on my neck, and the other on my mouth, and to do this three times, saying each time, 'Shame upon thee, shame upon thee! be humbled, son of Peter Bernardino, for thou art but a vile wretch; how darest thou be so proud, miserable servant of sin!'" On hearing this Brother Bernardo was much grieved, but out of holy obedience he did what St Francis had ordered him, but endeavoured to acquit himself of it as lightly as possible. St Francis, having promised obedience to Brother Bernardo, asked him what he wished him to do; the latter answered, "I command thee, in the name of holy obedience, that whenever we are together thou reprove and correct with great severity all my defects." This order much surprised St Francis, for Brother Bernardo was so holy that he held him in great reverence, and did not believe it possible to find any fault in him. From that time the saint avoided being much with Brother Bernardo, fearing lest, out of holy obedience, he might be obliged to reprove him. When he was obliged to see or to speak with him, he parted from him as soon as possible. And it was most edifying to hear with what charity, with what admiration and humility, St Francis, who was his superior, spoke of Brother Bernardo, who was his first son in God,—all to the praise and glory of Jesus Christ and his poor servant Francis. Amen.

CHAPTER FOUR

HOW THE ANGEL OF GOD PUT A QUESTION TO BRO-
THER ELIAS IN THE CONVENT OF VAL DI SPOLETO,
AND HOW BROTHER ELIAS, HAVING ANSWERED
PROUDLY, THE ANGEL DEPARTED FROM HIM, AND
TOOK THE ROAD TO SAN GIACOMO, WHERE HE MET
BROTHER BERNARDO AND TOLD HIM WHAT FOLLOWS

In the first beginning of the Order, when there were yet but few brothers and no convents established, St Francis went, out of devotion, to San Giacomo di Galicia, taking with him Brother Bernardo and one or two other brothers. As they travelled on together, they met by the way a poor sick man. St Francis, moved with compassion at the sight of his sufferings, said to Brother Bernardo, "My son, I wish thee to stay here, and take care of this sick man." And Brother Bernardo, meekly falling on his knees, received the order of his revered father, and remained behind, whilst St Francis and the others proceeded to San Giacomo. Arrived there, they spent the night in prayer in the church, and the Lord revealed to St Francis how he would found many convents all over the world, how his Order would increase and multiply, and how a great many brothers would join him. After this revelation St Francis founded his first convent in this part of the country, and then returned by the same way he had come. Finding Brother Bernardo with the sick man, who had quite recovered, he allowed him to go the following year to San Giacomo, whilst he returned to the Val di Spoleto, and took up his abode in a desert-place with Brother Masseo, Brother Elias, and others, who were very careful never to interrupt St Francis in his devotions; they did so out of the great respect they bore him, and because they knew that God revealed to him great things in prayer. It so happened one day, as St Francis was praying in the forest, that a handsome young man, in a traveller's dress, presented himself at the convent-gate, and knocked so loudly, so quickly, and so long, that the brothers were much surprised at such a strange and unusual way of knocking. Brother Masseo, who went and opened the gate, thus addressed the young man: "Whence comest thou, my son? The strange manner in which thou knockest makes me think thou hast never been here before." The young man asked, "How ought I, then, to knock?" Brother Masseo answered: "Thou shouldst knock three times, one after the other, and then wait time enough for the brother to say an 'Our Father' and come and open to thee; should he not arrive by that time, then thou mayest knock again." "I was in a great hurry," continued the stranger; "for I have made a long journey, and am come here to speak with St Francis, who at this hour is praying in the forest, wherefore I would not interrupt him. I pray thee, then, to call Brother Elias; for I wish to put a question to him, having heard that he is full of wisdom." Brother Masseo went to call Brother Elias; but the latter was angry, and refused to go, so that Brother Masseo was at a loss what answer to make the stranger. For if he told him Brother Elias could not wait on him, he would be saying an untruth; if he said he spoke in anger, he feared to give scandal. Whilst Brother Masseo was hesitating how he should act, whether he should return or not with the message, the stranger knocked again as he had knocked before. Brother Masseo hastened back to the convent-gate, and said reproachfully: "Thou hast not observed what I said to thee as to how thou shouldst knock." The young man answered: "As Brother Elias will not come to me, go and tell Brother Francis that I came here to speak with him; but, not wishing to interrupt his prayers, I beg him to order Brother Elias to come to me." And Brother Masseo went to St Francis, who was praying in the forest, with his eyes lifted up to heaven; he gave him the message of the young man, and the answer of Brother Elias. Now the young man was the angel of God, under the figure of a traveller. St Francis, without moving, and still looking up to heaven, said to Brother Masseo; "Go and tell Brother Elias, in the name of holy obedience, to go and speak with the young man." Brother Elias, having received the order of St Francis, went to the convent-gate in an angry mood, opened it with violence, and asked the young man what he wanted of him. The latter answered: "Beware of being angry, as thou appearest to be; for anger hurts the soul, and prevents it from discerning the truth." Brother Elias said again: "Tell me what thou wantest of me." "I want to know," answered the strang-

14

er, "if it is permitted to the followers of Holy
Scripture to eat whatever is served before
them, according to the words of Christ to his
disciples; and I wish to ask thee, likewise, if it
be allowed to any man to teach a doctrine contrary to the liberty preached in the Gospel."
Brother Elias answered proudly: "I know what
answer to make thee, but am not inclined to
give thee one; go about thy business." The
young man replied: "I know better than thou
dost what answer to make to these questions."
Then Brother Elias was much troubled; and,
feeling very angry, he shut the door with violence, and went his way. Considering, however,
the questions which had been put to him, he
doubted within himself whether he could answer them. Being vicar of the Order, he had
made a law which went even further than the
Scriptures, and passed the bounds of the rules
of St Francis, having ordered that none of the
brothers should eat flesh; so that the question
was put expressly against himself. Not knowing in what way to clear his doubts, and having been struck by the modest appearance of
the young stranger, remembering how he had
said that he could answer the questions better
than himself, he hurried back to the convent-
gate in hopes of finding him; but he had disappeared. The pride of Brother Elias made
him unworthy to converse with an angel. In
the mean time St Francis, to whom all had been
revealed by God, returned from the forest, and
addressed himself reproachfully to Brother

Elias, saying, "Thou doest wrong, proud Brother Elias; for thou hast sent away the holy angel of God, come to instruct us. I tell thee that I much fear thy pride will make thee end thy days out of the Order."* The same day and the same hour at which the angel had disappeared from the convent-gate, he appeared to Brother Bernardo, who was making his way homewards from San Giacomo along the bank of a large river. The angel, in the same disguise of a traveller, greeted him with the words, "God give thee peace, O good brother." Now Brother Bernardo, considering the beauty of the young man, who with such a sweet look pronounced the salutation of peace, according to the custom of his own country, asked him whence he came. "I come," answered the angel, "from the convent where St Francis resides. I went thither to speak with him, but was not able to do so, because he was in the forest contemplating divine things, and I would not disturb him. In the same convent were Brother Egidio, and Brother Elias, and Brother Masseo, who taught me how to knock at the convent-gate according to the custom of the brothers. Brother Elias would not answer the questions I put to him. He afterwards repented, sought to see and hear me; but it was too late." After these words, the angel asked Brother Bernardo why he did not cross the river. "Because, answered Brother Bernardo, "I fear to perish

* And so it happened as St Francis said, for he died out of the Order.

FLOWERS OF SAINT FRANCIS

in the waters, which are very deep." The angel said to him. "Let us cross together; fear naught." And, taking him by the hand, in an instant they were both on the other side of the river. Then Brother Bernardo knew it was the angel of God, and with great joy and great reverence he exclaimed: "Blessed angel of God, tell me thy name." The angel answered: "Why dost thou ask my name, which is Wonderful?" Having said these words, he disappeared, leaving Brother Bernardo greatly comforted; so that he ended his journey with much joy, and marked the day and the hour when the angel had appeared. On arriving at the convent, where St Francis was with his favourite companions, he related to them word for word his adventures; and they knew with a certainty that it was the angel who, on the same day and at the same hour, had appeared to them.

CHAPTER   FIVE

HOW THE HOLY BROTHER BERNARDO OF ASSISI WAS SENT TO BOLOGNA BY ST FRANCIS, AND HOW HE FOUNDED A CONVENT THERE

St Francis and his companions, having been called by God to carry the cross of Christ in their hearts, to practise it in their lives, and to preach it by their words, were truly crucified men both in their actions and in their works. They sought shame and contempt, out of love

B

to Christ, rather than the honours of the world, the respect and praise of men. Indeed they rejoiced to be despised, and were grieved when honoured. Thus they went about the world as pilgrims and strangers, carrying nothing with them but Christ crucified; and because they were of the true Vine, which is Christ, they produced great and good fruits in many souls which they gained to God. It happened that, in the beginning of the Order, St Francis sent Brother Bernardo to Bologna, there to accomplish many good works, according to the grace which God had given him. Brother Bernardo, making the holy sign of the cross, in the name of holy obedience, set out for Bologna; when he arrived in that city, the little children in the streets, seeing him dressed so strangely and so poorly, laughed and scoffed at him, taking him for a madman. Brother Bernardo accepted all these trials with great patience and with great joy, for the love of Christ; seeking to be even more despised, he went to the market-place, where, having seated himself, a great number of children and men gathered round him, and taking hold of his hood pushed him here and there, some throwing stones at him and others dust. Brother Bernardo submitted in silence, his countenance bearing an expression of holy joy. For several days he returned to the same spot to receive the same insults. Now, patience being a work of perfection and a proof of virtue, a learned doctor of the law, seeing such virtue and constancy in Brother Bernardo, who

had endured for so many days such contempt
and such injuries without losing his temper,
said within himself: "This man must be a great
saint"; and going up to him, he asked him who
he was, and whence he came. Brother Bernardo put his hand into his bosom, and taking out
the rules of St Francis, gave them to him to
read. The doctor, having read them, was struck
with wonder and admiration at the sublime perfection they prescribed; turning to his friends,
he said: "Truly here is the most perfect state
of religion I have ever heard of; this man and
his companions are the holiest men I have ever
met with in the world; guilty indeed are those
who insult him; we ought, on the contrary, to
honour him as a true friend of God." And addressing Brother Bernardo, he said to him: "If
it is thy wish to found a convent in this town,
in which thou mayest serve God according to
thy heart's desire, I will most willing help thee,
for the salvation of my soul." Brother Bernardo answered: "I believe it is our Saviour Jesus
Christ who has inspired thee with this good intention, and I most willingly accept thy offer,
to the honour of Christ." Then the doctor, with
much joy and great charity, conducted Brother
Bernardo to his house, and made him a present of a convenient building, which he arranged and furnished at his own expense, and from
that moment was a father to Brother Bernardo
and the especial defender of the Brothers Min-
or. Brother Bernardo, through the holiness of
his discourses, began to be much honoured by

19

the people, so much so that those who could see and touch him looked upon themselves as most especially blessed ; but he, like a true disciple of Christ, and a son of the humble Francis, fearing lest the honours of the world should disturb his peace and endanger the salvation of his soul, set out one day and returned to St Francis, whom he thus addressed : "Father, the convent is founded at Bologna, send other brothers there to keep it up, and reside there, as I can no longer be of any use; indeed I fear that the two great honours I receive might make me lose more than I could gain." Now St Francis, having heard, one after another, all the things which the Lord had wrought through Brother Bernardo, rendered thanks to God for having thus begun to spread abroad the poor disciples of the Cross; he sent other brothers to Bologna and to Lombardy, and these founded many convents in different countries.

CHAPTER SIX

HOW ST FRANCIS, WHEN ABOUT TO DIE, BLESSED THE HOLY BROTHER BERNARDO, AND NAMED HIM VICAR OF THE ORDER

The holiness of Brother Bernardo shone forth so brightly, that St Francis held him in great reverence, and was often heard to praise him. One day, as St Francis was in prayer, it was revealed to him by God that Brother Bernardo, by divine permission, would sustain many painful combats with the devil. St Francis felt great compassion for Brother Bernardo, for he loved him as a son; he wept and prayed for many days, imploring the Lord Jesus Christ to give him the victory over the evil one. As he was praying thus devoutly, the Lord answered his prayer, and said to him, "Fear not, Francis, for all the temptations which will assail Brother Bernardo are permitted by God, to increase his virtue and acquire for him a crown of merits; finally, he will gain the victory over all his enemies, because he is one of the ministers of the kingdom of heaven." This answer to prayer filled St Francis with joy; he thanked God; and Brother Bernardo from that moment became even dearer to St Francis than before, and many proofs of affection did he give him, not only during his life, but more especially at the hour of his death. When St Francis was about to leave this world, surrounded, like the holy prophet Jacob, by his devoted sons, all grieving at the departure of such a beloved father, he thus addressed them: "Where is my first-born son? let him come to me, that my soul may bless him before I die." Then Brother Bernardo said in an under voice to Brother Elias, who was vicar of the Order at that time, "Go to the right side of the saint, that he may bless thee"; and Brother Elias placed himself on the right side of St Francis, who had lost his sight through much weeping; and the saint, having put his right hand on the head of Brother Elias, said, "This is not the head of my first-born, Brother Bernardo." Then Brother Bernardo placed him-

self on the left side of St Francis, who crossed
his arms in the form of a cross, putting his right
hand on the head of Brother Bernardo and his
left on that of Brother Elias, and said to Brother Bernardo, "God, the Father of our Lord
Jesus Christ, bless thee with every spiritual and
celestial blessing, for thou art my first-born son
in God, chosen in this Order to set an example
of every virtue, and to follow Christ in evangelical poverty; for thou not only gavest all thy
possessions and distributed them freely and
liberally to the poor, but thou didst likewise
make an offer of thyself to God in this Order
as a sacrifice of love; blessed be thou, then, by
our Saviour Jesus Christ and by me His poor
servant with eternel blessings, both when thou
goest out and when thou comest in, both when
thou wakest and when thou sleepest, both living and dying; he that blesseth thee shall be
blessed, he that curseth thee shall not remain
unpunished. Thou shalt be at the head of all
thy brothers, and every one of thy commands
the brothers shall obey. I give thee power to
receive into this Order whomsoever thou willest; no brother shall rule over thee. Thou art
free to go where thou willest, and to remain
where it pleaseth thee best." After the death of
St Francis, the brothers loved and revered Brother Bernardo as their father. When it was his
turn to die, many brothers came from all parts
of the world to take leave of him; amongst them
was the angelic Brother Egidio, who when he
saw Brother Bernardo exclaimed, with great

joy, "*Sursum corda!* Brother Bernardo, *Sursum corda!*" and Brother Bernardo ordered secretly one of the brothers to prepare for Brother Egidio a place meet for contemplation, and it was done even as he ordered. When the last hour of Brother Bernardo was arrived, he begged to be raised in his bed, and thus addressed the brothers who surrounded him: "Beloved brothers, I have not many words to say to you; but I wish you to consider, that as the religious order which has been my choice has been yours also, the hour which is now come for me will come for you also; and this I find in my soul to tell you, that for a thousand worlds I would not have served another Lord than our Saviour Jesus Christ. Now I accuse myself before my Saviour and before you all of every offence I have committed; and I pray you, my dear brothers, to love one another." After having said these words, and given other good advice, he lay down on his bed; his face beamed with joy and shone with celestial brightness, of which all the brothers were witnesses. In that moment of ecstasy his holy soul, crowned with glory, passed from the present life to the beatific life of the angels.

CHAPTER SEVEN

The true servant of Christ, St Francis, was in certain things as it were a second Christ given to the world for the salvation of souls. This is why God the Father willed that in many points he should be conformed to His Son Jesus Christ, as we have already had an example in the calling of his twelve first companions, also in the mystery of the holy stigmatas, and in a fast of forty days which we are about to relate.

St Francis, one day of the Carnival, was near the Lake of Perugia, in the house of one of his devout children, with whom he had spent the night, when he was inspired by God to go and pass the time of Lent in an island on the lake. St Francis begged his friend, out of love to God, to conduct him in his boat to an island uninhabited by man, and to take him there in the night of Ash-Wednesday, so that none might know where he was. His friend, because of the great devotion he bore to St Francis, granted his request, and conducted him to a desert island. St Francis took naught with him but two small loaves. When they had reached the island, his friend left him and returned home; the saint earnestly entreated him to reveal to no one where he was, and not to come and fetch him before Holy Thursday; to which he consented. St Francis being quite alone, and there being no dwelling in the island in which

2 4

he could take shelter, he entered a thick part of the wood all overgrown with brambles and other creeping plants, and forming as it were a kind of hut, and there began to pray and enter into the contemplation of divine things. He passed the whole of Lent without drinking or eating aught but half of one of the small loaves he had taken with him, as we learnt from his friend, who went to fetch him on Holy Thursday, and found one of the loaves untouched and the other only half consumed. It is presumed that St Francis ate this half out of respect to our blessed Lord, who fasted forty days and forty nights without taking any material food; for by eating this bit of bread he put aside the temptation to vain-glory, and yet fasted forty days and forty nights in intimation of the Saviour. In later times God worked many miracles, through the merits of the saint, on the spot where St Francis had fasted so wonderfully; on which account people began to build there, and little by little a town rose up, with a convent called the Convent of the Isle, and even to this day the inhabitants of that town hold in great respect and great devotion the spot in which St Francis passed the time of Lent.

CHAPTER EIGHT

One day, as St Francis was going with Brother Leone from Perugia to Santa Maria degli Angioli, in the winter, and suffering a great deal from the cold, he called to Brother Leone, who was walking on before him, and said to him: "Brother Leone, if it were to please God that the Brothers Minor should give, in all lands, a great example of holiness and edification, write down, and carefully observe, that this would not be a cause for perfect joy." A little farther on, St Francis called to him a second time: "O Brother Leone, if the Brothers Minor were to make the lame to walk, if they could make straight the crooked, chase away demons, restore sight to the blind, give hearing to the deaf, speech to the dumb, and, what is even a far greater work, raise the dead after four days, write that this would not be a cause for perfect joy." Shortly after, he cried out again: "O Brother Leone, if the Brothers Minor knew all languages; if they were versed in all science; if they could explain all Scriptures; if they had the gift of prophecy, and could reveal, not only all future things, but likewise the secrets of all consciences and all souls, write that this would not be a cause for perfect joy." After proceeding a few steps farther, he cried out again with a loud voice: "O Brother Leone, little lamb of God! if the Brothers Minor could speak with the tongues of

26

angels; if they could explain the course of the stars; if they knew the virtues of all plants; if all the treasures of the earth were revealed to them; if they were acquainted with the various qualities of all birds, of all fish, of all animals, of men, of trees, of stones, of roots, and of waters,—write that this would not be a cause for perfect joy." Shortly after, he cried out again: "O Brother Leone, if the Brothers Minor had the gift of preaching so as to convert all infidels to the faith of Christ, write that this would not be a cause for perfect joy." Now this discourse having lasted for the space of two miles, Brother Leone wondered much within himself; and, questioning the saint, he said: "Father, I pray thee teach me where to find cause for perfect joy." St Francis answered: "If, when we shall arrive at Santa Maria degli Angioli, all drenched with rain and trembling with cold, all covered with mud and exhausted from hunger; if, when we knock at the convent-gate, the porter should come angrily and ask us who we are; if, after we have told him that we are two of his brothers, he should answer angrily, 'What you say is not the truth; you are but two impostors going about to deceive the world, and take away the alms of the poor; begone, I say'; if he refuses to open to us, and leaves us outside, exposed to the snow and rain, suffering from cold and hunger till night arrives,—then, if we accept such injustice, such cruelty, and such contempt with patience, without being ruffled, and without mur-

27

muring, believing with humility and charity that the porter really knows us, and that it is God who makes him speak thus against us, O Brother Leone, write down that this is a cause for perfect joy. And if we knock again, and the porter comes out in anger to send us away, as if we were vile impostors, with oaths and blows, and saying, 'Begone, miserable robbers! go to the hospital, for you shall neither eat nor sleep here!'—and if we accept all this with patience, with joy, and with charity, O Brother Leone, write that this is indeed a cause for perfect joy. And if, urged by cold and hunger, we knock again, calling and entreating with many tears, for the love of God, to the porter to open to us and give us shelter, and if he comes out more angry than before, exclaiming, 'These are but impertinent villains, I will deal with them as they deserve'; if he takes hold of a knotted stick, and, seizing us by the cowl, throws us on the ground, and, rolling us in the snow, beats and wounds us with the knots in the stick;—if we bear all these injuries with patience and joy, thinking of the sufferings of our blessed Lord, which we would share out of love to Him, O Brother Leone, write that here, finally, is cause for perfect joy. And now, brother, listen to the conclusion. Above all the graces and all the gifts of the Holy Spirit which Christ grants to His friends, is the grace of overcoming oneself, and accepting willingly, out of love to Christ, sufferings, injuries, discomforts and contempt; for in all the other gifts of God we cannot glory, because they do not proceed from ourselves, but from God, according to the words of the Apostle, 'What hast thou that thou hast not received from God? and if thou hast received it, why dost thou glory as if thou hadst not received it?' But in the cross of tribulation and affliction we may glory, because, as the Apostle says again, 'I will not glory save in the cross of our Sav iour Jesus Christ.' Amen."

CHAPTER   NINE

HOW ST FRANCIS WOULD TEACH BROTHER LEONE
WHAT TO ANSWER, AND HOW THE LATTER COULD
NEVER SAY AUGHT BUT THE CONTRARY TO WHAT
ST FRANCIS WISHED

St Francis was once, at the beginning of the order, with Brother Leone in a convent, where they had no books to say divine office. When the hour of Matins arrived, St Francis said to Brother Leone, "My beloved brother, we have no Breviary in which to say Matins, but in order to employ the time in praising God, I will speak with thee, and thou shalt answer me as I shall teach thee; beware thou do not change the words I shall order thee to say, Thus will I begin: 'O Brother Francis, thou hast done much evil, and hast committed so many sins in the world, that thou art only worthy of hell'; and thou, Brother Leone, shalt answer, 'It is very true thou art worthy of hell.'" And Brother Leone said, with the simplicity of a dove, "Willingly, father; begin, then, in the name of God." St Francis began thus: "O Brother Francis, thou hast done so much evil, and hast committed so many sins in the world, that thou art worthy of hell." And Brother Leone answered, "God will work so much good through thee, that thou wilt certainly go to heaven." "Do not speak thus, Brother Leone," said St Francis; "but when I say, 'Brother Francis, thou hast committed so many iniquities against God, that thou art worthy to be cursed by Him,' thou shalt answer thus: 'Yes, indeed, thou art worthy to be numbered among the cursed.'" And Brother Leone answered, "Most willingly, O my father." Then St Francis, with many tears and sighs, striking his breast, cried with a loud voice, "O Lord of heaven and earth, I have committed against Thee so many sins, that I deserve to be cursed by Thee." And Brother Leone answered, "O Brother Francis, the Lord will cause thee to be singularly blessed among the blessed." And St Francis, much surprised that Brother Leone answered quite the contrary to what he had ordered him, reproved him for it, saying: "Why dost thou not answer as I taught thee? I command thee, in the name of holy obedience, to do so. When I say, 'O wicked Brother Francis, how canst thou think God will have mercy on thee, when thou hast so sinned against the God of all consolation that thou art not worthy of finding mercy,' then thou, Brother Leone, my little lamb, thou shalt an-

swer: 'Thou art not worthy of finding mercy.'"
And St Francis began repeating, "O wicked
Brother Francis," and so on. Brother Leone
answered: "God the Father, whose mercy is
infinitely greater than thy sin, will have compassion on thee, and will likewise grant thee
many graces." At this answer St Francis, meekly angry, and ruffled without impatience, said
to Brother Leone, "How canst thou presume
to speak against obedience? Why hast thou so
often answered the contrary to what I ordered
thee?" Brother Leone answered, with great
humility and respect, "God knows, my father,
that I had resolved in my heart each time to
answer what thou commandest me, but the
Lord made me speak as it pleased Him, and
not as it pleased me." St Francis, greatly as-
tonished, said to Brother Leone, "I entreat
thee, beloved, to answer this time as I command thee." And Brother Leone said, "Speak,
in the name of God; for most certainly this
time I will answer thee as thou desirest." And
St Francis, weeping, said, "O wicked Brother
Francis, dost thou think that God will have
mercy on thee?" And Brother Leone answered, "Not only will He have mercy on thee, but
thou shalt receive from Him especial graces.
He will exalt thee and glorify thee to all eternity, because he that humbleth himself shall be
exalted; and I cannot speak otherwise, because
it is God who speaketh through me." After this
humble contestation, they watched till morning in tears and spiritual consolations.

CHAPTER   TEN

St Francis once resided at the Convent of the
Porziuncula, with Brother Masseo of Morig-
nano, a man of great sanctity and great dis-
cernment, who held frequent converse with
God; for which reason St Francis loved him
much. One day, as St Francis was returning
from the forest, where he had been in prayer,
the said Brother Masseo, wishing to try the
humility of the saint, went forth to meet him,
exclaiming: "Why after thee? Why after thee?"
St Francis asked him what he meant. Brother
Masseo answered: "I mean to ask thee why
all the world goes after thee; why all men wish
to see thee, to hear thee, and to obey thy word?
For thou art neither comely nor learned, nor
art thou of noble birth. How is it, then, that
men go after thee?" St Francis, hearing these
words, rejoiced greatly in spirit, and lifting up
his eyes to heaven, remained for a long space
with his mind wrapt in God; then, coming back
to himself, he knelt down and returned thanks
to God with great fervour of spirit, and addressing Brother Masseo, said to him, "Wouldst
thou learn the reason why all men come after
me, know that it is because the Lord, who is
in heaven, who sees the evil and the good in
all places—because, I say, His holy eyes have
not found among men a more wicked, a more
imperfect, or a greater sinner than I am; and

32

FLOWERS OF SAINT FRANCIS

to accomplish the wonderful work which He intends doing, He has not found a creature more vile than I am on earth; for this reason He has chosen me, to confound force, beauty, greatness, birth, and all the science of the world, that man may learn that every virtue and every good gift comes from Him, and not from the creature; that none may glory before Him; but if any one glory, let him glory in the Lord, to whom belongeth all glory in eternity." Then Brother Masseo, at such a humble answer, given with so much fervour, was greatly impressed, and learnt of a certainty that St Francis was well grounded in humility.

CHAPTER ELEVEN

HOW ST FRANCIS MADE BROTHER MASSEO TURN ROUND AND ROUND LIKE A CHILD, AND THEN WENT TO SIENNA

As St Francis was travelling one day with Brother Masseo, the latter walking on before, they arrived at a spot where three roads met, one led to Florence, the others to Sienna and to Arezzo. Brother Masseo asked St Francis which road they should take. "The one which pleaseth God," answered St Francis. "The one it pleaseth God," said Brother Masseo; "and how are we to know the will of God?" "By the sign I shall show thee," answered St Francis; "I order thee, by the merits of holy obedience, on the spot where thou art, to turn round and round, as children do in play, and not to stop or rest until I order thee"; and Brother Masseo began to turn round and round, until his head became dizzy and he fell down several times. As St Francis did not tell him to stop, he went on, out of obedience, till at last St Francis said, "Stand still, and do not move; but tell me towards which of the three roads thou art turned?" "Towards that which leads to Sienna," answered Brother Masseo. "That is the road," said St Francis, "which it pleaseth God we should take." As he went on his way, Brother Masseo wondered in himself why St Francis had made him turn round like a child, in the presence of all those who passed that way, but out of reverence to the saint he did not dare ask him. As they reached Sienna, the people of that city, having heard that the saint was approaching, went, out of devotion, to meet him, and taking him and Brother Masseo on their shoulders, carried them to the Bishop's palace, so that their feet had not touched the ground. In that same hour, some of the inhabitants of Sienna were fighting among themselves, and two of them had been killed. St Francis, hurrying to the spot, spoke to them so devoutly and in such holy words, that he constrained them all to make peace, and give over quarrelling. The Bishop, having heard the holy action of St Francis, invited him to his house, and received him with great honours; retaining him with him all that day and the following night. The next morning, St Francis, who in all his actions sought only the glory of God, rose very early, with his companion, and went his way, without even taking leave of the Bishop; at which Brother Masseo murmured within himself, saying, as he went, "What is this that this good man has done? He has made me turn round and round like a child, and he leaves the Bishop, who has received him with such honours, without saying a word, or even thanking him"; and it seemed to Brother Masseo that St Francis had acted indiscreetly; but, inwardly checked by a divine inspiration, he thus reproached himself for indulging in such thoughts: "Thou art too proud to dare to judge the operations of God's grace; thy indiscreet pride makes thee worthy of hell; for St Francis performed yesterday such holy actions, that they could not be more wonderful had they been accomplished by an angel of God; so that even were he to order thee to throw stones, thou shouldst do so, out of obedience; for that which he has done at Sienna is the work of God, as was proved by the result, for had he not pacified the men who were fighting together, not only many would have fallen victims, but the devil would have drawn many souls to hell. It is thy folly and thy pride which makes thee murmur at that which so manifestly proceeds from the will of God." All these things which Brother Masseo said in his heart were revealed to St Francis, who, coming up to him, said: "Hold fast the things which thou art thinking of at the present moment, for they are good and useful, and inspired by God; but thy murmurings, which preceeded them, were blind and vain and full of pride, sent to thy soul by the devil." Then Brother Masseo clearly saw that St Francis knew the secrets of his heart, and understood of a certainty how the spirit of divine wisdom directed all the actions of the saint.

CHAPTER TWELVE

HOW ST FRANCIS GAVE TO BROTHER MASSEO THE OFFICE OF PORTER, OF ALMONER, AND OF COOK; AND HOW, AT THE REQUEST OF THE OTHER BROTHERS, HE AFTERWARDS TOOK THESE FUNCTIONS FROM HIM

St Francis, wishing to mortify Brother Masseo, in order that pride should not enter into his soul, because of the many graces and gifts he had received from God, and also that through the grace of humility he should go on increasing from virtue to virtue, once when he was residing in a solitary convent with his first companions, who were all examples of holiness, of which number was Brother Masseo, he said to the latter, before all the brothers: "O Brother Masseo, all these thy companions have the grace of contemplation and of prayer; but thou hast the grace of preaching the word of God and of pleasing the people. I will, in order that they may give themselves to contemplation, that thou fill the office of porter, of almoner, and of cook, and when the other monks shall be at their meals, thou alone shalt eat outside the convent, so as to be ready to say a few godly words to those who come to the convent, before they knock at the gate, and that none other be obliged to go out but thee; this thou shalt accomplish, through the virtue of holy obedience." Then Brother Masseo uncovered himself, bowed his head, and meekly received and executed this order; filling for some days the office of porter, of almoner, and of cook. His companions, who were all men enlightened by the Spirit of God, seeing him so employed, began to feel in their hearts great remorse, considering how Brother Masseo had reached a far greater state of perfection than any of them, and how all the work of the convent fell to his share, and not to theirs. They went to implore their father, St Francis, to divide among them those charges, as they could not in conscience allow Brother Masseo to bear all the burden of the convent. St Francis listened to their request, and granted what they asked. Calling Brother Masseo, he said to him, "Brother Masseo, thy brothers wish to share the charges I have given thee, and I will that the charges be divided among you." Brother Masseo said, with great humility and patience, "Father, whatever charge thou dost put upon me, be it small or be it great, I accept it as ordained by the Lord." Then St Francis, seeing the charity of the brothers and the humility of Brother Masseo, made them a most wonderful sermon on holy humility, teaching them that the greater the

37

gifts and graces we have received from God, so much greater must be our humility; for without humility no virtue can be acceptable to Him. Having finished this sermon, he distributed the charges among them with great charity.

CHAPTER   THIRTEEN

HOW ST FRANCIS AND BROTHER MASSEO PLACED THE BREAD THEY HAD COLLECTED ON A STONE NEAR A FOUNTAIN ; AND HOW ST FRANCIS PRAISED THE VIRTUE OF HOLY POVERTY, AND PRAYED ST PETER AND ST PAUL TO MAKE HIM GREATLY LOVE HOLY POVERTY. HOW ST PETER AND ST PAUL APPEARED TO HIM

The wonderful servant and follower of Christ, St Francis, wishing to be in all things conformed to his Master, who, as the Gospel relates, sent His disciples two by two in all the cities and all the lands whither He intended to go to prepare the way for Him, after he had assembled his twelve companions, sent them forth into the world two by two to preach the truth. In order to set them an example of holy obedience, he first began to act himself, like the Saviour Jesus Christ. Having sent his companions to different parts of the world, he took with him Brother Masseo, and set out towards the province of France. Arriving in a certain town, and being very hungry, they went, according to their rule, begging their bread for the love of God. St Francis took one street, and Brother Masseo the other. St Francis, being a little man, with a mean exterior, did not attract much attention, and only collected a few bits of dry bread, whereas Brother Masseo, being tall and good-looking, received a great many large pieces of bread, with several whole loaves. When they had ended their task of begging, they met on a spot outside the city where was a beautiful fountain and a large stone, on which each placed what they had collected. St Francis, seeing that the pieces of bread which Brother Masseo had collected were much larger and better ones than those he had received, rejoiced greatly, and said, "O Brother Masseo, we are not worthy of this great treasure"; and he repeated these words several times. Brother Masseo answered, "Father, how canst thou talk of a treasure where there is so much poverty, and indeed a lack of all things? for we have neither cloth, nor knife, nor dish, nor table, nor house to eat in, nor servant or maid to wait upon us." St Francis answered, "And this is just the reason why I look upon it as a great treasure, because man has had no hand in it, but all has been given to us by Divine Providence, as we clearly see in this bread of charity, in this beautiful table of stone, and in this so clear fountain. Wherefore let us beg of God to make us love with all our hearts the treasure of holy poverty." Having spoken thus, they returned thanks; and when they had refreshed themselves with the bread and water, they rose and went on their way to France. Meeting with a church on the road, St Francis said to his companion, "Let us enter this

39

church and pray." During his prayer the Lord visited him with a great increase of fervour, which so inflamed his soul with affection for holy poverty, that it seemed as if flames played round his head, and proceeded from his mouth; and going thus, all shining and burning with divine love, to his companion, he said to him, "Ah! ah! ah! thou must give thyself to me"; and repeated these words three times. The third time he breathed on Brother Masseo, who, to his great surprise, was raised above the earth, and fell at some distance before the saint. He told his companion afterwards how, during this ravishment, he had felt such a sweet sensation in his soul, and had received such consolations from the Holy Spirit, as he had never before experienced. After this St Francis said to his companion, "Let us go to St Peter and St Paul, and let us pray them together that they may teach and help us to possess the unbounded treasure of holy poverty, for it is a treasure so great and so divine, that we are not worthy of possessing it in these vile bodies of ours. It is this celestial virtue which teaches us to despise all earthly and transitory things, and through which every hindrance is removed from the soul, so that it can freely commune with God. Through this virtue the soul, whilst still on earth, is able to converse with the angels in heaven. It is this virtue which accompanied Christ on the cross, which was buried with Christ, rose again with Christ, and went up to heaven with Christ. It is this virtue which even

40

in this world enables the souls who are inflamed with love of Him to fly up to heaven; it is also the guardian of true charity and true humility. Let us pray the holy Apostles of Christ, who were perfect lovers of this evangelical pearl, that they may obtain for us from the Saviour Jesus the grace, through His great mercy, to become true lovers, strict observers, and humble disciples of this most precious, most beloved, and most evangelical grace of poverty." Conversing thus they arrived at Rome, and entered the church of St Peter. St Francis knelt in prayer in one corner of the church, and Brother Masseo in another. After praying some time with great devotion and many tears, the most holy Apostles Peter and Paul appeared to St Francis in much splendour, and thus addressed him: "As it is thy request and wish to observe that which Christ and His holy Apostles observed, the Lord Jesus sends us to thee to let thee know that thy prayer has been heard, and that it is granted to thee and to all thy followers to possess the treasure of holy poverty. We also tell thee from Him, that whosoever, after thy example, shall embrace this holy virtue shall most certainly enjoy perfect happiness in Heaven; and thou and all thy followers shall be blessed by God." Having said these words they disappeared, leaving St Francis full of consolation. He rose from prayer, and, returning to Brother Masseo, asked him if God had revealed anything to him in prayer. He answered, "No." Then St Francis told him how the holy Apostles had appeared to him, and what they had said. And both were filled with joy, and resolved to return to the Valley of Spoleto, giving up the journey to France.

CHAPTER FOURTEEN

HOW THE LORD APPEARED TO ST FRANCIS AND TO HIS BROTHERS AS HE WAS SPEAKING WITH THEM

St Francis, in the beginning of the Order, having assembled his companions to speak to them of Christ, in a moment of great fervour of spirit commanded one of them, in the name of God, to open his mouth and speak as the Holy Spirit should inspire him. The brother, doing as he was ordered, spoke most wonderfully of God. St Francis then commanded him to be silent, and ordered another brother to speak in the same way, which having done with much penetration, St Francis ordered him likewise to be silent, and commanded a third brother to do the same. This one began to speak so deeply of the things of God, that St Francis was convinced that both he and his companions had spoken through the Holy Spirit. Of which he received a manifest proof; for whilst they were thus talking together, our Blessed Lord appeared in the midst of them, under the form of a beautiful young man, and blessed them all. They were ravished out of themselves, and fell on the ground as if they had been dead, and were quite unconscious of all external things. When they

42

recovered from their trance, St Francis said to them, "My beloved brothers, let us thank God, who has deigned to reveal to the world, through His humble servants, the treasures of divine wisdom. For the Lord is He who openeth the mouth of the dumb, and maketh the tongues of the simple to speak wisdom."

CHAPTER FIFTEEN
HOW ST CLARE ATE WITH ST FRANCIS AND HIS COM-
PANIONS AT SANTA MARIA DEGLI ANGIOLI

When St Francis resided at Assisi he often visited St Clare, giving her holy counsel. And she, having a great desire to eat once with him, often begged him to grant her this request; but the saint refused to allow her this consolation. Her companions, being aware of the refusal of St Francis, and knowing how great was the wish of Sister Clare to eat with him, went to seek him, and thus addressed him: "Father, it seems to us that the severity on thy part in not granting so small a thing to Sister Clare, a virgin so holy and so dear to God, who merely asks for once to eat with thee, is not according to holy charity, especially if we consider that it was at thy preaching that she abandoned the riches and pomps of this world. In truth, if she were to ask of thee a greater grace than this one, thou shouldest grant it to thy spiritual daughter." St Francis answered: "It seems to you, then, that I ought to grant her this request?" "Yes, father, it is meet that thou grant her this favour and this consolation." St Francis answered: "As you think so, let it be so, then; but, in order that she may be the more consoled, I wish the meal to take place in front of Santa Maria degli Angioli, because, having been for a long time shut up in San Damiano, it will do her good to visit Santa Maria degli Angioli, where she took the veil, and where she was made a spouse of Christ. We will, then, eat there together in the name of God." The day appointed having arrived, St Clare left her convent with great joy, taking with her one of her sisters, and followed by the companions of St Francis. She arrived at Santa Maria degli Angioli, and having devoutly saluted the Virgin Mary, before whose altar her hair had been cut off, and where she had received the veil, they conducted her to the convent, and showed her all over it. In the meantime St Francis prepared the meal on the bare ground, as was his custom. The hour of dinner being arrived, St Francis and St Clare, with one of the brothers of St Francis and the sister who had accompanied the saint, sat down together, and all the other companions of St Francis were humbly seated round them. When the first dish was served, St Francis began to speak of God so sweetly, so sublimely, and in so wonderful a manner, that the grace of God visited them abundantly, and all were ravished in Christ. Whilst they were thus ravished, with their eyes and hearts raised to heaven, the people of Assisi and of Bettona, and of all the country round about, saw Santa Maria degli Angioli as it were on fire, as well as the convent and the woods adjoining. It seemed to them as if the church, the convent, and the woods were all enveloped in flames; and the inhabitants of Assisi hastened with great speed to put out the fire. On arriving at the convent, they found no fire; and entering within the gates they saw St Francis, St Clare, with all their companions, sitting round their humble meal, but absorbed in contemplation; and they then knew of a certainty, that what they had seen was a celestial, not a material, fire, which God had miraculously sent to bear witness to the divine flame of love which consumed the souls of these holy monks and nuns; and they returned home with great consolation in their hearts, and much holy edification. After a long lapse of time, St Francis, St Clare, and their companions came back to themselves; and, being fully restored by the spiritual food, cared not to eat that which had been prepared for them; so that, the holy meal being finished, St Clare, well accompanied, returned to San Damiano, where the sisters received her with great joy, as they had feared that St Francis might have sent her to rule some other convent, as he had already sent St Agnes, the sister of the saint, to be Abbess of the Convent of Monticelli, at Florence; for St Francis had often said to St Clare, "Be ready, in case I should send thee to some other convent"; and she, like a daughter of holy obedience, had answered, "Father, I am always ready to go whithersoever thou shalt send me." For which reason the sisters greatly rejoiced when she returned to them, and St Clare was from that time much consoled.

CHAPTER   SIXTEEN

HOW ST FRANCIS, HAVING BEEN TOLD BY ST CLARE AND THE HOLY BROTHER SILVESTER THAT HE SHOULD PREACH AND CONVERT MANY TO THE FAITH, FOUNDED THE THIRD ORDER, PREACHED TO THE BIRDS, AND REDUCED TO SILENCE THE SWALLOWS

The humble servant of Christ, St Francis, a short time after his conversion, having already assembled and received into the Order many brothers, was much troubled and perplexed in mind as to what he was to do, whether to give himself entirely to prayer, or now and then to preach the Word. Through great humility, he had no opinion of himself or of the virtue of his prayers; and wishing to know the will of God, he thought to seek it through the prayers of others. Wherefore he called to him Brother Masseo, and thus addressed him: "Go to Sister Clare, and tell her from me to set herself to pray with some of the holiest of her sisters, and ask the Lord to show me clearly whether He wills that I should preach or only keep to prayer. Then go to brother Silvester, and ask of him the same favour." Brother Silvester had been in the world, and was the same who had seen in a vision a golden cross come out of St Francis's mouth and reach up to heaven and to the farthest extremities of the world. Brother Silvester was so holy, that whatever he asked

46

of God was granted to his prayer, and very often he held converse with the Lord; so that St Francis revered him greatly. Brother Masseo did as St Francis had commanded him; he carried the message first to St Clare, and then to Brother Silvester, who set about praying immediately; and, having received the answer from the Lord, returned to Brother Masseo, and said to him: "The Lord commands thee to go and tell Brother Francis that he has not called him to this state merely to save his own soul, but that he may produce fruits in those of others, and that many through him should be saved." Having received this answer, Brother Masseo returned to Sister Clare, to ask her what she had learnt from God; and she told him that she and all her companions had received from God the same answer as the Lord had given to Brother Silvester. Then Brother Masseo hastened to St Francis to bring him these answers; and St Francis received him with great charity, washing his feet, and serving him at dinner. When the repast was over, he called Brother Masseo into the forest, and, kneeling down before him, took off his hood; and crossing his arms on his breast, he said to him: "What answer dost thou bring me? what has the Lord Jesus Christ ordered me to do?" Brother Masseo answered: "The Lord Jesus Christ has revealed both to Brother Silvester and to Sister Clare, that it is His will thou shouldest go about the world to preach; for thou hast not been called for thyself alone, but for

the salvation of others." St Francis, having received this answer, and knowing it to be the
will of the Lord Jesus Christ, arose with fervour, saying, "Let us go in the name of God";
and taking with him Brother Masseo and Brother Agnalo, both holy men, he let himself be
guided by the Spirit of God, without considering the road he took. They soon arrived at a
town called Savenniano, where St Francis began to preach, ordering first the swallows, who
were singing, to keep silence until he had finished; and the swallows obeyed his voice. He
preached with such fervour, that the inhabitants of the town wished to follow him, out of
devotion; but St Francis would not allow them,
saying, "Do not be in such a haste; you need
not leave your homes. I will tell you what you
must do to savey our souls." Thereupon he
founded the Third Order for the salvation of
all; and leaving them much consoled and well
disposed to do penance, he went from thence,
and reached a spot between Cannajo and Bi-
vagno. And as he was going on, with great fervour, he lifted up his eyes, and saw on some
trees by the wayside a great multitude of birds;
St Francis was much surprised, and said to his
companions, "Wait for me here by the way,
whilst I go and preach to my little sisters the
birds"; and he entered into the field, and began to preach to the birds which were on the
ground. All of a sudden those which were on
the trees came round him, and all listened while
St Francis preached to them, and did not fly

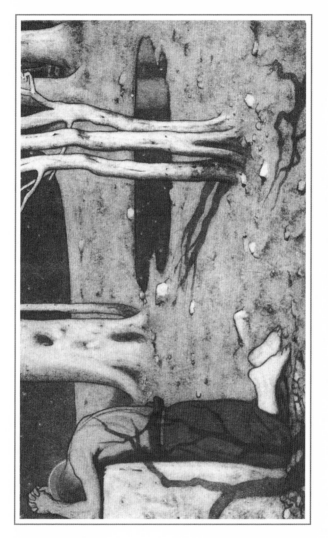

SAINT FRANCIS IN PRAYER

SAINT FRANCIS PREACHING TO THE BIRDS

away until he had given them his blessing. And Brother Masseo related afterwards to Brother James of Massa how St Francis went among them and even touched them with his garments, and how none of them moved. The substance of the sermon was this: "My little sisters the birds, you owe much to God, your Creator, and ought to sing His praise at all times and in all places, because He has given you liberty and the air to fly about in; and though you neither spin nor sew, He has given you a twofold and a threefold clothing for yourselves and for your offspring; and He sent two of your species into the Ark with Noah that you might not be lost to the world; besides which, He feeds you, though you neither sow nor reap. He has given you fountains and rivers to quench your thirst, mountains and valleys in which to take refuge, and trees in which to build your nests; so that your Creator loves you much, having thus favoured you with such bounties. Beware, my little sisters, of the sin of ingratitude, and study always to praise the Lord." As he said these words, all the birds began to open their beaks, to stretch their necks, to flap their wings, to bow their heads to the ground, and by their motions and by their songs endeavoured to manifest their joy to St Francis. And the saint rejoiced with them; he wondered to see such a multitude of birds, and was charmed with their beautiful variety, with their attention and familiarity, for all which he devoutly returned thanks to the Lord. Having fin-

ished his sermon, St Francis made the sign of
the cross, and allowed them to fly away. Then
all those birds rose up into the air, singing most
sweetly; and, following the sign of the cross,
which St Francis had made, they divided themselves into four companies. One company flew
towards the east, the others towards the west,
towards the south, and towards the north, and
each company went away singing most wonderfully; signifying thereby, that as St Francis, the
bearer of the Cross of Christ, had preached to
them, and had made upon them the sign of the
cross, after which they had divided among themselves the four parts of the world, so the preaching of the Cross of Christ, renewed by St Francis, would be carried by him and by his brothers all over the world, and that the humble
monks, like little birds, should possess nothing in this world, but cast all the care of their
lives on the providence of God.

CHAPTER   SEVENTEEN

HOW A LITTLE CHILD WHO HAD ENTERED THE
ORDER SAW ST FRANCIS IN PRAYER ONE NIGHT, AND
SAW THE SAVIOUR, THE VIRGIN MARY, AND MANY
OTHER SAINTS TALK WITH HIM

A pure and innocent child was received into
the Order during the lifetime of St Francis, and
the convent in which he lived was so small that
the monks were obliged to sleep on camp-beds.
St Francis came one day to that convent. In
the evening, after Compline, he went to bed,

so as to rise up early to pray, as was his custom, when all the other monks were asleep. The little child made up his mind carefully to watch St Francis, so as to know something of his ways, and find out more especially what he did in the night when he got up; and in order that he might not be overtaken by sleep, he lay down by St Francis, and tied the end of the cord he wore round his waist to the one which the saint wore, so that he was sure of being awoke when the latter got up in the night; he did it so gently, that St Francis was not aware of his contrivance. When all the other monks were fast asleep, St Francis rose from his bed, and finding what the child had done, he carefully untied the knot so as not to awake him, and went alone into the wood which was near the convent. Entering into a little cell which was there, he began to pray. Shortly after, the child awoke, and found St Francis gone, and that he had untied his cord; he got up quickly and went to seek him. Finding the door open which led to the wood, he thought St Francis had gone that way; and entering into the wood, and hurrying on to the little cell, he heard the noise of many voices. Approaching near to hear and see whence they came, he saw a great and wonderful light all round the saint, and in the light was Jesus Christ, the Virgin Mary, St John the Baptist, and St John the Evangelist, with a great multitude of angels, who were all talking with St Francis. The child, on seeing this, fell to the ground as if he had been dead. When the mir-

51

FLOWERS OF SAINT FRANCIS

acle of the holy vision was ended, St Francis rose to return to the convent, and stumbling on the way against the child, who appeared to be dead, with great compassion he took him up in his arms and carried him in his bosom as the good shepherd carries his lambs. Having learnt from him how he had seen the vision, he ordered him to tell no man as long as he, St Francis, lived. The little child grew up in the grace of God, and had a great devotion to St Francis. He became one of the most distinguished men of the Order. After the death of St Francis, he related the vision to the other monks.

CHAPTER   EIGHTEEN
OF THE WONDERFUL CHAPTER HELD BY ST FRANCIS AT SANTA MARIA DEGLI ANGIOLI, AT WHICH MORE THAN 5000 MONKS WERE PRESENT

The faithful servant of Christ, St Francis, once held a general chapter at Santa Maria degli Angioli, at which chapter more than 5000 monks were present. Amongst them was St Dominic, the head and founder of the Order of Preaching Friars, who happened to be on his way from Bologna to Rome. Having heard of the chapter which St Francis had called together in the plain of Santa Maria degli Angioli, he went there with seven friars of his Order. A Cardinal, much devoted to St Francis, and to whom the saint had foretold he would one day be Pope, came expressly from Perugia to Assisi. Every day he went to visit St Francis and his monks.

FLOWERS OF SAINT FRANCIS

Sometimes he sang Mass and preached to them; and each time the said Cardinal visited the holy college he experienced much pleasure and much devotion. Seeing the monks all seated in the plain round Santa Maria degli Angioli, in groups here of forty, there of a hundred, and elsewhere of eighty, all occupied in conversing about God, or in prayer, or in works of charity; seeing them all so silent and so grave, and wondering how such a multitude could be so orderly, he was moved to tears, and exclaimed, with great devotion, "Truly this is the field of God; this is the army, and these are the knights, of the Lord." Not one vain or useless word was to be heard in all that multitude; each group of monks was engaged either in prayer, or saying their office, in weeping over their sins and those of their benefactors, or in reasoning on the salvation of souls. Many tents made of mats had been pitched in that field, divided in groups, according to the different provinces from whence the monks came; and that chapter was called the "chapter of the mats."

The monks had no other beds but the bare ground, with here and there a little straw; for pillows they had stones or pieces of wood. For all this they were held in much devotion; and so great was the fame of their sanctity, that many came to see and hear them from the court of the Pope which was at Perugia, and from other parts of the Valley of Spoleto. Many counts, many barons, many knights and other gentlemen, many Cardinals and Bishops and abbots, many priests and much people, came to see this great and holy and humble congregation; for the world had never yet witnessed so many holy men assembled together; and most especially they went to see the saintly founder and father of the Order, who had taken from the world so many gifted men, and had formed such a beautiful and devout flock to follow the steps of the true Pastor, Jesus Christ. The chapter being assembled, St Francis, the father of all those holy men, expounded with great fervour of spirit the Word of God, and spoke to them in a loud voiçe that which the Holy Spirit dictated. The subject he took for his sermon was this: "My children, we have promised great things to God, and God has promised even greater things to us. If we observe what we have promised to Him, we shall certainly receive what He has promised to us. The pleasures of this world pass quickly away, but the punishment which follows them is eternal. The sufferings of this world are trifling, but the glory of the next is without bounds." And, preaching on these words most devoutly, he comforted the monks, encouraging them to holy obedience, to reverence towards the holy Mother Church, to charity among themselves, to pray God for all people, to bear with patience the adversities of life, to be temperate in prosperity, to keep angelic purity and chastity, to be at peace with God, with men, and with their own conscience, to love, to observe, and to practice holy proverty. He then added, "I command you all here present, through holy obedience, to take no thought what you shall eat or what you shall drink, or of aught else that is necessary to the body, but only to meditate, to pray, and to praise God, casting on Him the thought of all the rest, for He has you all in His especial care; and let each of you receive this command with a happy heart and a joyful countenance." And St Francis having finished his sermon, all the monks began to pray. St Dominic, who was present, wondered much at this order of St Francis, considering it as indiscreet, for he could not understand how such a great multitude could exist without taking any thought for the body. But the heavenly Pastor, our Blessed Saviour, wishing to show what care He takes of His lambs, and with what singular love He loves His poor servants, put into the hearts of all the people of Perugia, of Spoleto, of Foligno, of Spello, of Assisi, and of all the neighbouring country, to take meat and drink to that holy congregation; and presently men came from all these places with horses, and asses, and carts, laden with bread and wine, with beans and cheese, and other good things of which the poor of Christ had need. Besides all this, they brought napkins, and knives, and jugs, and glasses, and all that was needed for such a multitude; and those who could carry most and serve the best greatly rejoiced, and the knights and the barons and other noblemen, who were present, waited on the brothers with great devotion and humility. St Dominic, seeing this, and knowing of a certainty that it was the divine

providence of God which had provided for them
thus, acknowledged most humbly that he had
unjustly accused St Francis of having given indiscreet orders; and going to him, he humbly
knelt before him and confessed his fault, adding, "The Lord truly hath especial care of these
holy servants of poverty. I knew it not till now,
and henceforth I promise to observe holy evangelical poverty; and I condemn, in the name of
God, all the friars of my Order who shall seek
to have possessions of their own." And St Dominic was greatly edified by the faith of the most
holy Francis, by the obedience and poverty of
such a large and well-ordered chapter, and blessed the providence of God, who had given them
every grace in such abundance. In that same
chapter it was revealed to St Francis that many
brothers wore on their flesh small hearts and
bands of iron, for which reason many were ill
and hindered in their prayers; and St Francis,
like a discreet father, ordered all those who wore
such things to take them off and place them
before him; and more than five hundred little
hearts and bands of iron were placed before
him,—some destined to be worn round the
arms, and others round the waist,—and all put
together formed a large heap, which St Francis
ordered to be left in that field. The chapter being ended, he encouraged them all in well-do-
ing, and, warning them how to avoid sin in this
wicked world, sent them back to their respect-
ive homes, with his blessing and that of God,
and full of spiritual joy and consolation.

CHAPTER NINETEEN

HOW THE VINE OF THE PRIEST OF RIETI, IN WHOSE
HOUSE ST FRANCIS ENTERED TO PRAY, WAS TRAM-
PLED UNDER FOOT BY THE GREAT NUMBERS WHO
CAME TO SEE HIM, AND HOW IT PRODUCED A GREATER
QUANTITY OF WINE THAN USUAL, AS ST FRANCIS
HAD PROMISED; AND HOW THE LORD REVEALED TO
THE SAINT THAT HEAVEN WOULD BE HIS PORTION
WHEN HE LEFT THIS WORLD

St Francis at one time being grievously tormented with a disease in his eyes, the Cardinal
Ugolino, the protector of his Order, who loved him dearly, wrote to him to come to Rieti,
where there were some excellent oculists. St
Francis, having received the Cardinal's letter, set off first to San Damiano, where Sister
Clare, the devout spouse of Christ, was to give
her some spiritual consolation, intending afterwards to go on to the Cardinal. On arriving at
San Damiano, the following night his eyes grew
so much worse that he could not see the light,
and was obliged to give up going any farther.
Sister Clare made him a little cell of reeds, in
order that he might repose better; but St Francis, owing partly to the pain he suffered, and
partly to the multitude of rats, which much annoyed him, could not rest either day or night.
After suffering for several days this pain and
tribulation, he began to think that it was sent
to him by God as a punishment for his sins,
and he thanked the Lord in his heart and with
his lips, crying out with a loud voice, "My God,
I am worthy of this, and even worse. My Lord
Jesus Christ, the Good Shepherd, Thou hast
shown Thy mercy to us poor sinners in the
various bodily pains and sufferings it pleas-

57

eth Thee to send us; grant to me, Thy little lamb, that no pain, however great, no infirmity, and no anguish, shall ever separate me from Thee." Having made this prayer, a voice came from heaven, which said, "Francis, if all the earth were of gold, if all the seas and all the fountains and all the rivers were of balm, if all mountains, all hills, and all rocks were made of precious stones, and if thou couldest find a treasure as much more precious again as gold is more precious than earth, and balm than water, and gems than mountains and rocks, if that precious treasure were offered to thee in the place of thy infirmity, wouldst thou not rejoice and be content?" St Francis answered, "Lord, I am unworthy of such a treasure." And the voice of God said again, "Rejoice with all thy heart, Francis, for that treasure is life eternal, which I have in keeping for thee, and even now promise to thee; and this thy infirmity and affliction is a pledge of that blessed treasure." And St Francis was filled with joy at such a glorious promise; then calling his companion, he said to him, "Let us go to the Cardinal." He humbly took leave of Sister Clare, after having comforted her with holy words, and took the road to Rieti. When he approached the town, such a multitude came out to meet him, that he would not go into the city, but went to a church which was about two miles off. The people, hearing where he was gone, went thither to see him; so that the vine which surrounded the church was greatly injured, and all the grapes were gathered; at which the priest, to whom it belonged, was very grieved in his heart, and repented of having received St Francis in his church. The thought of the priest having been revealed to the saint, he called him to him and said, "Dear father, tell me, how many measures of wine does this vine produce when the year is a fertile one?" He answered, "Twelve measures." St Francis added, "I pray thee, father, have patience and put up with my presence here a few days longer, as I find great rest in this church; and, for the love of God and of me His poor servant, let the people gather the grapes off thy vine; and I promise thee, in the name of my Saviour Jesus Christ, that it shall produce every year twenty measures of wine." And St Francis remained there for the benefit of the souls of all those who went to see him, for many went away filled with divine love, and gave up the world. The priest had faith in the promise of St Francis, and left the vineyard open to all those who came to see him. And, O wonder! The vine was entirely ruined, so that there scarcely remained, here and there, a few small bunches of grapes; but the time of the vintage having arrived, the priest gathered the few bunches which were left, and put them into the winepress; and, according to the promise of St Francis, these few little bunches did not fail to produce twenty measures of excellent wine. This miracle teaches us that, as in consequence of the merits of St Francis, the vine, though de-

59

spoiled of its grapes, produced an abundance of grapes, so in the same way many Christians, whose sins had made them barren of virtue, through the saint's preaching and example, often came to abound in the good fruit of repentance.

CHAPTER   TWENTY

OF A BEAUTIFUL VISION WHICH APPEARED TO A YOUNG MAN WHO SO HATED THE HABIT OF ST FRANCIS, THAT HE WAS ON THE POINT OF LEAVING THE ORDER.

A young man, of noble birth and of delicate habits, who had entered the Order of St Francis, was seized after a few days, through the devil's suggestions, with a violent dislike to the dress of the friars minor: he hated the shape of the sleeves; he felt a horror for the cowl, for the length of the dress, and the coarseness of the material; so that it seemed to him as if he carried about him an insupportable weight; and, disliking the Order more and more, he decided to leave it and return to the world. It was the custom of this young man, at whatever hour he passed before the altar in the convent where the Blessed Sacrament was reserved, to kneel down with great respect, and, covering his head with his hood and crossing his arms on his breast, to prostrate himself, as he had been taught to do by the master of the novices. It so happened, that the night when he had made up his mind to leave the convent, he passed before the altar, and kneeling down prostrated himself to the ground, and, being ravished in spirit, the Lord sent him a most wonderful vision. He saw before him a great multitude of saints ranged in procession, two by two, clothed in vestments made of the most precious materials: their faces and their hands shone like the sun; they sang, as they walked, to the sound of celestial music. Two of them were more nobly and more richly dressed than the rest, and surrounded by such a blaze of light that none could look on them without being dazzled. At the end of the procession was one so gloriously adorned, that he seemed to be more favoured than the others. Now the young man, seeing such a beautiful procession, was struck with wonder, and endeavoured to guess the meaning of the vision; he dared not ask, and seemed struck dumb with amazement. The procession having passed away, he took courage, and addressing himself to those who were in the rear, he said, "O beloved, I pray you tell me who are those wonderful beings who form this venerable procession." They answered, "Know, my son, that we are all friars minor, who are come from the glories of Paradise; and those two who shine forth brighter than the rest, are St Francis and St Anthony; and the last one you saw so especially honoured is a holy monk, lately dead, who having fought with courage against temptation, and having persevered to the end, we lead in triumph to the glories of Paradise: and

61

these splendid vestments which adorn us have been given to us by God, in exchange for the coarse tunic we wore with so much patience in religion; and the glorious light which shines upon us has been given in reward for the humility, the holy poverty, the obedience, and chastity we had observed to the end of our lives. Now, my son, do not find the robe of religion so rough to wear; for if, clothed in the sackcloth of St Francis, and out of love to Christ, thou dost despise the world, and mortify thy flesh and fight valiantly against the devil, thou too shalt receive these splendid vestments, and shine with this glorious light." On hearing these words the young man came to his senses, and feeling himself much strengthened, he put far from him all temptations to leave the Order, confessed his sin to the guardian and to the brothers, and from that moment dearly loved the coarse vestment of St Francis and the severity of penance, and ended his life in the Order, a great example of sanctity.

CHAPTER TWENTY-ONE
OF THE MOST HOLY MIRACLE OF ST FRANCIS IN
TAMING THE FIERCE WOLF OF AGOBIO

At the time when St Francis was living in the city of Agobio, a large wolf appeared in the environs, so terrible and so fierce, that he not only devoured other animals, but made a prey of men; and as he often approached the town, all the people were in great alarm, and never went out but armed, as if they were going to battle. Notwithstanding these precautions, if any of the inhabitants ever met him alone, he was sure to be devoured, as all defence was useless; and, out of fear of the wolf, they did not dare go beyond the city walls. St Francis, feeling great compassion for the people of Agobio, resolved to go and meet the wolf, though all advised him not to do so. Making the holy sign of the cross, and putting all his confidence in God, he went out of the city, taking his brothers with him; but these fearing to go any farther, St Francis bent his steps alone toward the spot where the wolf was known to be, and many people followed at a distance, and witnessed the miracle. The wolf, seeing all this multitude, ran towards St Francis with his jaws wide open. As he approached, the saint, making the sign of the cross, cried out, "Come hither, brother wolf; I command thee, in the name of Christ, neither to harm me nor any body else." And, O miracle! no sooner had St Francis made the sign of the cross, than the terrible wolf closed his jaws, stopped running, and coming up to St Francis, lay down at his feet as meekly as a lamb. And the saint addressed him: "Brother wolf, thou hast done much evil in this land, destroying and killing the creatures of God without His permission; thou hast not only destroyed animals, but thou hast dared devour even men, made after the image of God; for which thing thou art worthy of being hung like a robber and a murderer. All men cry against thee, the dogs

FLOWERS OF SAINT FRANCIS

pursue thee, and all the inhabitants of this city are thy enemies; but I will, O brother wolf, make peace between them and thee, so that thou no more offend them, and they forgive thee all thy past offences, and neither men nor dogs pursue thee any more." Having listened to these words, the wolf bowed his head, and, by the movements of his body, of his tail, and of his eyes, made signs that he agreed to what St Francis said; and St Francis added, "As thou art willing to make this peace, I promise thee that thou shalt be fed every day by the inhabitants of this land as long as thou shalt live among them; thou shalt no longer suffer hunger, as it is hunger which has made thee do so much evil; but if I obtain all this for thee, thou must promise, on thy side, never again to attack any animal or any human being. Dost thou make this promise?" and the wolf, bowing his head, made a sign that he consented. St Francis said again: "Brother wolf, wilt thou pledge thy faith that I may trust to this thy promise?" and St Francis put out his hand to receive the pledge of the wolf; the latter lifted up his right paw and placed it familiarly in the hand of St Francis, giving him thereby the only pledge which was in his power; and St Francis, addressing him again, said: "Brother wolf, I command thee, in the name of Christ, to follow me immediately, without hesitation or doubting, that we may go together to ratify this peace which we have concluded in the name of God"; and the wolf, obeying him, walked by his side as meekly as a lamb, to the great astonishment of all the people. The news of this most wonderful miracle spread quickly through the town, and all the inhabitants, both men and women, small and great, young and old, flocked to the market-place to see St Francis and the wolf. All the people being assembled, the saint got up to preach, saying, amongst other things, "How for our sins God permits such calamities, and how much greater and more dangerous are the flames of hell, which last for ever, than the rage of the wolf, which can only kill the body; and how much we ought to dread the jaws of hell, if the jaws of so small an animal as a wolf can make a whole city tremble through fear." The sermon being ended, St Francis added these words: "Listen, my brethren: the wolf which is here before you has promised and pledged his faith that he consents to make peace with you all, and no more offend you in aught, and you must promise to give him each day his necessary food; to which, if you consent, I promise in his name that he will most faithfully observe the compact." Then all the people promised with one voice to feed the wolf to the end of his days; and St Francis, addressing the latter, said again: "And thou, brother wolf, dost thou promise to keep the compact, and never again to offend either man or beast, or any other creature?" And the wolf knelt down, bowed his head, and, by the motions of his tail and of his ears, endeavoured to show that he was willing, as far as was in his power, to hold to the com-

E

pact. And St Francis continued: "Brother wolf, as thou gavest me a pledge of this thy promise when we were outside the town, so now I will that thou renew it in the sight of all this people, and assure me that I have done well to promise in thy name"; and the wolf lifted up his paw and placed it in the hand of St Francis. Now this event caused great joy in all the people, and a great devotion towards St Francis, both because of the novelty of the miracle, and because of the peace which had been concluded with the wolf; and they lifted up their voices to heaven, praising and blessing God, who had sent them St Francis, through whose merits they had been delivered from such a savage beast. The wolf lived two years at Agobio; he went familiarly from door to door without harming any one, and all the people received him courteously, and fed him with great pleasure, and no dog barked at him as he went about. At last, after two years, he died of old age, and the people of Agobio felt his loss greatly; for when they saw him going about so tamely amongst them all, he reminded them of the virtue and sanctity of St Francis.

CHAPTER TWENTY-TWO
STORY OF HOW ST FRANCIS TAMED THE WILD DOVES

A young man having one day caught a great number of doves, as he was going to sell them he met St Francis, who always felt a great compassion for such gentle animals; and, looking at the doves with eyes of pity, he said to the young man, "O good young man, I entreat thee to give me those harmless birds, emblems in Scripture of humble, pure, and faithful souls, so that they do not fall into cruel hands, which would put them to death." And the young man, inspired by God, gave them immediately to St Francis, who placed them in his bosom, and addressed them thus sweetly: "O my little sisters the doves, so simple, so innocent, and so chaste, why did you allow yourselves to be caught? I will save you from death, and make you nests, that you may increase and multiply, according to the command of God." And St Francis made nests for them all, and they began to lay their eggs and hatch them in presence of the brothers, and were as familiar and as tame with St Francis and the monks as if they had been hens brought up amongst them, and never did they go away until St Francis had given them his blessing. And St Francis said to the young man who had given them to him, "My son, thou shalt become a monk in this Order; thou shalt serve most fervently the Lord Jesus Christ"; and so it was, for the young man became a monk, and lived in the Order most holily.

CHAPTER TWENTY-THREE

HOW ST FRANCIS DELIVERED THE BROTHER WHO,
BEING IN SIN, HAD FALLEN INTO THE POWER OF
THE DEVIL

St Francis, being one day in prayer in the Convent of the Porziuncula, saw, by the revelation of God, that all the convent was surrounded and besieged by devils, as by a great army; but none could penetrate into the convent, because the brothers were so holy that the demons could not enter into them. They remained, however, on the watch, and one day one of the brothers, having been offended by another, thought in his heart how he could accuse and do him harm. Having yielded to this evil thought, the devil, seeing a way open to him, entered the convent and took possession of the brother. St Francis, like a vigilant pastor, ever watching over his flock, seeing that the wolf had entered in to devour one of his lambs, called the brother, and commanded him to confess immediately the hatred he had nourished in his heart towards his neighbour, and which had caused him to fall into the power of the enemy. The brother, much alarmed, and seeing that his saintly father had penetrated into his deepest thoughts, confessed the evil feeling which had entered into his heart, and humbly asked for mercy and for penance. When he had done so, and been absolved of his sin and accepted his penance, St Francis saw the devil go away; and the brother, being freed from such a cruel monster through the charity of his good shepherd, thanked God, and returned to the little flock of the

68

saintly pastor corrected and strengthened, and lived afterwards in great sanctity.

CHAPTER TWENTY-FOUR

HOW ST FRANCIS CONVERTED TO THE FAITH THE
SULTAN OF BABYLON

St Francis, urged by zeal for the faith of Christ and by a wish to suffer martyrdom, took with him twelve of his most holy brothers, and went one day beyond the sea with the intention of going straight to the Sultan of Babylon. They arrived in a province belonging to the Saracens, where all the passes were guarded by men so cruel, that none of the Christians who went that way could escape being put to death. Now it pleased God that St Francis and his companions should not meet with the same fate; but they were taken prisoners, and, having been bound and ill-treated, were led before the Sultan. St Francis stood before him, and inspired by the Holy Spirit he preached most divinely the faith of Christ; and to prove the truth of what he said, professed himself ready to enter into the fire. Now the Sultan began to feel a great devotion towards him, both because of the constancy of his faith, and because he despised the things of this world (for he had refused to accept any of the presents which he had offered to him), and also of his ardent wish to suffer martyrdom. From that moment he listened to him willingly, and begged him to come back often, giving both him and his companions leave to preach wherever they pleased; he likewise gave them a sign of his protection, which would preserve them from all molestation.

At last St Francis, seeing he could do no more good in those parts, was warned by God to return with all his brothers to the land of the faithful. Having assembled his companions, they went together to the Sultan to take leave of him. And the Sultan said to him: "Brother Francis, most willingly would I be converted to the faith of Christ; but I fear to do so now, for if the people knew it, they would kill both me and thee and all thy companions. As thou mayest still do much good, and I have certain affairs of great importance to conclude, I will not at present be the cause of thy death and of mine. But teach me how I can be saved, and I am ready to do as thou shalt order." And St Francis answered: "My lord, I will take leave of thee for the present; but after I have returned to my own country, when I shall be dead and gone to heaven, by the grace of God, I will send thee two of my monks, who will administer to thee the holy baptism of Christ, and thou shalt be saved, as the Lord Jesus has revealed to me; and thou in the mean time shalt free thyself from every hindrance, so that, when the grace of God arrives, thou be found well disposed to faith and devotion." The Sultan promised so to do; and did as he had promised. St Francis returned to the venerable college of his saintly brethren, and after a few years ending his mortal life, he gave up his soul to God. The Sultan, having fallen ill, awaited the fulfilment of the promise of St Francis, and placed guards in all the passes, ordering them if they met two brothers in the habit of St Francis to conduct them immediately to him. At the same time St Francis appeared to two of his monks, and ordered them without delay to go to the Sultan and save his soul, according to the promise he had made him. The monks set out, and having crossed the sea, were conducted to the Sultan by the guards he had sent out to meet them. The Sultan, when he saw them arrive, rejoiced greatly, and exclaimed, "Now I know of a truth that God has sent His servants to save my soul, according to the promise which St Francis made me through divine revelation." Having received the faith of Christ and holy baptism from the brothers, he was regenerated in the Lord Jesus Christ; and having died of his disease, his soul was saved, through the merits and prayers of St Francis.

CHAPTER   TWENTY-FIVE

HOW ST FRANCIS HEALED MIRACULOUSLY A LEPER BOTH IN HIS BODY AND IN HIS SOUL, AND WHAT THE SOUL SAID TO HIM ON GOING UP TO HEAVEN

The true disciple of Christ, St Francis, as long as he lived in this miserable life, endeavoured with all his might to follow the example of Christ the perfect Master; whence it happened often, through the operation of grace, that he healed the soul at the same time as the body, as we read that Jesus Christ did; and not only he willingly served the lepers himself, but he willed that all the brothers of his Order, both when they were travelling about the world and when they were halting on their way, should serve the lepers for the love of Christ, who was for our sakes willing to be treated as a leper. It happened once, that in a convent near the one in which St Francis then resided there was a hospital for leprosy and other infirmities, served by the brothers; and one of the patients was a leper so impatient, so insupportable, and so insolent, that many believed of a certainty (and so it was) that he was possessed of the devil, for he ill-treated with blows and words all those who served him; and, what was worse, he blasphemed so dreadfully our blessed Lord and His most holy Mother the blessed Virgin Mary, that none was found who could or would serve him. The brothers, in order to gain merit, endeavoured to accept with patience the injuries and violences committed against themselves, but their consciences would not allow them to submit to those addressed to Christ and to His Mother; and they determined to abandon this leper, but would not do so until they signified their intention, according to the rule of St Francis. Having done so, St Francis visited himself this perverse leper, and said to him, "May God give thee peace, my beloved brother!" and the leper answered, "What peace can I look

7 2

for from God, who has taken from me peace and every other blessing, and made me a putrid and disgusting object?" And St Francis answered: "My son, be patient; for the infirmities of the body are given by God in this world for the salvation of the soul in the next; there is great merit in them when they are patiently endured." The sick man answered: "How can I bear patiently the pain which afflicts me night and day? And not only am I greatly afflicted by my infirmity, but the monks thou has sent to serve me make it even worse, for they do not serve me as they ought." Then St Francis, knowing through divine revelation that the leper was possessed by the malignant spirit, began to pray, and prayed most earnestly for him. Having finished, he returned to the leper and said to him: "My son, I myself will serve thee, as thou art not satisfied with the others." "Willingly," answered the leper; "but what canst thou do more than they have done?" "Whatsoever thou wishest I will do for thee," answered St Francis. "I will that thou wash me all over; for I am so disgusting that I cannot bear myself." Then St Francis heated some water, in which he put a great many odoriferous herbs; he then undressed him, and began to wash him with his own hands, whilst another brother threw the water upon him, and, by a divine miracle, wherever St Francis touched him with his holy hands the leprosy disappeared, and his flesh was perfectly healed; and as his body began to be healed, so likewise his soul was healed also. And the leper, seeing the leprosy beginning to disappear, felt a great sorrow and repentance for his sins, and began to weep bitterly. Whilst his body was being purified externally of the leprosy through the cleansing of the water, so the soul internally was purified from sin by the washing of tears and repentance. Feeling himself completely healed both in his body and in his soul, he humbly confessed his sins, crying out in a loud voice, with many tears, "Unhappy me! I am worthy of hell for the wickedness of my conduct to the brothers, and for the impatience and blasphemy I have uttered against the Lord"; and for fifteen days he never ceased to weep bitterly for his sins, .mploring the Lord to have mercy on him, and made a general confession to a priest. St Francis, perceiving this evident miracle which the Lord had enabled him to work, returned thanks to God, and set out for a distant country; for out of humility he wished to avoid all glory, and in all his actions he sought only the glory of God, and not his own. It pleased God that the leper, who had been healed both in his body and in his soul, after having done penance for fifteen days, should fall ill of another infirmity; and having received the sacraments of the Church, he died most holily. His soul on its way to heaven appeared in the air to St Francis, who was praying in a forest, and said to him, "Dost thou know me?" "Who art thou?" asked the saint. "I am the leper whom our Blessed Lord healed through thy merits, and to-day

FLOWERS OF SAINT FRANCIS

I am going to life eternal, for which I return
thanks to God and to thee. Blessed be thy soul
and thy body, blessed be thy holy words and
works, for through thee many souls are saved
in the world; and know that there is not a single
day in which the angels and other saints do
not return thanks to God for the holy fruits of
thy preaching and that of thy Order in various
parts of the world. Be comforted, then, and
thank the Lord, and may His blessing rest on
thee." Having said these words, he went up to
heaven, and St Francis was much consoled.

CHAPTER   TWENTY-SIX

HOW ST FRANCIS CONVERTED CERTAIN ROBBERS
AND ASSASSINS, WHO BECAME MONKS ; AND OF THE
WONDERFUL VISION WHICH APPEARED TO ONE OF
THEM WHO WAS A MOST HOLY BROTHER

St Francis went one day down the desert of Bor-
go to San Sepolcro, and passing by a castle called Monte Casale, he saw a young man of noble
mien, but slender and delicate in appearance,
coming towards him, who thus addressed him:
"Father, I would willingly be one of thy monks."
St Francis answered, "My son, thou art young,
noble, and delicate; perhaps thou wouldst not
be able to endure poverty and hardships." The
young man said again, "Father, are you not
men, like me? If you, then, can support these
things, through the grace of God I shall be
able to do so likewise." This answer greatly
pleased St Francis, and giving the young man

his blessing, he received him immediately into the Order, and gave him the name of Brother Angel. And this young man was so remarkable and so distinguished, that he was shortly after named Guardian of the Convent of Monte Casale. At that time there were three famous robbers in that part of the country, who did much evil in all the neighbourhood. They came one day to the said convent, and asked Brother Angel, the guardian, to give them something to eat. The guardian, reproving them harshly, answered them thus: "Cruel robbers and murderers, you are not ashamed to deprive others of the fruits of their labours, and you have the courage to come here to devour that which is given in charity to the servants of God,—you who are not worthy of the earth which bears you, for you neither respect man nor the Lord who made you. Go away about your business, and do not appear here again." And much troubled by these words, the robbers went away in anger. Shortly after, St Francis arrived at the convent with a sack of bread and a little vessel of wine, which he and his companion had begged; and the guardian related to him how he had sent away the robbers. St Francis reproved him sharply, saying that he had behaved most cruelly, for sinners are brought back to God more easily by kindness than by harsh words. "Wherefore," said he, "our Master Jesus Christ, whose Word we have promised to observe, says that the whole need not a physician, but the sick, and the He came not to call the just, but sinners, to repentance; and for this reason He often sat down to meat with them. As, then, thou hast acted against charity, and against the Gospel of Christ, I command thee, in the name of holy obedience, to take with thee this sack of bread, which I have begged, and this little vessel of wine, and go after the robbers, over the hills and across the valleys, until thou meat with them. And when thou hast found them, give them from me this bread and wine; and then, kneeling down before them, thou shalt humbly confess thy fault, and then beg them, in my name, not to do any more evil, but to fear God and never again offend Him. If they consent to this, I promise to provide them for all their wants, and to give them continually both meat and drink; and when thou hast told them this, thou shalt humbly come back here." Whilst the guardian went on the errand of St Francis, the latter began to pray, and asked of God to touch the hearts of the robbers and bring them to repentance. The obedient guardian, having found out their retreat, presented to them the bread and wine, and said and did what St Francis had commanded; and it pleased God that, as the robbers ate the bread of charity which St Francis had sent them, they reasoned thus among themselves: "Alas for us, miserable men that we are! What pains await us in hell; for we not only have robbed and beaten and wounded our neighbours, but we have likewise taken away our lives, and yet for all these cruel deeds we feel no remorse of conscience, and no fear of

God! and behold this holy monk who is come
to us, for a few unkind words, which we merited
most justly, has humbly confessed that he was
wrong, and has likewise brought us bread and
wine, with a most gracious promise from the
holy St Francis. These are indeed holy religious of God who merit His Paradise, and we are
sons of perdition, who are worthy of the pains
of hell; and each day we add to our perdition,
and we know not if, because of the sins we have
committed hitherto, we can ever find mercy in
the sight of God." One of them having spoken
thus, the other two answered, saying, "Most
certainly thou speakest truly; but what are we
to do?" "Let us go," said one of the others, "to
St Francis; and if he gives us a hope that our
sins may find mercy in the sight of God, we will
do what he shall command us to save our souls
from the punishment of hell." This counsel
pleased the others, and they agreed to go immediately to St Francis; and having found him,
they thus addressed him: "Father, because of
the multitude of our sins we dare not look for
mercy from God; but if thou hast a hope that
He may have pity on us, we are ready to do what
thou shalt order, and do penance for our sins
with thee." Then St Francis bade them stay, and
with much kindness and charity comforted
them by giving them many proofs of the mercy
of God, and promising them to ask the Lord to
have pity on their sins. He told them that His
mercy knows no bounds, and that were their
sins without number the mercy of God is even

FLOWERS OF SAINT FRANCIS

greater, according to the word of the Gospel
and of the Apostle St Paul, who says, our blessed Lord "came into the world to save sinners."
The three robbers on hearing the words resolved to renounce the devil and his works; and St
Francis received them into the Order, in which
they did great penance. Two of them died shortly after their conversion, and went to heaven;
but the third survived, and, reflecting on his
sins, he did penance during fifteen years. Besides the ordinary fasts which he observed with
the brothers, he fasted at other times three days
in the week on bread and water, went always
barefooted, wore no other vestment but his tunic, and never slept after matins. During this time
St Francis passed from this miserable life. The
converted robber having continued to do penance for many years, it so happened that one
night, after matins, he was visited by such a
strong temptation to sleep, that he could neither
pray nor watch as was his custom. At last, finding
it impossible to resist any longer, he threw himself on his bed to sleep. No sooner had he laid
down his head than he was ravished, and led
in spirit on a very high mountain, on the side
of which was a deed precipice bordered with
sharp stones and large rocks all broken to pieces,
so that the precipice was frightful to look at;
and the angel who conducted the brother pushed him with such violence, that he fell into the
abyss, and, rolling down from stone to stone and
from rock to rock, he reached the bottom shattered to pieces, as it seemed to him. As he lay

on the ground in a pitiable condition, the angel said to him, "Arise, for thou hast a much longer journey to take." And the brother answered, "Thou art both cruel and unreasonable. Thou seest that I am about to die from my fall, which has shattered me to pieces, and thou tellest me to arise." And the angel, coming near him, touched him and healed all his wounds. He then showed him an immense plain, full of sharp and pointed stones, and covered with thorns and brambles, and told him that he was to run all over the plain, and cross it barefooted till he reached the other end, where was a burning furnace, into which he was to enter. And the brother having crossed the plain with great pain and suffering, the angel ordered him to enter the furnace, as it was meet for him to do. The brother exclaimed, "Alas, what a cruel guide thou art! Thou seest that I am nearly dead, having crossed this horrible plain; and to rest me thou commandest me to enter this burning furnace"; and looking up, he saw all around many demons with iron pitchforks in their hands; and as he hesitated to obey the angel, they pushed him into the furnace. When he was in the furnace, he looked around and saw one who had formerly been his companion burning all over from head to foot; and he said to him, "O my unhappy companion, how camest thou here?" And he answered, "Go a little further, and thou shalt find my wife; she will tell thee why we are damned." And the brother went a little further, and saw the said woman surround-

MEETING OF SAINT LOUIS OF FRANCE
AND BROTHER GILES

SAINT CLARE BLESSING THE BREAD

ed with flames; and he said to her, "O unfortunate and miserable woman, why art thou condemned to suffer such a cruel torment?" "Because," she answered, "at the time of the great famine which St Francis had foretold, my husband and I cheated the people, and sold the wheat and oats in a false measure. It is for this I am condemned to burn in this dreadful place." Having heard these words, the angel who conducted the brother pushed him out of the furnace, and said to him, "Prepare thyself now for a very horrible journey." And the brother answered him sorrowfully, "O cruel guide, thou hast no compassion on me. Thou seest how I am almost burnt to death in this furnace, and thou preparest for me another horrible and dangerous journey." Then the angel touched him, and he became whole and strong; after which he conducted him to a bridge, which it was impossible to pass without great danger, for it was slightly built, very narrow, and very slippery, without any parapets, and underneath flowed a terrible river full of serpents and scorpions and dragons, and which produced a great stench. And the angel said to him, "Go over the bridge, as by all means thou must cross it." And the brother answered, "How can I cross it without falling into that dangerous river?" The angel said to him, "Follow me, and place thy foot where thou shalt see me place mine, and thou shalt cross it safely." The brother walked behind the angel as he had ordered him, and reached the middle of the bridge, and all of a sudden the angel flew away; and leaving the brother, he went on to a very high mountain at a great distance from the bridge. And the brother saw where the angel had flown to, and being without his guide, and looking down, he saw all those terrible animals with their heads out of the water, and their mouths open ready to devour him, if he were to fall into the river; and he trembled much with fear, not knowing what to do or what to say, as he could neither go back nor go forward. Seeing himself in such tribulation, and having no refuge but in God, he bent down, and clinging to the bridge, with all his heart and with many tears he recommended himself to the Lord, praying Him to have mercy on him. Having finished his prayer, it seemed to him as if wings were growing out of his back, and he waited with great joy till they should be large enough to enable him to fly away from the bridge, and to go the spot where the angel had flown to. After having waited a little time, his impatience to leave the bridge was so great, that he tried to fly; but his wings not having reached their growth, he fell on the bridge, and the feathers came off; upon which he clung again to the bridge as he had done before, and recommended himself to God. Having finished his prayer, it seemed to him as if the wings were growing again; and losing patience a second time, he tried to fly before the wings were fully grown, and falling down on the bridge as before, the feathers came off. And seeing that it was his impatience to fly away which made him fall down thus, he said within himself, "If my wings begin to grow a third time, I will most certainly wait until they are large enough to enable me to fly away without falling." And having come to this decision, he saw the wings begin to grow for the third time, and waited so long that they might attain their growth, that it seemed to him as if more than a hundred and fifty years had elapsed between the first growth of his wings and the third. At last he arose for the third time, and exerting all his strength, he flew up to the spot where the angel had flown before him; and knocking at the gate of the palace into which he had entered, the porter asked him who he was and whence he came. And he answered, "I am one of the Friars Minor." The porter said to him, "Wait a little whilst I go and fetch St Francis, to see if he knows thee." As the porter was gone to fetch St Francis, the brother began to examine the wonderful walls of the palace, which appeared so luminous and so transparent, that he could see through them the choirs of saints, and what they were doing. As he was struck with wonder at this sight, St Francis came towards him, with Brother Bernard and Brother Giles, followed by a great multitude of saints, both men and women, who had followed him in life, and they appeared to be innumerable. And St Francis said to the porter, "Let him come in, for he is one of my friars." As soon as he had entered, he felt such consolation and such sweetness, that he forgot all the tribulations he had gone through, as if they had never

83

been. And St Francis, taking him inside, showed him many wonderful things, and said to him, "My son, it is meet that thou return to the world: thou shalt remain there seven days, during which thou shalt prepare thyself with great devotion and great care; for after the seven days I will go and fetch thee, and then thou shalt come with me to this abode of the blessed." St Francis wore a most wonderful cloak, adorned with beautiful stars, and his five stigmata were like five stars, so bright that all the palace was illuminated by their rays. And Brother Bernard had on his head likewise a crown of stars, and Brother Giles was adorned with a blazing light, and he saw many other holy brothers he had not known in the world. Having taken leave of St Francis, he returned, much against his will, to the world. When he awoke and came back to himself, the brothers were singing prime; so that the vision had lasted only from matins to prime, though it had seemed to him as if many years had elapsed. He related to the guardian all the vision from beginning to end. After seven days he fell ill of a fever, and on the eighth day St Francis came to him, as he had promised, with a great multitude of glorious saints, and conducted his soul to the kingdom of the blessed, to eternal life.

CHAPTER TWENTY-SEVEN

HOW ST FRANCIS CONVERTED AT BOLOGNA TWO
SCHOLARS WHO BECAME BROTHERS, AND HOW HE
DELIVERED ONE OF THEM FROM A GREAT TEMPT-
ATION

St Francis coming one day to the city of Bologna, all the inhabitants went out to meet him,
and the crowd was so great that it was with
much difficulty he made his way to the market-
place, which was filled with men, women, and
scholars. And St Francis, on arriving there,
stood upon an elevated spot, and began to
preach that which the Holy Spirit put it into
his mind to say; and he preached so wonderfully that he appeared to be an angel, not a
man; and his words were like sharp arrows,
which pierced through the hearts of those who
listened to them. And many men and women
were brought to repentance through that sermon; of this number were two noble students of
the March of Ancona—one named Pellegrino,
and the other Rinieri. These two being touched in their hearts by divine inspiration, through
the said sermon, went to St Francis, saying
that they wished to give up the world and become friars in his Order. And it having been
revealed to St Francis that they had been sent
by God to be examples of virtue in the Order,
and on account of the great fervour they showed, he received them joyfully, saying to them:
"Thou, Pellegrino, shalt follow in the Order
the ways of humility; and thou, Rinieri, shalt
serve the brothers,"—and so it was; for Brother Pellegrino would never be treated as a
cleric but as a layman though he was learned

85

FLOWERS OF SAINT FRANCIS

and deeply versed in the Sacred Canons. And
through his humility he reached a high degree
of perfection in virtue; so that Brother Bernard, the first son of St Francis, said of him
that he was one of the most perfect friars in
the world; and finally Brother Pellegrino passed from this world full of virtue, having done
many miracles both before and after his death.
And Brother Rinieri served the brothers most
devoutly and most faithfully, living in great
sanctity and great humility; and he became
very intimate with St Francis; having been
named minister of the province of the March
of Ancona, he governed it for a long time with
much discretion and most peaceably; and St
Francis revealed to him many secrets. After
some time the Lord allowed a great temptation
to take possession of his soul, which greatly
grieved and troubled him; he observed severe
penance, subjected himself to much rigorous
discipline, and endeavoured day and night,
with prayers and tears, to drive away the temptation; not succeeding, he believed that God
had abandoned him. Being in a state of great
despair, he determined, as a last remedy, to go
to St Francis, thinking thus within himself, "If
the Saint receives me kindly and is familiar
with me, as is his custom, I may hope that God
will have pity on me; if not, this will be the
sign that I am abandoned by the Lord." And
setting out, he went to St Francis, who was at
that time dangerously ill, in the palace of the
Bishop of Assisi; and God revealed to him the

whole temptation which had assailed Brother Rinieri, and his intention of coming to him. St Francis called immediately Brother Leo and Brother Masseo, and said to them, "Go forth to meet my beloved Brother Rinieri, and having embraced him, salute him from me, and tell him that of all the brothers scattered abroad in the world I love him most particularly." And they set out; and meeting Brother Rinieri on the way, they embraced him, telling him what St Francis had ordered them to say. The message brought such sweetness and such consolation to him, that he was quite beside himself with joy; and then thanking God with all his heart, he reached the place where St Francis was lying ill. Now though St Francis was grievously ill, yet when he heard that Brother Rinieri was approaching, he arose and went to meet him; and embracing him with much affection he said to him, "My very dear Brother Rinieri, of all the brothers in the world I love thee most especially"; and making the holy sign of the cross on his forehead, he kissed him, and added, "My beloved son, the Lord hath permitted this temptation that thou mayest gain a great increase of merits; but if thou dost not wish this gain, the temptation shall be removed"; and, O miracle! no sooner had St Francis pronounced these words than immediately the temptation left him, and it seemed to him as if in all his life he had never been tempted, and he was greatly comforted.

CHAPTER   TWENTY-EIGHT

Brother Bernard of Quintavalle was an example of the manifestation of the grace of God in the poor followers of the Gospel, who gave up the world to follow Christ. Since he had taken the habit of St Francis, he was often rapt in God through the contemplation of celestial things. It happened one day, as he was in a church hearing Mass, his mind was so raised to God that he was transfixed and ravished, so as not to be aware of the moment of the elevation of the Body of Christ; for he neither knelt down nor removed his cowl, as did the others, but remained motionless, with his eyes intently gazing upwards, and remained so from the morning till the ninth hour. On coming back to himself, he went about the convent crying out with a loud voice, "O brothers! O brothers! O brothers! there is not a man in all this land, however great and however noble he may be, who, if a palace full of gold were offered him, would not willingly carry on his back a sack of copper to acquire such a rich treasure." Now this celestial treasure, promised to the lovers of Christ, had been revealed to Brother Bernard; and his mind was so fixed upon it, that for fifteen years his heart and countenance were always raised to heaven. In all that time he never satisfied his hunger, though he ate a little of whatever was set before him; wherefore he said, that if a man does

88

not taste what he eats his abstinence has no merit, for true abstinence is to moderate oneself in those things which are agreeable to the palate. His intelligence became so enlightened that many great divines had recourse to him to solve difficult questions and explain obscure passages of Scripture, which he did with the greatest facility. His mind was so completely detached and abstracted from all terrestial things, that he soared like the swallows above the earth, and remained sometimes twenty, sometimes thirty days on the top of a high mountain contemplating divine things. For which reason Brother Giles said that he had received a gift from God which had been given to no other human being, namely, that in his divine flight he was fed like the swallows. And, because of this wonderful grace of contemplation which he had received from God, St Francis willingly and frequently held converse with him day and night; and they were often found together in a state of ecstasy, in the wood where they had met to talk together on divine things.

CHAPTER TWENTY-NINE

HOW THE DEVIL OFTEN APPEARED TO BROTHER
RUFFINO IN THE FORM OF A CRUCIFIX, TELLING HIM
THAT ALL THE GOOD HE DID WAS OF NO USE, AS HE
WAS NOT OF THE NUMBER OF THE ELECT OF GOD;
WHICH HAVING BEEN REVEALED TO ST FRANCIS, HE
MADE KNOWN TO BROTHER RUFFINO THE ERROR
INTO WHICH HE HAD FALLEN

Brother Ruffino, one of the most noble men of
the city of Assisi, a companion of St Francis
and a man of great sanctity, was one day strongly tempted in his mind on the subject of pre-
destination, so that he grew quite melancholy
and sorrowful; for the devil put it into his heart
that he was damned, and not of the number of
those predestined to life eternal, making him
believe that all he did in the Order was completely lost. During several days he was tormented by this temptation, without having the
courage to reveal it to St Francis, though he
never ceased to pray and fast. The enemy of
his soul added sorrow to sorrow, not only fighting inwardly but likewise outwardly, taking
various forms in order better to deceive him.
One day he appeared to him under that of a
crucifix; and said to him, "O Brother Ruffino,
why dost thou inflict on thyself penance and
prayer, as thou art not of the number of the
predestinate to life eternal? Believe me,—for
I know whom I have chosen and predestined,
—and do not believe the son of Peter Bernardino if he tells thee contrary; do not take his
advice in this matter, as neither he nor any
other knows the truth but I, who am the Son of
God. Know of a certainty that thou art of the

90

number of the damned; and the son of Peter Bernardino, thy father, and his father, are likewise damned, and whosoever followeth them is damned." On hearing these words, Brother Ruffino was so blinded by the spirit of darkness, that he lost all the faith and love he had hitherto professed for St Francis, and did not even wish to communicate to him what was passing within him. But that which Brother Ruffino did not reveal to his saintly father was revealed to him by the Holy Spirit. When the Saint learned to what dangers his son was exposed, he sent to him Brother Masseo; but Brother Ruffino refused to listen to him, saying "What have I to do with Brother Francis?" And Brother Masseo, enlightened by the Spirit of God, knowing the deceits of the devil, answered, "O Brother Ruffino, thou knowest that St Francis may be compared to an angel of God who has made known the truth to many souls in the world, and through whom we have received the grace of God; wherefore I will at all events that thou come with us to him, for I clearly see that thou art deceived by the devil." On hearing these words, Brother Ruffino arose and went to St Francis. The Saint, perceiving him at a distance, exclaimed, "O Brother Ruffino, whom hast thou believed?" When he came near him, he related to him one by one all the temptations, both internal and external, to which he had been exposed, showing him clearly that he who had appeared to him was the devil and not Christ, and that he was by no means to listen to his suggestions; but if he appeared to him again and told him he was damned, he was to say to him these words, "Open thy mouth!" and by this sign he would clearly know if he was the devil or not; for no sooner would he have uttered the words than he would immediately disappear. "Thou oughtest to have known," added the Saint, "with whom thou wast dealing, when he hardened thy heart against all that was good; for such is his especial office. Christ the Blessed never hardens the heart of the faithful; on the contrary His office is to soften the heart of man, according to the words of the prophet: 'I will take away the heart of stone, and give thee a heart of flesh.'" And Brother Ruffino, seeing that St Francis was acquainted with all his temptations in the order they had come to him, was deeply touched by his exhortations, and began to weep bitterly, and confess humbly his guilt in concealing from him his trouble. He was greatly consoled and comforted by the admonitions of his saintly father, which St Francis ended by saying, "My son, go to confession, and do not give up the practice of thy accustomed prayers; know of a certainty that the temptation will be to thee a source of great consolation and humility, as thou shalt shortly see." Brother Ruffino returned to his cell in the wood; and as he was praying and weeping bitterly the enemy approached, bearing in his exterior the semblance of Christ Himself. He thus addressed him, "O Brother Ruffino, did I not tell thee not to listen to the son of Peter

Bernardino, or to weary thyself with prayer and fasting, inasmuch as thou art damned? What is the use of inflicting on thyself privations in this world, as thou hast no hope of salvation after death?" And immediately Brother Ruffino said, "Open thy mouth!" upon which the devil left him in such a rage and in such a fury, that the Mount Subassio, which was close by, was shaken to every foundation, and large stones rolled down the sides, knocking against each other as they fell, and producing a great fire in all the valley; and the noise they made was so terrible, that St Francis and all his companions went out to see what had taken place: and even to this day those large stones are to be seen lying in great confusion. And Brother Ruffino plainly saw that it was a devil who had deceived him. Returning to St Francis, he threw himself at his feet, and acknowledged his fault. St Francis comforted him with kind words, and sent him back to his cell full of consolation. As he was praying there most devoutly Christ the Blessed appeared to him; and filling his soul with the fire of divine love, He thus addressed him, "Thou didst well, My son, to believe in St Francis; for he who made thee so unhappy was the devil. But I am Christ, thy Master; and in order to prove to thee that I am He, I promise thee that thou shalt never again be troubled in this way." Having said these words, He departed, leaving the brother so happy, and enjoying such peace and sweetness of spirit, with his mind so raised above the things of this world,

that day and night he was ravished in God, and
from that moment he had no doubts as to his
salvation, and became quite a new man. Most
willingly would he have remained day and
night in prayer and in the contemplation of divine things, had he been permitted to do so.
Wherefore St Francis said of him that he had
been canonised during his lifetime by Christ,
and that, excepting in his presence, he would
not hesitate to call him St Ruffino even though
he were still on earth.

CHAPTER   THIRTY

OF THE BEAUTIFUL SERMON WHICH ST FRANCIS AND
BROTHER RUFFINO PREACHED AT ASSISI

The said Brother Ruffino, through constant
contemplation, was so absorbed in God that
he had grown almost insensible to all external
things, and very seldom spoke; added to which
he never had possessed the gift of speech, neither was he eloquent nor self-possessed. Notwithstanding this, St Francis ordered him one
day to go to Assisi, to preach to the people that
which God should dictate to him; and Brother
Ruffino expostulated, saying, "Reverend father, I pray thee excuse me, and send some other
brother in my stead; for thou knowest that I
have not the grace of preaching: I am simple
and ignorant." St Francis answered, "Inasmuch
as thou hast not obeyed immediately, I command thee to take off thy cloak and thy hood

and go to Assisi, where thou shalt enter a church and preach to the people; and this shalt thou do out of holy obedience." Having received this order, Brother Ruffino took of his mantle and his hood and proceeded to Assisi; and entering the church, after having bowed before the altar, he mounted into the pulpit and began to preach to the people, who, seeing him in such a strange costume, laughed at him, saying, "These men do such penance that they are quite out of their mind." In the mean time St Francis, reflecting how promptly Brother Ruffino, who was one of the most noble men of Assisi, had obeyed the harsh commandment he had given him, reproached himself, saying, "How couldst thou, who art but the humble son of Peter Bernardino, send one of the most distinguished men to Assisi to preach to the people as if he were a mad man? May God forgive thee! But thou shalt do the same thing thou hast ordered him to do." And immediately he took off his cloak and his hood with great fervour of spirit, and went to Assisi, taking with him Brother Leo, who carried his mantle and that of Brother Ruffino. The inhabitants of Assisi, seeing him thus accoutred, reviled him, believing that both he and Brother Ruffino were out of their minds through much penance. St Francis entered the church as Brother Ruffino was saying these words, "O beloved, flee from the world, and leave sin; render to all men that which is their due, if thou wilt avoid hell; keep the commandments of God, love the Lord and thy neighbour, if thou wilt possess the

95

kingdom of Heaven." Then St Francis ascended the pulpit, and began to preach in such a wonderful way on holy penance, on the world, on voluntary poverty, on the hope of life eternal, on the nakedness of Christ, on the shame of the Passion of our Blessed Saviour, that all those who heard him, both men and women, began to weep bitterly, being moved to devotion and compunction; and in all Assisi the Passion of Christ was commemorated as it never had been before; so that the people were greatly edified by this action of St Francis and of Brother Ruffino. And St Francis put on the cloak of Brother Ruffino and his own, and returned to the convent of the Porziuncula, praising and glorifying God, who had given them grace to conquer and despise themselves, to the edification of the flock of Christ, and enabled them, by their example, to show how the world ought to be despised. And from that day the people greatly revered them; those who could touch the hem of their garments esteemed themselves most happy.

CHAPTER   THIRTY-ONE
HOW ST FRANCIS WAS ACQUAINTED WITH THE SECRETS OF THE CONSCIENCES OF ALL HIS BROTHERS

As our Lord Jesus Christ says in His Gospel, "I know My sheep, and Mine know Me," so the holy St Francis, like a good shepherd, knew, through divine revelation, all the merits and virtues of his companions, and also their defects and faults, and was enabled to deal with them according to their needs,—humbling the proud and exalting the humble, rebuking vice and praising virtue,—as we read in the wonderful revelations which were made to him by God with regard to his first children. Amongst others, we are told that St Francis was once with his companions in a convent talking of God, and Brother Ruffino was absent, being in contemplation in the forest; as the Saint was conversing with them, Brother Ruffino passed by at some distance, and St Francis asked them whom they believed to be the holiest soul in the world. They answered immediately, that they believed it to be St Francis. The Saint reproved them, saying, "Beloved brothers, I am the most unworthy and the vilest of all men in the world; but see there Brother Ruffino, who is now coming out of the forest; the Lord has revealed to me that his soul is one of three most holy on earth; and I tell you candidly, I should not hesitate to call him St Ruffino even during his lifetime, his soul being full of grace, and sanctified and canonised in Heaven by our Lord Jesus Christ." St Francis never expressed this opinion in the presence of Brother Ruffino. That he was equally acquainted with the defects of his brothers, we learn in the case of Brother Elias, whom he often reproved for his pride; and of Brother John della Cappella, to whom he foretold that he would hang himself; and of that brother who was seized by the devil as a punishment for his disobedience; and of many others whose defects and virtues were clearly revealed to him by Christ.

CHAPTER   THIRTY-TWO

HOW BROTHER MASSEO OBTAINED FROM CHRIST THE GRACE OF HUMILITY

The first companions of St Francis endeavoured with all their might to follow holy poverty with regard to earthly things, and to acquire every other virtue, as the sure means of obtaining celestial and eternal riches. It so happened one day, as they were assembled together to speak of divine things, one of them related the following example. "There was a man, a great friend of God, to whom had been given the grace of a life contemplative as well as active. He was at the same time so humble, that he looked upon himself as a very great sinner; and his humility was to him a means of sanctification, and confirmed him in the grace of God; for it caused him to increase in virtue, and saved him from falling into sin." And Brother Masseo, hearing such wonderful things of humility, and knowing it to be one of the greatest treasures of life eternal, was so inflamed with a love and desire of this virtue of humility, that he lifted his eyes to Heaven with much fervour, and made a vow and firm resolution never again to rejoice until he should feel the said virtue to be firmly established in his soul. From that moment he was constantly shut up in his cell, macerating his body with fasts and vigils and prayers, weeping before the Lord, and earnestly imploring Him to grant him this virtue, without which he felt that he was only worthy of hell, and with which the friend of God of whom he had heard was so richly endowed. Brother Masseo having passed several days in this state of mind, as he was entering the forest and asking the Lord, who willingly listens to the prayers of the humble, with cries and tears, to grant him this divine virtue, he heard a voice from Heaven, which called him twice: "Brother Masseo! Brother Masseo!" And he, knowing in his spirit that it was the voice of Christ, answered, "My Lord." And Christ answered, "What wilt thou give in exchange for this virtue which thou askest for?" And Brother Masseo answered, "Lord, I will willingly give my eyes." And Christ answered, "I grant thee the virtue, and command at the same time that thou keep thy eyes." And having said these words, the voice was silent; and Brother Masseo was so filled with the grace of humility, that from thenceforward he was constantly rejoicing. And often as he was in prayer he was heard to utter a joyful sound, like the song of a bird, resembling "U-u-u," and his face bore a most holy and happy expression. With this he grew so humble that he esteemed himself less than all other men in the world. And Brother James of Fallerone having asked him why he always rejoiced in the same way, he replied gaily, that when a way was good he saw no reason to change it.

99

CHAPTER THIRTY-THREE

St Clare, a most devout servant of the Cross of
Christ, and one of the sweetest flowers of St
Francis, was so holy, that not only the Bishops
and Cardinals, but the Pope himself wished to
see and hear her, and often went to visit her
in person. One day, amongst others, the Holy
Father went to her convent to hear her speak
of celestial things; and having long reasoned
together, St Clare ordered the table to be laid
and bread to be placed upon it, in order that
the Holy Father might bless it. The spiritual
conversation being at an end, St Clare, kneeling down with great reverence, begged him to
bless the bread which had been placed on the
table. The Holy Father answered, "Most faithful sister, I will that thou bless this bread by the
sign of the cross, to which thou hast devoted
thyself." St Clare said, "Most Holy Father, excuse me. I should indeed be worthy of reproof
if I, a miserable woman, were to presume to
give such a blessing in the presence of the Vicar
of Christ." And the Pope answered, "In order
that such an act be not looked upon as presumptuous, but that it may bear on it the marks
of obedience, I command thee, in the name of
holy obedince, to make on this bread the sign
of the cross, and to bless it in the name of God."
And St Clare, like a true daughter of obedience,
blessed the loaves most devoutly, making on
them the sign of the holy cross; and, oh, won-

derful to relate, on all those loaves appeared a cross, most clearly marked; and some of them were eaten, but the rest were put aside, in order to testify of the miracle. And the Holy Father, having seen the miracle, thanked God; and taking some of the bread, went away, leaving his blessing with Sister Clare. At that time Sister Ortolana, mother of St Clare, and Sister Agnes, her sister, were living together in the convent with St Clare, both most virtuous women, full of the Holy Spirit, likewise many other nuns; to whom St Francis sent a great number of sick persons, who were all healed through prayer and by the sign of the most holy cross.

CHAPTER   THIRTY-FOUR

HOW ST LOUIS, KING OF FRANCE, WENT IN PERSON IN A PILGRIM'S GARB TO VISIT THE HOLY BROTHER GILES

St Louis, king of France, went on a pilgrimage to visit the different sanctuaries in the world. Having heard of the fame of the sanctity of Brother Giles, who was one of the first companions of St Francis, he determined in his heart to go and visit him in person; for which object he set out for Perugia, where the said brother then lived. He arrived at the convent-gate as if he had been a poor unknown pilgrim, and asked with great importunity for Brother Giles, without telling the porter who it was who wished to see him; and the porter went to Brother

Giles, and told him there was a pilgrim at the gate who asked for him. And the Lord having revealed to Brother Giles that the pilgrim was the king of France, he left his cell in haste, and ran to the gate without asking any questions. They both knelt down and embraced each other with great reverence and many outward signs of love and charity, as if a long friendship had existed between them, though they had never met before in their lives. Neither of them spoke a word; and after remaining clasped in each other's arms for some time, they separated in silence, St Louis to continue his journey, and Brother Giles to return to his cell. As the king departed, one of the brothers inquired of one of the persons who accompanied him who it was who had embraced Brother Giles, and he answered that it was Louis, king of France; and when the other brothers heard this, they were all sorrowful because Brother Giles had not spoken to him; and giving vent to their grief, they said, "O Brother Giles, why hast thou been so uncivil as not to say a word to such a holy king, who has come from France to see thee, and hear from thee some good words?" Brother Giles answered, "Beloved brothers, be not surprised at this, as neither I could say a word to him nor he to me; for no sooner had we embraced each other than the light of divine wisdom revealed his heart to me, and mine to him; and by a divine operation we saw into each other's hearts, and knew far better what we had to say than if we had explained in words that which we experienced in our souls. The tongue of man reveals so imperfectly the secret mysteries of God, that words would have been to us rather a hindrance than a consolation. Know, then, that the king went away satisfied with me, and greatly comforted in mind."

CHAPTER THIRTY-FIVE

HOW ST CLARE, BEING ILL, WAS MIRACULOUSLY CARRIED, ON CHRISTMAS-NIGHT, TO THE CHURCH OF ST FRANCIS, WHERE SHE ASSISTED AT THE OFFICE

St Clare was at one time so dangerously ill, that she could not go to church with the other nuns to say the Office on the night of the Nativity of Christ. All the other sisters went to matins; but she remained in bed, very sorrowful because she could not go with her sisters to receive spiritual consolation. But Jesus Christ, her Spouse, would not leave her comfortless, and carried her miraculously to the church of St Francis, so that she was present at the Office in the morning, assisted at the midnight Mass, received the Holy Communion, and was carried back to her bed. When the nuns returned to their convent, the ceremonies being ended at St Damiano, they went to St Clare and said to her, "O our mother, Sister Clare, what great consolations we have experienced at this feast of the Holy Nativity! Oh, if it had but pleased God that you should have been with us!" And St Clare answered, "Praise and glory be to our Lord Jesus Christ

103

FLOWERS OF SAINT FRANCIS

the Blessed, my beloved sisters and daughters; for I have not only assisted at all the solemnities of this most holy night, but I have experienced in my soul even greater consolations than those which have been your share; for by the intercession of my father, St Francis, and through the grace of our Saviour Jesus Christ, I have been personally present in the church of my venerable father St Francis, and with the ears of my body and those of my spirit have heard all the Office, and the sounds of the organ, and the singing, and have likewise received there the most Holy Communion. Rejoice, then, because of these graces which I have received, and return thanks to our Lord Jesus Christ."

CHAPTER   THIRTY-SIX

HOW ST FRANCIS EXPLAINED TO BROTHER LEO A BEAUTIFUL VISION HE HAD SEEN

St Francis being once grievously ill, Brother Leo, as he was in prayer by his bedside, was rapt in ecstasy, and carried in spirit to a great, wide, and rapid river; and watching those who crossed it, he saw some brothers heavily laden enter the river, who were carried away by the current and were drowned; some contrived to reach one third of the way; others arrived as far as the middle of the stream; yet none could resist the rapidity of the waters, but fell down and were drowned. Presently he saw other brothers arrive; these carried nothing on their backs, but all bore upon them the marks of holy poverty. They entered the river, and passed over to the other side without any danger to themselves. Having seen this, Brother Leo came to himself; and St Francis, knowing in spirit that he had had a vision, called him to him, and asked him what he had seen. When Brother Leo had related to him the vision, St Francis said, "What thou hast seen is perfectly true. The great river is the world; the brothers who were drowned are those who do not follow their evangelical profession, or practise the great virtue of poverty; but those who passed the river are those who neither seek nor possess in this world any earthly riches, who having food and raiment are therewith content, and follow Christ naked on the cross, bearing joyfully and willingly His sweet and easy yoke, and loving holy obedience: these pass easily from life terrestrial to life eternal."

CHAPTER   THIRTY-SEVEN

HOW JESUS CHRIST THE BLESSED, AT THE PRAYER OF ST FRANCIS, CONVERTED A RICH NOBLEMAN WHO HAD MADE GREAT OFFERS TO ST FRANCIS, AND INSPIRED HIM WITH A WISH TO BECOME A RELIGIOUS

St Francis, the servant of Christ, arriving late one evening at the house of a rich and powerful nobleman with one of his brothers, was received by him as if they had been angels of God, with so much courtesy and respect that the Saint felt himself drawn to love him greatly; for he considered how on entering his house he had embraced him with much affection; how he had

105

washed his feet, and humbly wiped and kissed them; how he had lighted a great fire, and prepared a supper composed of the choicest meats, serving him himself with a joyful countenance. When the supper was ended, the noblemen thus addressed St Francis: "Behold, my father, I offer thee myself and all I possess. If ever thou art in want of a tunic, or a mantle, or any other thing, purchase them, and I will pay thee. And see, I am ready to provide for all thy wants, as, through the grace of God, it is in my power to do so; for I abound in all temporal riches, and out of love to God, who gave them to me, most willingly do I bestow my goods on His poor." St Francis, seeing so much courtesy and generosity, felt great affection towards him; and having taken leave of him, he said to his companion, "Truly this nobleman would be a great gain to our Order, he is so grateful to God, and so kind to his neighbour and to the poor. Know, dear brother, that courtesy is one of the attributes of God, who sends His rain on the just and on the unjust; courtesy is the sister of charity, it extinguisheth hatred and kindles love. I have discovered in this good man such divine virtues, that I would most willingly have him as a companion. On some future day we will pay him another visit, as possibly the Lord may touch his heart, and induce him to follow us in His service; in the mean time we will pray God to put this desire into his heart, and give him grace to execute it." And a few days after St Francis had made this prayer, the Lord touched the heart of the nobleman; and the Saint said to his companion, "Let us go, my brother, to the dwelling of that courteous nobleman, as I hope in God that, amongst his temporal gifts, he will offer himself and join our Order"; and they set out accordingly. As they arrived near the house, St Francis said to his companion, "Wait for me a little, that I may first ask the Lord to prosper our journey, and pray that it may please our Saviour Jesus Christ, through His holy Passion, to take from the world this virtuous nobleman, and confide him to us, His poor weak servants." Having said this, he knelt down in a spot where he could be seen by the nobleman, who was walking to and fro in his rooms; and it pleased God that he should perceive St Francis as he prayed in the presence of Christ, who appeared in great glory and stood before him; and he saw that the Saint was raised above the earth. On seeing this he felt in his heart such a desire to leave the world, that he hastened out of his palace, and with great fervour of spirit ran to St Francis, and kneeling at his feet implored him earnestly and devoutly to receive him into his Order, and allow him to do penance with him. And the Saint, seeing that his prayer was granted, and that the nobleman asked of him the accomplishment of his wish, arose and embraced him joyfully, devoutly returning thanks to God, who had made such a present to his Order. And the nobleman said to St Francis, "What wilt thou have me to do, my father? I am ready to obey thee, and give all I possess to the poor, in order to follow Christ with thee, without any hindrance from temporal things." And he followed the advice of the Saint, distributed all he possessed to the poor, entered the Order, and lived a life of holiness and penance, speaking always of divine things.

CHAPTER   THIRTY-EIGHT

HOW IT WAS REVEALED TO ST FRANCIS THAT BRO-
THER ELIAS WAS DAMNED, AND WAS TO DIE OUT OF
THE ORDER; AND HOW AT THE DESIRE OF THE SAID
BROTHER HE PRAYED TO CHRIST FOR HIM, AND HOW
HIS PRAYER WAS GRANTED

As St Francis and Brother Elias were living together in a convent, it was revealed by God to St Francis that Brother Elias was damned, as he was about to apostatise, and that he would die out of the Order. In consequence of this revelation, the Saint took such a dislike to him that he neither spoke to him nor conversed with him; and when Brother Elias went towards him, he turned away and took another direction, in order not to meet him; which Brother Elias perceiving, and seeing that St Francis disliked him, wished to know the reason. As the brother accosted him one day to speak with him, the Saint endeavoured, as usual, to avoid him; but Brother Elias retained him courteously, and begged him to tell him why he avoided his company, and refused to speak to him. St Francis answered, "This is the reason: it has been revealed to me by God that thou wilt apostatise, and die out of the Order; also that, because of thy sins, thou art damned." On hearing this Brother Elias said, "My reverend father, I implore thee, by the love of Christ Jesus, not to despise me for this reason, nor send me from thee; but, like a good shepherd, follow the example of thy Master: seek and receive the lamb which will perish without thy help. Pray to God for me, that, if possible, He may revoke the sentence of my damnation; for it is written, that the Lord will forgive the sinner if he repent of his sin; and I have such faith in thy prayers, that were I even in hell and thou wert to pray for me, I should find refreshment. I implore thee, then, that thou recommend me, a sinner, to God, who came into the world to save sinners, that He may have mercy on me." Brother Elias made this request with so much fervour and many tears, that St Francis had compassion on him; and promised to pray for him, which he did, and as he prayed most devoutly, the Lord revealed to him that his prayer was granted; that the sentence of damnation pronounced on Brother Elias had been revoked; that his soul would be finally saved; but that he would leave the Order and die out of it; and so it happened. Frederick, king of Sicily, having rebelled against the Church, was excommunicated by the Pope, with all those who gave him aid or counsel. Brother Elias being looked upon as one of the most learned men in the world, King Frederick, wishing to see him, sent for him. He obeyed the summons, and thus rebelled against the Church;

for which reason he was excommunicated by the Pope, and deprived of the habit of St Francis. Shortly after the excommunication he fell dangerously ill; and a lay brother who belonged to the Order, a man of holy life, having heard of his illness, went to visit him, and amongst other things said to him, "My dear brother, I grieve to see thee thus excommunicated and out of thy Order, and that probably thou wilt die in this state. If there is any way by which I can deliver thee from this danger, most willingly would I undergo any trouble and fatigue to help thee." Brother Elias answered, "My brother, I see no other way but that thou go to the Pope and entreat him, for the love of God and of St Francis His servant, upon whose teaching I gave up the world, to absolve me from this excommunication, and restore to me my religious habit." And the lay brother said he would most willingly undertake the journey for his salvation; and taking leave of him, he went to the Pope, and humbly kneeling before him implored him to take pity on Brother Elias, for the love of Christ and of St Francis His servant. And it pleased God that the Holy Father granted his request, telling him to return to him, and if he found him alive to tell him from him that he was absolved from the excommunication, and the habit of his Order was restored to him. He hurried back with this joyful news to Brother Elias; and finding him on the point of death he gave him the message of the Pope, telling him that he was absolved from the excommun-

ication, and giving him his habit; and Brother
Elias departed from this world. His soul was
saved by the merits and by the prayers of St
Francis, in which he had such faith.

CHAPTER   THIRTY-NINE

OF THE WONDERFUL DISCOURSE WHICH ST ANTHONY
OF PADUA, A FRIAR MINOR, MADE IN THE CONSISTORY

That wonderful vessel of the Holy Spirit, St
Anthony of Padua, one of the chosen disciples
and companions of St Francis, whom the latter
called his Vicar, was preaching once before the
Pope and the Cardinals in the Consistory; and
there were present men of divers nations,—
Greeks, Latins, French, Germans, Slavonians,
English, and others; and he was so inflamed
by the Holy Spirit, and explained the word of
God so devoutly, so sweetly, so clearly, and in
a manner so efficacious and so learned, that all
those who were in the Consistory, though they
spoke different languages, understood what he
said as perfectly as if he had spoken the language of each. And they were all full of wonder,
for it seemed to them as if the miracle of the
Apostles at the time of Pentecost had been renewed, when the Holy Spirit taught them to
speak all languages; and they said among themselves, "Does not he that preacheth come from
Spain? How is it, then, that we each hear in his
words our own tongue spoken?" And the Pope,
as much surprised as the others, considering
the deep meaning of his words, exclaimed, "In

truth this man is the ark of the Testament, and the treasure of the Holy Scriptures."

CHAPTER   FORTY

OF THE MIRACLE WHICH GOD PERFORMED WHEN ST ANTHONY, BEING AT RIMINI, PREACHED TO THE FISH OF THE SEA

Christ the Blessed was pleased to show forth the great sanctity of His most faithful servant St Anthony, and how men ought devoutly to listen to his preaching, by means of creatures without reason. On one occasion, amongst others, He made use of fish to reprove the folly of faithless heretics, just as we read in the Old Testament how in ancient times He reproved the ignorance of Balaam by the mouth of an ass. St Anthony being at one time at Rimini, where there were a great number of heretics, and wishing to lead them by the light of faith into the way of truth, preached to them for several days, and reasoned with them on the faith of Christ and on the Holy Scriptures. They not only resisted his words, but were hardened and obstinate, and refused to listen to him. At last St Anthony, inspired by God, went down to the sea-shore, where the river runs into the sea, and having placed himself on a bank between the river and the sea, he began to speak to the fish as if the Lord had sent him to preach to them, and said, "Listen to the word of God, O you fish of the sea and of the river, as the faithless heretics refuse to do so." No sooner

FLOWERS OF SAINT FRANCIS

had he spoken these words than suddenly a
great multitude of fish, both small and great,
approached the bank on which he stood, and
never before had so many been seen in the sea
or in the river; all kept their heads out of the
water, and seemed to be attentively looking on
St Anthony's face; all were ranged in perfect
order and most peacefully, the smaller ones in
front near the bank, after them came those a
little bigger, and last of all, where the water was
deeper, the large ones. When they had placed
themselves in this order, St Anthony began to
preach to them most solemnly, saying, "My
brothers the fish, you are bound, as much as
it is in your power, to return thanks to your
Creator, who has given you such a noble element for your dwelling; for you have at your
choice sweet water and salt water; you have
many places of refuge from the tempest; you
have likewise a pure and transparent element
for your nourishment. God, your bountiful and
kind Creator, when He made you, ordered
you to increase and multiply, and gave you His
blessing. In the universal deluge, all other creatures perished; you alone did God preserve
from all harm. He has given you fins to enable you to go where you will. To you was it
granted, according to the commandment of
God, to keep the prophet Jonas, and after three
days to throw him safe and sound on dry land.
You it was who gave the tribute-money to our
Saviour Jesus Christ, when, through His poverty, He had nothing to pay. By a singular mys-

113   H

tery you were the nourishment of the Eternal King, Jesus Christ, before and after His resurrection. Because of all these things you are bound to praise and bless the Lord, who has given you so many and so much greater blessings than to other creatures." At these words the fish began to open their mouths, and bow their heads, and endeavoured as much as was in their power to express their reverence and show forth their praise. St Anthony, seeing the reverence of the fish towards their Creator, rejoiced greatly in spirit, and said with a loud voice, "Blessed be eternal God; for the fish of the sea honour Him more than men without faith, and animals without reason listen to His word with greater attention than sinful heretics." And whilst St Anthony was preaching, the number of the fish increased, and none of them left the place he had chosen. And the people of the city, hearing of the miracle, made haste to go and witness it. With them came the heretics of whom we have spoken above, who, seeing such a wonderful and manifest miracle, were touched in their hearts; and all threw themselves at the feet of St Anthony to hear his words. The Saint then began to expound to them the Catholic faith. He preached so eloquently, that all those heretics were converted and returned to the true faith of Christ; the faithful were filled with joy, and greatly comforted, and strengthened in faith. After this St Anthony sent away the fish, with the blessing of God; and they all departed, rejoicing as they went, and the people returned to the city. St Anthony remained at Rimini for several days, preaching and reaping much spiritual fruits in the souls of his hearers.

CHAPTER   FORTY-ONE

HOW THE VENERABLE BROTHER SIMON DELIVERED A BROTHER FROM A GREAT TEMPTATION, ON AC-COUNT OF WHICH HE WAS ON THE POINT OF LEAV-ING THE ORDER

About the beginning of the Order, and during the lifetime of St Francis, a young man from Assisi took the habit whose name was Simon; and the Lord adorned him with such graces and such elevation of mind, that all his life he was a mirror of sanctity, as I heard from those who had lived with him for a long time. He very sel-dom left his cell, and whenever he was in com-pany with the brothers he always spoke of God. He had never learnt grammar, and yet he talk-ed of divine things and of the love of Christ in a way so elevated and with such profound wis-dom, that his words seemed to be supernatural. One evening he went into the wood with Bro-ther James of Massa to speak of God, and they spent the whole night conversing sweetly on divine love. When morning dawned they seem-ed to have been together but a few minutes, as the said Brother James told me himself. Bro-ther Simon was so completely absorbed by these divine communications with God, and his spirit was so overflowing with love, that he was often obliged to lie down, as the tranquil sweetness which came over him with the Holy Spirit required not only the repose of the soul, but likewise that of the body; and during these divine visitations he was often rapt in God, and quite insensible to all outward things. On one occasion, as he was thus rapt in God, and insensible to the world, his heart was so burning with divine love that all bodily sensations were deadened. A brother wishing to convince himself if this really was the case, as it appeared to be, took a piece of burning coal out of the fire, and put it on his foot; and Brother Simon neither felt it, nor did it leave any mark, though it was left there some time, until it went out of itself. The said Brother Simon, when he sat down to his meals, before nourishing his body took and gave to those around him the nourishment of the soul, by speaking of God. A young man of San Severino, who had been excessively vain and worldly, and who was of noble blood and of delicate habits, was converted by one of the holy conversations of Brother Simon, and entered the Order. When he received him into the convent he took from him his secular dress, and the young man remained with Brother Simon to be instructed in the rules. The devil, who is ever on the watch to do evil, tempted him so strongly in the flesh, that he felt it was impossible to resist; and he went to Brother Simon, and said to him, "Give me back my clothes which I wore in the world, as I cannot resist this temptation of the flesh. "Brother Simon, feeling for him great compassion, said to him, "Sit down here awhile with me, my son"; and he spoke to him of God so earnestly, that the temptation left him. Shortly after, however, it returned, and he again went and asked for his clothes, and Brother Simon delivered him from it by speaking to him of God; and he did the same thing several times. At last, one night the same temptation assailed him again with such force, that he felt it was quite impossible to resist; and he went to Brother Simon, and implored him to give him back his scholar's dress, as he could no onger remain in the convent. Brother Simon, as usual, made him sit down by his side, and talked to him of God; the young man listened, and bowing his head sorrowfully, laid it on Brother Simon's breast. The latter, filled with compassion, raised his eyes to Heaven, and prayed that the Lord would have pity on him. As he prayed he was rapt in ecstasy, and his prayer was granted. When he came back to himself, he found the young man quite freed from the temptation, and as calm as if he had never been assaulted; the evil spirit which had raged in his heart was, as it were, converted into the Spirit of God, for he had approached the burning coal of divine love,—that is to say, Brother Simon,— and his heart henceforth was enflamed with the love of God and of his neighbours. Finding himself on one occasion with a malefactor who had been condemned to have both his eyes torn out, he felt such compassion for him that he went boldly to the governor, and in full council implored him with tears and prayers to allow him to give one of his eyes, so that the malefactor might not lose both. The governor and all those who composed his council were so touched by the charity of the monk, that they forgave the culprit. Brother Simon being one day in prayer in the forest, and being greatly annoyed by a flock of crows who disturbed him in his meditations by their cries, he ordered them, in the name of Christ, to go away, and never to return again; and the birds flew away at his command, and were never again seen or heard in all the country round about. And all the farmers of Fermo, where the convent was situated, bore testimony to this miracle.

CHAPTER   FORTY-TWO

OF SEVERAL WONDERFUL MIRACLES WHICH THE LORD PERFORMED THROUGH THE MEANS OF THE HOLY BROTHERS, BROTHER PETER OF MONTICELLO, AND BROTHER CONRAD OF OFFIDA, AND HOW BROTHER BENTIVOGLIO CARRIED A LEPER FIFTEEN MILES IN A VERY SHORT TIME ; HOW ST MICHAEL SPOKE TO ANOTHER BROTHER ; AND HOW THE VIRGIN MARY APPEARED TO BROTHER CONRAD AND PLACED HER DIVINE SON IN HIS ARMS

As the sky is adorned with stars, so the province of the Marsh of Ancona was in former times adorned with Saints and exemplary monks; these, like the bright luminaries in heaven, ornamented the Order of St Francis, and enlightened the world by their doctrine and example. Foremost amongst these was Brother Lucido Antico, in whom indeed shone forth the light of divine charity and holiness; taught by the Spirit of God, his preaching produced innumerable fruits. Another brother, Bentivoglio of Severino, was seen by Brother Masseo raised above the earth as he was praying in the forest, at the sight of which miracle Brother Masseo became a Friar Minor, and grew so holy that he worked many miracles, both during his lifetime and after his death: he is buried at Murro. The said Brother Bentivoglio being once all alone at Trave Bonanti, nursing and serving a leper, received an order from his superior to go to another convent fifteen miles off. Not wishing to abandon the poor leper, he placed him carefully on his back, and charitably took him with him. Between the dawn of day and the rising of the sun he accomplished the fifteen miles, and arrived with his burden at the convent to which he had been sent, which was called the Convent of Mount Sancino. Had he been an eagle, he would not have flown as quickly, and such a miracle caused great wonder and surprise in the country. Another brother, Peter of Monticello, who was the guardian of the old Convent of Ancona, was raised several feet above the earth, to the foot of the crucifix before which he was in prayer. This same Brother Peter, having once observed the Lent of St Michael with great devotion, as he was praying on the last day of the fast in the church, was heard to speak with St Michael by a young man who had hidden himself behind the high altar, in hopes of seeing something wonderful; and

119

the words which he heard were these. The Saint said to Brother Peter, "Thou hast suffered faithfully for my sake, and during many days hast mortified thy body; wherefore I am come to comfort thee, and whatever grace thou wishest to ask of God, I will obtain for thee." Brother Peter answered, "Most holy prince of the celestial hosts of Saints, faithful servant of divine love, and pious protector of souls, this is the grace I ask of thee, namely, that thou obtain from God the pardon of my sins." And St Michael answered, "Ask some other grace, as this I will most easily obtain." And as Brother Peter asked for nothing else, the Archangel added, "Through the faith and devotion which thou hast to me, I will not only obtain for thee this grace, but likewise many others." And when the conversation, which had lasted some time, was ended, the archangel Michael departed, leaving Brother Peter greatly comforted. At the same time lived Brother Conrad of Offida in the Convent of Forano in the province of Ancona, where resided Brother Peter. Having gone one day into the forest to meditate on God, Brother Peter followed him to see what would befall him; and Brother Conrad began to implore the Virgin Mary, with great fervour and devotion, to obtain from her Blessed Son that he might experience somewhat of the sweetness which St Simeon experienced the day of the Purification, when he held in his arms Christ the Blessed. Having finished his prayer, the Virgin Mary obtained his request; and, behold, the Queen of

FLOWERS OF SAINT FRANCIS

Heaven appeared with her Blessed Son in her arms in great splendour, and approaching Brother Conrad placed the Holy Child in his arms. He received Him most reverently, and embracing Him clasped Him to his breast, his heart overflowing and burning with divine love and inexpressible consolation. Brother Peter, who witnessed this scene at a distance, felt likewise in his soul great sweetness and joy. And the Virgin Mary having departed from Brother Conrad, Brother Peter hastened back to the Convent that he might not be seen; but when Brother Conrad arrived, full of joy and happiness, Brother Peter said to him, "O brother, thou hast been greatly comforted to-day!" And Brother Conrad answered, "What sayest thou, Brother Peter? How dost thou know? Hast thou seen me?" "I know," answered Brother Peter, "that the Virgin Mary, with her Blessed Son, has visited thee." And Brother Conrad, who, through great humility, wished to keep secret the graces with which God had favoured him, entreated Brother Peter not to tell any one what he had witnessed; and from henceforth so great was the love which existed between these two brothers, that they seemed to have but one soul and one heart and one mind in all things. The said Brother Conrad, being once in the Convent of Siruolo, delivered a woman who was possessed by the devil, by praying for her a whole night; and her mother having known it, he left the place in the morning, that he might not be discovered and honoured by the people.

CHAPTER FORTY-THREE

HOW BROTHER CONRAD OF OFFIDA CONVERTED A
YOUNG BROTHER, WHO WAS A STUMBLING-BLOCK
TO THE OTHER BROTHERS; AND HOW AFTER DEATH
HIS SOUL APPEARED TO BROTHER CONRAD, BEGGING
HIM TO PRAY FOR HIM; AND HOW THROUGH HIS
PRAYERS HE WAS DELIVERED FROM THE GREAT
PAINS OF PURGATORY

The life of the said Brother Conrad of Offida,
the great advocate of evangelical poverty and of
the rule of St Francis, was so exemplary and so
meritorious in the sight of God, that Christ the
Blessed honoured him with many miracles, not
only after death, but likewise during his life.
Amongst others, being once on a visit to the convent of Offida, the brothers begged him, for the
love of God and holy charity, to reprove a young
brother, who was in the said convent, and whose
conduct was so puerile, so disordered, and his
manners so dissolute, that he distracted both
the young and old brothers at Divine Office, and
cared but little to observe any of the rules of the
Order. At the request of the brothers, and out
of compassion to the said young man, Brother
Conrad called him to him, and reproved him
with so much charity, that the most complete
change took place in his heart, and the dissolute
young man was converted into an edifying brother; he became so obedient, so meek, so devout, so anxious to do what was right, so ready
to serve others, and so zealous in the practice of
every virtue, that the brothers to whom he had
hitherto been a stumbling-block found in him
such comfort and such satisfaction, that they
loved him dearly. Shortly after his conversation

it pleased God to take him out of the world; and his death caused great sorrow to the brothers. A few days after his soul had left his body, it appeared to Brother Conrad as he was in prayer before the altar of the convent, and saluted him as his father. Brother Conrad asked him who he was, and he answered, "I am the soul of the young brother who died a few days ago." And Brother Conrad said to him, "My beloved son, how is it with thee?" And the soul answered, "By the grace of God, and through thy teaching, I have cause to be thankful, for I am not damned; but because of certain sins of which I had not time to repent when I was in the world, I am suffering the pains of Purgatory; and I pray thee, father, as thou hadst compassion on me when I was in life, to help me now by thy prayers, and say for me some Paters, for thy prayers are most acceptable to God." And Brother Conrad, continuing his devotions, said for him a Pater with a Requiem. And the soul said, "O dear father, I am greatly refreshed already, and I pray thee to repeat thy prayer for me." Brother Conrad did as he was begged, and the soul said again, "As thou prayest for me, my sufferings are relieved; wherefore I implore thee not to cease to pray for me." And Brother Conrad, seeing that the soul of the young man was relieved by his prayers, said in his intention a hundred Paters; and when they were finished the soul said to him, "I thank thee, dearest father, in the name of God, for thy great charity towards me; through thy prayers I have been delivered from

123

the pains of Purgatory, and am going to Heaven." And the soul departed. Brother Conrad, in order to comfort and console the brothers, related to them the vision. And the soul of the young brother went to Heaven, through the merits and prayers of Brother Conrad.

CHAPTER   FORTY-FOUR

HOW THE MOTHER OF CHRIST AND ST JOHN THE EVANGELIST APPEARED TO BROTHER CONRAD, AND TOLD HIM WHO HAD SUFFERED THE GREATEST SORROW AT THE PASSION OF CHRIST

When Brother Conrad and the above-mentioned Brother Peter, who were the two shining lights of the province of Ancona, lived together in the Convent of Forano, such love and charity existed between them that they seemed to have but one heart and one soul; and they made a pact between themselves that they would make known to each other and share every mercy which the Lord should send them. Having made this agreement, it happened one day, as Brother Peter was praying and meditating devoutly on the Passion of Christ, and how His Blessed Mother, and St John the Evangelist, and St Francis, were represented at the foot of the cross, as having been crucified with Christ in mental sufferings, he felt a great wish to know which of the three had suffered the greatest sorrow on account of the Passion of Christ—the Mother who had given Him birth, the disciple who had laid his head on His

124

bosom, or St Francis, who was crucified, as it were, with Him. As he was meditating on this, the Virgin Mary appeared to him, with St John the Evangelist and St Francis, all clothed in the celestial vestments of the beatified; and St Francis seemed to be more richly dressed than St John. And Brother Peter was greatly terrified by this vision; but St John comforted him by saying, "Do not fear, dear brother; for we are come to enlighten thy doubts: know, then, that the Mother of Christ, and I, His disciple, have suffered above every other creature at His Passion, and after us St Francis has suffered more than all others; and this is why thou seest him in such glory." And Brother Peter said, "Most holy Apostle of Christ, why are the vestments of St Francis more beautiful than thine?" "Because," answered St John, "when he was in the world, he wore a more humble dress than mine." And having said these words, he gave to Brother Peter a glorious vestment he had in his hand, saying, "Take this dress which I have brought for thee"; and St John being about to put it on him, Brother Peter fell down in terror, and began to cry out, "Brother Conrad, Brother Conrad, haste thou to help me! come and see most wonderful things!" And as he said these words, the vision disappeared. And Brother Peter related to Brother Conrad all he had seen, and they returned thanks to God together.

CHAPTER FORTY-FIVE

OF THE CONVERSION, LIFE, MIRACLES, AND DEATH
OF THE HOLY BROTHER JOHN DELLA PINNA

When Brother John della Pinna was a little
child in the province of Ancona, a beautiful
child appeared to him one night, and calling
him, said, "John, go to Santo Stefano, where
one of my Friars Minor is preaching; listen to
his words, and believe the doctrines he teaches,
for I have sent him to thee. After that thou shalt
make a great journey, and then come to me."
And the child John arose, and was greatly
troubled in mind. On reaching Santo Stefano,
he found a great multitude of men and women
waiting to hear a sermon; and he who was about
to preach was a monk named Philip, who was
one of the first monks who had visited Ancona,
as there were but few convents established in
the province. And the said Brother Philip stood
up to preach; and he did so most devoutly, not
with words of wordly wisdom, but, inspired by
the Spirit of Christ, he announced the kingdom
of eternal life. And the sermon being ended,
the child went to Brother Philip, and said to
him, "Father, if thou wilt receive me into the
Order, most willingly will I do penance, and
serve our Lord Jesus Christ." And Brother
Philip seeing the great innocence of the child,
and his earnest desire to serve God, said to him,
"Come to me on such a day at Ricanati, and I
will receive thee." Now a provincial chapter was
to be held at Ricanati, and the child in his simplicity fancied that was the journey he was to
make according to the vision, and that after hav-

ing accomplished it he would go to Heaven,
which he thought likewise would be as soon as
he had been received into the Order. He went
accordingly to Ricanati, where he was received
into the Order by Brother Philip. Seeing that
it did not happen to him as he had expected,
and the head of the chapter having said that if
any one wished to go to the province of Provenza, for the merit of holy obedience, he would
most willingly give him permission, and Brother John feeling a great desire to go there,—
thinking in his heart that that would be the
journey he was to make before he went to Heav-
en, but not having courage to say so,—he confided his wish to Brother Philip, and entreated him to obtain for him permission to go to
the province of Provenza. And Brother Philip,
seeing his purity and the holiness of his intentions, obtained for him the permission he wished for; and the little Brother John set out on his
way most joyfully, as he believed that, the journey being ended, he would go to Heaven. But
it pleased God that he should remain in the
said province twenty-five years, always looking
forward to the day of his departure, and living
in great sanctity; setting a most holy example,
and increasing in virtue, and in favour with God
and man; he was much beloved by seculars as
well as by the brothers. And Brother John being one day in prayer, weeping and lamenting
that his wish was never accomplished, and his
pilgrimage here below so lengthened, Christ
the Blessed appeared to him, and he felt his

soul melt within him; and the Lord said to him, "My son, Brother John, ask Me what thou wilt." And he answered, "My Lord, I have naught else to ask Thee but Thyself, as I desire naught else; but I ask Thee to forgive my sins, and to grant me the grace that I may see Thee once more, when I shall have the greatest need of Thy presence." And Christ the Blessed answered, "Thy request is granted"; and having said these words He departed, and Brother John was greatly comforted. At last the brothers of the province of Ancona, having heard of the fame of his sanctity, persuaded the General of the Order to command him, out of holy obedience, to return to Ancona. No sooner had the order reached him than he set out most joyfully, hoping that on arriving he would go to Heaven, according to the promise of Christ. On arriving in the province he lived there thirty years, and was not recognised by any of his relations; every day he expected that, through the mercy of God, the promise would be accomplished. During this time he often filled the office of guardian with much discretion, and the Lord performed many miracles for him. Amongst the other gifts he had received from God was the spirit of prophecy. Being once absent from the convent, one of his novices was so strongly tempted by the devil that he determined to leave the Order as soon as Brother John should return. And Brother John having been informed, by the spirit of prophecy, of the temptation, and of the decision of the novice, hastened back to the convent, and having called the novice, ordered him to go to confession; but before he did so he related to him all his temptations, as the Lord had revealed them to him, and ended by saying, "My son, as thou hast waited for me, and wouldst not go away without my blessing, the Lord has had pity on thee, and thou not only wilt not leave the Order, but thou shalt die in it, in the grace of God." And the said novice remained in the Order, and became a holy brother. And these things were related to me by Brother Ugolino. The said Brother John, whose mind was so happy and so calm, very seldom spoke; he was a man of prayer, and very seldom returned to his cell after the night's devotions, but remained in the church till morning. One night after prayers the angel of God appeared to him, and said, "Brother John, thy life is ended, and the moment thou hast so ardently desired is arrived; and I make known to thee from God that thou mayst ask of Him what grace thou wilt. I likewise announce to thee that thou mayst choose between one day in Purgatory, or seven days of sufferings in this world." And Brother John, having chosen the seven days of sufferings in this world, fell ill immediately, and was afflicted with diverse diseases; for he had a great fever, and the gout in his hands and feet, also a pain in his side, and many other sufferings; but what was worse than all this was a devil who stood before him, holding a large paper on which were written all the sins he had ever committed in thought or deed. And the devil said to him, "Because of these sins which thou hast committed, in thought, word, and deed, thou art condemned to the depths of hell." And it seemed to him as if he had never done any good actions; he even forgot that he was in the Order, or had ever been in it, and believed he was damned, as the devil said he was; so that when the brothers asked him how he was, he answered, "I am most unhappy, because I am damned." The brothers seeing this, sent for an aged brother named Brother Mathew of Monte Robbiano, who was a holy man and a great friend of Brother John. When the said Brother Mathew arrived, the seventh day of his sufferings was approaching, and going near him he asked him how he was. "Very ill," was the answer; "and very unhappy, because I am damned." And Brother Mathew said to him, "Dost thou not remember that thou hast often confessed to me, and I have absolved thee of all thy sins? Dost thou not likewise remember that thou hast served God for many years in this holy Order? Dost thou not know that the mercy of God is greater than all the sins in the world, and that Jesus Christ the Blessed, our Saviour, gave Himself for our salvation? Have good hope; for I know of a certainty that thou wilt be saved." And as he spoke the end of the trial arrived, and the temptation disappeared, and Brother John was greatly comforted; and he said to Brother Mathew, "My dear brother, thou art tired, and it is late; I pray thee go and take a little rest." But Brother Mathew would not leave him.

Yielding, however, at last to his prayers, he went to take a little rest, and Brother John remained alone with the monk who served him. And Christ the Blessed appeared in great glory, as He had promised to appear to him once more when he should be in great need of Him, and He healed him of all his infirmities. And Brother John joined his hands, and thanked God for having permitted him to end the long journey of the present miserable life in the arms of Jesus Christ, to whom he confided his soul, passing from this mortal life to life eternal with Christ the Blessed, whom he had so long wished and desired to see. Brother John was buried in the Convent della Pinna di San Giovanni.

CHAPTER   FORTY-SIX

HOW BROTHER PACIFICO, BEING IN PRAYER, SAW THE SOUL OF BROTHER UMILE, HIS BROTHER IN THE FLESH, GO UP TO HEAVEN

After the death of St Francis, two brothers of the province of Ancona entered the Order; one was named Brother Umile, and the other Brother Pacifico; both attained a great degree of perfection and sanctity. Brother Umile lived in the Convent of Saffiano, and died there; Brother Pacifico lived in another convent, at some distance. It pleased God that Brother Pacifico, being one day in prayer in a solitary place, was rapt in ecstasy, and saw the soul of his brother, which had just left his body, go

131

straight to Heaven without any hindrance.
Many years after this, Brother Pacifico was
sent to the Convent of Saffiano, where his brother had died, at the time when the monks, at
the demands of the Lords of Bruforte, changed their convent for another, and were removing the remains of the holy brothers who had
died there. When the grave of Brother Umile
was opened, his brother took his bones, and
having washed them in wine, wrapped them
carefully in a white napkin, and weeping over
them, kissed them with great devotion. The
other brothers were much surprised that he
should set them such a bad example, and could
not understand how a man so holy could show
such an early affection towards his brother,
and honour his remains so far above those
of the other monks, who, not having been less
holy than Brother Umile, were worthy of the
same honour. And Brother Pacifico, knowing
how he was misjudged by the brothers, humbly explained to them his conduct, saying, "My
most dear brothers, do not be surprised if I
have honoured the bones of my brother above
those of the other monks; for, thanks be to God,
it is not through carnal affection that I have
done so, but because when my brother left this
life I was praying in a solitary place, very far
from the convent where he lay dead, and I saw
his soul go straight up to Heaven; wherefore I
am sure that his bones are holy, and will be
honoured in Heaven. If the Lord had revealed
to me the same thing of the other monks, I

should have treated their remains with equal reverence." And the brothers being convinced that his intentions were holy and just, were greatly edified by what he had told them, and praised God, who did such wonderful things for His holy monks.

CHAPTER FORTY-SEVEN

OF A HOLY BROTHER TO WHOM THE MOTHER OF CHRIST APPEARED WHEN HE WAS ILL, AND BROUGHT HIM THREE VASES OF HEALING OINTMENT

In the above-mentioned Convent of Saffiano lived formerly a Friar Minor so holy that there appeared to be something supernatural about him, and he was often rapt in God. He possessed the grace of contemplation; and often when he was ravished and raised above the earth in ecstasy, all kinds of birds came and perched on his head, on his arms, and on his hands, and sang most wonderfully. He was very fond of solitude, and rarely spoke; but when any one asked him a question, he answered so wisely and so graciously that he seemed to be rather an angel than a mortal. He was a man of prayer and contemplation, and the brothers held him in great reverence. Having finished the course of virtuous life, it was the will of God that he should fall dangerously ill, so that he could take no nourishment; and he refused all human remedies, placing all his hope in the celestial Physician, Jesus Christ the Blessed, and His divine Mother, by whom

133

through the mercy of God, he was visited and healed. As he was lying on his bed, preparing for death with all his heart and with great devotion, the glorious Virgin Mary, Mother of Christ, appeared to him with a great multitude of angels and holy virgins, and surrounded by much splendour; she approached his bed, and seeing her, he experienced great comfort and joy both in his body and in his soul, and began to pray to her humbly, to ask of her Divine Son to deliver his soul from its miserable prison of flesh. And as he went on praying, with many tears, the Virgin Mary called him by his name, and said to him, "My son, have no doubts; for thy prayer is granted, and I am come to comfort thee a little before thou leavest this world." By the side of the Virgin Mary were three holy virgins, holding in their hands three vases filled with a sweet ointment; and the Virgin Mary took one of the vases and opened it, and all the house was filled with the odour thereof; and taking a spoonful of the contents, she gave it to the sick brother. No sooner had he tasted it than he experienced such a sweet sensation, that it seemed as if his soul could no longer remain in his body, and he cried out, "No more, O blessed Virgin Mary; no more, O blessed physician, whose pleasure it is to save the human race from perishing; I cannot endure such sweetness." But the compassionate Mother of God continued to give him the ointment, until the vase was emptied. The first vase being emptied, the blessed Virgin took the second, and was about to give him the contents; but he said, "O blessed Mother of God, if my soul is, as it were, melted by the sweetness and virtue of the ointment thou hast already given me, how shall I ever be able to support the effect of the second vase? I pray thee, O Virgin, blessed above all the Saints and all the Angels, not to give me any more." The glorious Virgin Mary answered, "Taste, my son, a little of the second vase"; and having given him a little, she said, "Thou hast sufficient, my son, for today; I will come again shortly to conduct thee to the kingdom of my Son, whom thou hast always sought and desired"; and having said these words, she took leave of him, and departed. And the brother was so strengthened and comforted by the medicine she had given him, that he lived several days in perfect health, without taking any nourishment. Shortly after, as he was gaily talking with the brothers, he passed from this miserable life most joyfully.

CHAPTER FORTY-EIGHT

HOW BROTHER JAMES DELLA MASSA SAW IN A VISION
ALL THE FRIARS MINOR IN THE WORLD IN THE FORM
OF A TREE ; AND HOW THE VIRTUES, THE MERITS
AND THE VICES OF ALL WERE MADE KNOWN TO HIM

Brother James della Massa, to whom the Lord revealed many secrets, and to whom He gave a perfect knowledge of the Holy Scriptures and of the future, was so holy, that Brother Giles of Assisi, Brother Mark of Montino, Brother Juniper, and Brother Lucido said of him, that they knew no one in the world who was greater in the sight of God than this Brother James. I had a great wish to see him; for having asked Brother John, the companion of Brother Giles, to explain to me certain spiritual things, he said to me, "If thou will be well directed in spiritual things, try to speak with Brother James della Massa; for his words being the words of the Holy Spirit, one can neither add nor take away any thing from them, and there is not a man on earth I have a greater wish to see." When Brother John was superior of the convent, this Brother James was once, in prayer, ravished in God, and remained three days in ecstasy, quite insensible to all corporal sensations, so that the brothers thought he was dead; and during this ecstasy many things which regarded the Order were revealed to him; and having learnt this, my wish to speak to him and to hear him greatly increased. When the Lord permitted me to see him, I thus addressed him: "If that which I have heard of thee be true, I pray thee not to conceal it from me. I have heard that when thou wast three days as if thou hadst been dead, amongst other things, the Lord revealed to thee what was to take place in our Order; and this was told me by Brother Mathew, to whom thou hadst revealed it out of obedience." Brother James confessed most humbly that what Brother Mathew had said was true. And this is what Brother Mathew told me: "I know a brother to whom the Lord has made known that which will take place in our Order; for Brother James della Massa has told me that after the Lord had revealed to him many things concerning the Church militant, he saw in a vision a large and beautiful tree, the root of which was of gold, and all the branches were men, and these men were all Friars Minor; and there were as many large branches as there were provinces in the Order, and each branch was composed of as many brothers as there were in each province; and he was informed of the number of brothers in the Order and in each province, of their names, their ages, their rank, and the different offices they filled; also their various merits and defects. And he saw Brother John of Parma at the summit of the highest branch o the tree, and round him were the ministers of each province; and he saw Christ the Blessed sitting on a throne, who calling St Francis to Him, gave him a chalice full of the spirit of life, saying, 'Go to thy brothers, and give them to drink of this spirit of life, as Satan will rise up against them, and many will fall and not rise again." And Christ the Blessed gave to St Francis two angels to accompany him; and St Francis took the chalice to his brothers, and offered it first to Brother John of Parma, who taking it drank all its contents in haste and with great reverence, and having done so he became luminous like the sun. And after him St Francis offered it to all the others; and very few there were who took it, and drank with devotion: those who did so, were filled with light, like the sun; but those who took the chalice and threw away its contents most irreverently, became black and deformed, and horrible to look at; those who drank a part of the contents and threw away the rest, were partly bright and partly dark, in proportion to the quantity they had drunk or thrown away. The brightest of all was the said Brother John, who, having emptied to the dregs the cup of life, had seen by the aid of a celestial light the tempests and troubles which were about to rise against the tree, and shake and tear its branches; for which reason the said Brother John left the top of the tree where he was, and placing himself under its branches hid himself close to the roots. A brother who had partly drunk and partly thrown away the contents of the chalice, took possession of the place on the branch he had left; no sooner was he there, than the nails of his fingers became like points of iron; on seeing this, he hastened to leave the place he had taken, and in his fury sought to vent his rage on Brother John; and Brother John perceiving his intention, cried out to Christ the Blessed, who was seated on His throne, to help him; and Christ the Blessed, hearing his cry, called St Francis, and giving him a sharp stone, said, 'Take this stone, and go and cut the nails of the brother, who seeks to tear Brother John, so that he may not be able to do him any harm." And St Francis did as he was ordered In the mean time a great tempest arose, and the wind shook the tree in such a way that all the brothers fell to the ground.

FLOWERS OF SAINT FRANCIS

First fell those who had thrown away the contents of the chalice of the spirit of life: these were carried by devils to dark regions, full of pain and anguish; but Brother John, and others who had drunk of the chalice, were carried by angels to the regions of life eternal, full of light and splendour. And Brother James, who witnessed this vision, saw clearly the names, the condition, and the fate of each brother. And the tempest did not cease till the tree was blown down, and carried away by the wind; and immediately another tree arose out of the golden roots of the old one, and it was entirely composed of gold, and its leaves and fruits; and we will not describe for the present the beauty, the virtues, and the delicious fragrance of this wonderful tree."

CHAPTER FORTY-NINE
HOW CHRIST APPEARED TO BROTHER JOHN OF ALVERNIA

Amongst the learned and holy brothers and sons of St Francis, who, as Solomon says, form the glory of their fathers, was the venerable and holy Brother John of Fermo, of the province of Ancona, who lived in our times. Having spent the greater part of his life in the Convent of Vernia, he died there, and was known by the name of Brother John of Alvernia; he was a man of great holiness and great sanctity. This Brother John, when he was a child, greatly loved the ways of penance, which preserve the purity of the body and of the soul; and at a very tender age he began to wear a belt of iron, and observed great fasting and abstinence; more especially he used these mortifications when he was residing with the Canons of San Pietro di Fermo, who lived in great luxury; he avoided all pleasures, and macerated his body with great severity. His companions, being against such penitential ways, tried by every means to turn him from them, taking from him his instruments of penance, and preventing him from fasting; the holy child, inspired by God, resolved to leave the world and its worshipers, and put himself in the arms of his crucified Lord, taking the habit of the crucified St Francis; which he did. Having been received into the Order so young, and confided to the care of the master of the novices, he grew so spiritual and so devout, that whenever he heard the said master speak of God, he felt his heart burn within him, as if it had been on fire, so that it was impossible for him to remain quiet, and he ran to and fro in the garden, in the forest, and even in the church; so sweet was the sensation he experienced, that it seemed to him as if his heart melted like wax before the fire. As time went on, this holy youth advanced from virtue to virtue, and his soul was adorned and enriched with spiritual gifts; he was often rapt in ecstasy, so that his mind was at times raised to the splendours of the cherubim, at times to the ardour of the seraphim and the joys of the beatified. At one time this ecstasy of divine love, which seemed, as it were, to set his heart on fire, lasted three years, and this took place on the holy mountain of Alvernia. But as God takes especial care of His children, sending them at different times consolations and tribulations, adversity and prosperity, according to their need, in order to preserve in them the grace of humility, or to awaken in their hearts a greater thirst after spiritual things, so it pleased His divine bounty, when the three years were ended, to withdraw from Brother John this flame of celestial love, and take from him every spiritual consolation. Brother John was most disconsolate and sorrowful, and this great trial made him so miserable, that he wandered about the forest, crying out with sighs and tears for the beloved Spouse of his soul, as his soul without His presence could enjoy neither peace nor rest. And nowhere could he find his Beloved, or recover those sweet spiritual sensations to which the love of Christ had accustomed him. And this trial lasted several days, during which he persevered in prayer, weeping and sighing, and imploring the Lord to take pity on his soul, and restore to him his Beloved. At last, his patience having been sufficiently tried, as he was wandering one day sorrowfully in the forest he sat down, overcome with fatigue; and as he was gazing up to Heaven, with his eyes full of tears, Jesus Christ the Blessed appeared to him, standing in silence in the path by which he had come himself. Brother John knew Him to be the Christ, and throwing himself at His feet he burst into a flood of tears, and thus addressed Him: "Help me, O my Lord! for without Thee, my sweet Saviour, I am in sorrow and in darkness; without Thee, gentle Lamb, I am in anguish and in fear; without Thee, Son of the most high God, I am in confusion and in shame; without Thee, I am despoiled of every good, for Thou, Jesus Christ, art the true light of my soul; without Thee, I am lost and damned, for Thou art the life of souls, the life of life; without Thee, I am sterile and unfruitful, for Thou art the fountain of every grace; without Thee, I can have no consolation, for Thou, Jesus, art our Redeemer, our love, our desire, the bread of comfort, the wine which rejoices the hearts of Angels and of Saints; enlighten me, O pitying Shepherd, for I am Thy lamb, though most unworthy." When the Lord delays to grant the desires of holy men, their love towards Him greatly increaseth; for this reason Christ the Blessed left Brother John, going from him without granting his request, and without speaking to him. Then Brother John rose, and running after Him threw himself again at His feet, imploring Him not to leave him, and crying out, "O Jesus Christ, most sweet Saviour, have mercy on me in my trouble; by the truth of Thy salvation and the multitude of Thy mercies, restore to me the joy of Thy countenance, and cast upon me a look of pity; for the earth is full of Thy mercy." But the Lord Jesus went from him without saying a word, or leaving him any consolation; and Brother John followed Him with greater fervour, and when he came up to Him, Christ the Blessed turned round, and looking at him most sweetly, He opened His holy and merciful arms and embraced him; and when He opened His arms Brother John saw rays of light come from His holy bosom, which lighted up all the forest, as well as His own soul and body. Then Brother John knelt down at the feet of Christ the Blessed, who, as He had given His foot to Mary Magdalene to kiss, so He gave it to Brother John. And Brother John, taking it with great reverence, bathed it with his tears like another Magdalene, saying most devoutly, "I pray Thee, my Lord, not to look at my sins, but by Thy holy Passion, and by the precious Blood which Thou hast shed, awaken my soul to the grace of Thy love, as Thou hast commanded us to love Thee, with all our heart and with all our strength; which commandment none can fulfil without Thy help. Help me, then, beloved Son of God, that I may love Thee with all my heart and all my strength." And as Brother John was thus praying at the feet of Christ, his prayer was granted, and the flame of divine love which he had lost was restored to him, and he felt himself greatly comforted. Knowing that the gift of divine grace had been restored to him, he began to return thanks to Christ the Blessed, and devoutly kiss His feet. Then standing up, and looking on the Saviour's face, Jesus Christ gave him His holy hands to kiss; having kissed them, Brother John approached the bosom of Christ, and embraced Him. Christ the Blessed received him in His arms; and as Brother John embraced the Saviour, and was embraced by Him, the air was filled with the sweetest perfumes, so sweet that no other perfume in the world could be compared with them. And Brother John was consoled, and enlightened, and rapt in ecstasy, and this sweet perfume lasted in his soul many months; and from thenceforth from his lips, which had drunk at the fountain of divine wisdom on the sacred bosom of the Saviour, fell the most wonderful and celestial words, which changed the hearts of those who heard them, and produced great fruits in souls; and for a long time, whenever Brother John followed the path in the forest where the blessed feet of Christ had passed, he saw the same wonderful light and breathed the same sweet odour. When Brother John came back to himself after this vision, though the corporal presence of Christ had disappeared, his mind was so enlightened and so imbued with divine wisdom, that although he was not a learned man, or versed in human studies, he explained most wonderfully the most difficult questions on the Holy Trinity and the profound mysteries of Holy Writ; and when speaking before the Pope, the Cardinals, the king, the barons, the masters, and doctors, they were surprised at his sublime discourse, and at the words of wisdom which he pronounced.

SAINT FRANCIS IN MEDITATION

SAINT FRANCIS REVEALS HIMSELF, AFTER
HIS DEATH, TO A HOLY BROTHER

CHAPTER FIFTY

As Brother John was saying Mass on the day after All Saints, for the souls of the dead, as the
Church has ordered, he offered with such charity and such compassion the holy sacrifice, which
the dead desire above every thing else we can
give them, that he seemed to be overwhelmed
and consumed by the ardour of the feelings
which filled his heart; and when he lifted up
devoutly the Body of Christ and offered it to
God the Father, entreating Him, for the love of
His blessed Son Jesus Christ, who had died on
the cross for the souls of men, to deliver from
the pains of Purgatory the souls of the dead
which He had created and redeemed, he saw
immediately an immense number of souls go
out of Purgatory, like innumerable sparks of
fire coming out of a burning oven; and he saw
them go up to Heaven, through the merits of
the Passion of Christ, who is daily offered for
the living and the dead in that most holy sacrifice, which is worthy to be adored for ever and
ever.

CHAPTER FIFTY-ONE

At the time that Brother James of Fallarone, a
man of great sanctity, was dangerously ill in the

FLOWERS OF SAINT FRANCIS

Convent of Moliano, which was under the jur-
isdiction of Fermo, Brother John of Alvernia,
who was then living in the Convent of Massa,
hearing of his illness, and loving him as his
dear father, began to pray for him, imploring
God most devoutly in mental prayer to restore
to Brother James the health of the body, if it
were for the good of his soul. As he prayed he
was rapt in ecstasy, and he saw in the air a great
army of Angels and Saints above his cell, which
was in the forest; they were surrounded by such
splendour and glory, that all the country round
about was illuminated. Amongst the Angels he
saw the said Brother James, for whom he was
praying, clothed in white and shining raiments;
he also saw the holy father St Francis, with the
marks of the cross on his hands and feet, looking most glorious; he likewise recognised Brother Lucido Santo, and Brother Mathew of
Monte Robbiano, and many other brothers he
had neither seen nor known in this life. And as
he contemplated with great delight that holy
band of Saints, it was revealed to him that the
sick brother for whom he had been praying
would die of the disease of which he was lying
ill, and that his soul would be saved; but that
he would not go straight to Heaven after death,
as it was necessary he should be purified for a
time in Purgatory. And this revelation made to
Brother John filled his heart with such joy that
he did not grieve over the death of Brother
James, but experienced great sweetness in his
soul, and said within himself, "Brother James,

my sweet father; Brother James, my sweet brother; Brother James, faithful servant and friend of God; Brother James, companion of the Angels and one of the army of Saints!" And as he was thus rejoicing he came to himself; and he left the convent immediately, and went to visit Brother James at Moliano, and found him so much worse that he could scarcely speak. And he announced to him the death of his body and the salvation and glory of his soul, of which he was certain through divine revelation; and Brother James received him most joyfully, thanking him for the good news he brought him, and praying him devoutly not to forget him. And Brother John begged him after death to come to him and tell him where he was and how it fared with him, which Brother James promised, should it please the Lord. The moment of his death approaching, Brother James began to repeat with great devotion the verse of the psalm, "In pace in idipsum dormiam et requiescam"; which signifies, "I will go to sleep in peace in life eternal, and will rest"; and having said these words, he left this world, with a joyful countenance. When he was buried, Brother John returned to the Convent of Massa, and there awaited the accomplishment of the promise of Brother James that he would appear to him after death. As he was in prayer on that same day, Christ the Blessed appeared to him surrounded by a multitude of Angels and Saints; but Brother James was not with them, which greatly surprised Brother John, who recommended him most devoutly to Christ the Blessed. The following day, as he was again praying in the forest, Brother James appeared in the company of Angels, his countenance beaming with joy; and Brother John said to him, "O most dear father, why didst thou not appear to me on the day thou promised?" Brother James answered, "Because it was necessary that I should be purified in Purgatory; but at the same hour that Christ appeared to thee, and in which thou didst recommend me to Him, He granted thy prayer and I was free from all suffering, and I appeared to Brother James of Massa, a holy lay brother, who was serving Mass; and I saw the consecrated wafer, when the priest lifted it up, converted into a beautiful living child; and I said to him, This day I shall go with Him to life eternal, where none can go without Him." And having said these words, Brother James disappeared, and went up to Heaven with the holy company of Angels, and Brother John was greatly comforted. The said Brother James of Fallarone died on the night of St James the Apostle, in the month of July, in the above-mentioned Convent of Moliano; and through his merits the Lord did many miracles after his death.

CHAPTER   FIFTY-TWO

OF THE VISION OF BROTHER JOHN OF ALVERNIA, BY
WHICH HE BECAME ACQUAINTED WITH ALL THE
ORDER OF THE HOLY TRINITY

The said Brother John of Alvernia having renounced all worldly joys and temporal consolations, and having placed all his hopes in God,
the divine bounty granted him many consolations, especially in the days which commemorated some act of Christ the Blessed. As the
Nativity of Christ was approaching, in which
he expected some great consolation from God,
the Holy Spirit filled his heart with such love
to Christ, who had humbled Himself so as to
take upon Him our humanity, that it seemed
truly as if his soul were a burning furnace; and
the great love which consumed his heart agit-
ated him so violently, that he could not resist
the ardour of the Holy Spirit, or prevent himself from crying out. At the same time that he
experienced this great fervour he felt such a
security of his salvation, that it seemed to him,
had he died at that moment, that he would not
have suffered in Purgatory; and this state lasted six months, though he did not always feel
the same degree of fervour, but it increased at
certain hours of the day. During that time he
received many wonderful visitations and consolations from God, and was often ravished in
ecstasy, as was seen by the brother who wrote
these things. One night especially he was so rapt
in God, that he saw in Him all things created,
both celestial and terrestrial, with all their per-
fections and their various orders and degrees;

and he knew most clearly how every thing created presents itself to its Creator, and how God is above, and in, and around all things created. He was likewise made acquainted with one God in Three Persons and Three Persons in one God, and the infinite love which made the Son of God become man out of obedience to the Father. He was likewise informed in this vision how there is no other way by which the soul can go to God, and have life eternal, but through Christ the Blessed, who is the way, the truth, and the life of the soul.

CHAPTER   FIFTY-THREE

HOW, AS HE WAS SAYING MASS, BROTHER JOHN OF ALVERNIA FELL DOWN, AS IF HE HAD BEEN DEAD

A most wonderful thing befell Brother John in the above-mentioned Convent of Moliano, as is related by the brothers who were present. The first night after the Octave of St Laurence, within the Octave of the Assumption of our Lady, having said Matins in the church with the other brothers, his heart was filled with divine grace, and he went into the garden to meditate on the Passion of Christ, and prepare himself most devoutly to celebrate Mass, which it was his turn to sing the next morning. As he was meditating on the words of the consecration of the Body of Christ, and contemplating the boundless charity of Jesus, who not only bought us with His precious Blood, but left as food for our souls His Body and His Blood, the love of the sweet Jesus so filled his heart that he could not contain himself, and cried out several times, *Hoc est Corpus meum.* As he said these words Christ the Blessed appeared to him, with the Virgin Mary and a multitude of angels, and the Spirit of God made known to him the mysteries of that great sacrament. When day dawned he entered the church, so absorbed by all he had seen that he repeated aloud the above words, with great fervour of spirit, not believing he was seen or heard by any one; but there was a brother praying in the choir who saw and heard everything; and he remained in this state till the hour came to say Mass. He approached the altar, and began the sacrifice; as he proceeded his heart was overflowing with love to Christ, and the sensation he experienced was so ineffable that he could not express it in words, and he doubted whether he ought to leave off the celebration of Mass or to go on. The same thing having happened to him before, and the Lord having moderated the sensation, so that he was enabled to finish the sacrifice, trusting that He would do so again, he proceeded, with great fear and trembling. When he arrived at the Preface of our Lady, the divine illumination and the sensation of ardent love towards God so increased in his heart, that when he reached the *qui pridie* he could scarcely resist any longer. When he came to the Consecration, and had pronounced over the Host half of the words, that is to say, *Hoc est,* it was quite impossible for

151

him to go on, but he repeated over and over the same words, *Hoc est enim*; and the reason why he could not proceed was, that he saw before him Christ Himself, with a multitude of angels, and he could not endure His Majesty. He saw that Christ would not enter the Host, nor would it be changed into the Body of Christ, unless he pronounced the other words of the Consecration, namely, *Corpus meum*. Being greatly perplexed and unable to go on, the guardian, with the other brothers, and the people who were in the church to hear Mass, approached the altar, greatly alarmed to see and consider the actions of Brother John; and many were moved to tears by his devotion. At last, after a long time, it pleased God that Brother John should pronounce in a loud voice the words, *enim Corpus meum*; and immediately the form of bread was changed, and Jesus Christ the Blessed appeared in the Host, in His bodily shape, and in great glory; showing thereby the humility and charity which made Him to take flesh of the Virgin Mary, and which now places Him daily in the hands of the priest when he consecrates the Host. When Brother John had elevated the Host and the consecrated chalice, he was ravished out of himself, and all corporal sensations being suspended, his body fell back. If he had not been supported by the guardian, who was behind him, he would have fallen to the ground; and all the brothers and the men and women who were in the church collected round him, and he was carried to the sacristy as dead, for

his body was quite cold, and his fingers so stiff-
ened that they could not be opened or moved;
and he remained in this state till the third hour,
and it was summer. When he came back to himself, I, who was present, feeling a great desire
to know what he had experienced, went to him,
and begged him, for the love of God, to tell me
every thing. As he greatly trusted me, he related all that had happened to him; amongst
other things he told me that as he was consecrating the Body and Blood of Christ, his soul
seemed to melt within him like wax, and his
body to be without bones, so that he could not
lift his arms or his hands, or make the sign of
the cross on the wafer or on the chalice. He
likewise told me that, before he became a priest,
it had been revealed to him by God that he
should faint away when saying Mass; but having
said many Masses, and no such thing having yet
happened to him, he thought that the revelation could not have come from God. Nevertheless, about fifty days before the Assumption
of our Lady, when this thing befell him, it had
been again revealed to him by God that it should
so happen to him about the time of the Feast
of the Assumption. But he had afterwards for-
gotten this vision or revelation from our Lord.

OF THE SACRED AND HOLY STIG-
MATA OF ST FRANCIS,

AND CERTAIN CONSIDERATIONS THEREUPON

In this part we will treat concerning sundry
devout considerations of the glorious, sacred

FLOWERS OF SAINT FRANCIS

and holy stigmata of our blessed father St Francis, which he received from Christ on the holy mountain of Alvernia. And inasmuch as the said stigmata were five, according to the five Wounds of our Lord Jesus Christ, therefore this treatise shall contain five considerations.

The first consideration shall be of the manner in which St Francis came to the holy mountain of Alvernia.

The second consideration shall be of his life and conversation with his companions on that same holy mountain.

The third consideration shall be of the seraphical apparition, and the impression of the sacred stigmata.

The fourth consideration shall be of the descent of St Francis from Mount Alvernia after he had received the sacred stigmata, and of his return to St Mary of the Angels.

The fifth consideration shall be of certain apparitions and divine revelations vouchsafed, after the death of St Francis, to certain holy friars and other devout persons, concerning these sacred and glorious stigmata.

1. OF THE FIRST CONSIDERATION OF THE SACRED STIGMATA

Concerning the first consideration, be it known that in the year 1224 St Francis, being in his forty-third year, went, by the inspiration of God, from the Valley of Spoleto into Romagna, taking with him Brother Leo as his companion; and on their way they passed by the Castle of Montefeltro, where was a great concourse of people, and a solemn banquet held, by reason that one of the Counts of Montefeltro was that day to receive his knighthood. And when St Francis heard of it, and that many gentlemen of various countries were gathered together there, he said to Brother Leo, "Come, let us go up unto this festival; for, by God's help, we shall gather some rich spiritual fruit therefrom."

Now, among other men of high degree who had come together to this feast, there was a certain gentleman of Tuscany who was both rich and mighty. He was called Orlando da Chiusi di Casentino; and for the marvellous things which he had heard of the holiness and the miracles of St Francis, he bore him great devotion, and had an exceeding desire to see him and to hear him preach.

St Francis, then, being come to this castle, entered into the courtyard where all these gentlemen were assembled; and, in fervour of spirit, he mounted on a low wall, and began to preach, choosing for the theme of his discourse these words in the vulgar tongue:

"So great is the joy which I expect,
That all pain is joy to me."

And upon this theme, by the direction of the Holy Ghost, he preached so profoundly and so devoutly, proving it by the divers pains and sufferings of the holy apostles and martyrs, and by the manifold tribulations and temptations of holy virgins and all other saints, that all that multitude of men hung upon his words both

155

with their ears and hearts, and hearkened to him as to an angel of God. Among whom the said Orlando, being touched in heart by God through the miraculous preaching of St Francis, was led to speak to him after the sermon touching the state of his soul. So he took him aside, and said to him, "O father, I would fain take counsel with thee concerning the salvation of my soul." And St Francis answered him. "It pleaseth me well: but go now and pay respect to thy friends, who have bidden thee to this feast, and dine with them; and after dinner we will speak together as much as it shall please thee."

Orlando, therefore, went to dine, and after dinner he returned again to St Francis, and discoursed fully with him concerning the state of his soul, and in the end he said to him, "I have a mountain in Tuscany, a devout and solitary place, called Mount Alvernia, far from all concourse of men, well fitted for one who would do penance for his sins, or who desires to lead a solitary life; if it please thee, I will freely give it to thee and thy companions for the welfare of my soul."

When St Francis heard this bountiful offer of a thing which he had greatly desired, he was exceeding glad, and thanking and praising God in the first place, and after Him Orlando, he thus replied: "Orlando, as soon as thou shalt have returned to the house, I will send some of our brethren to thee, to whom thou shalt show this place; and if it shall seem to them well fitted for prayer and penance, I will at once accept thy charitable offer."

Having said thus, St Francis departed, and returned to St Mary of the Angels; and Orlando likewise returned to his castle, which was called Chiusi, and was about a mile's distance from Mount Alvernia. St Francis then sent two of his companions to the said Orlando, who received them with much charity and gladness; and he sent with them to Mount Alvernia full fifty armed men, to be their defence against wild-beasts. And these brethren, being thus accompanied, ascended the mount, and searched diligently, until at last they came to a spot well fitted for devout contemplation; and this they chose for their habitation, and, with the help of the armed men in their company, they made some little cells of branches of trees; and thus they accepted this Mount Alvernia, and took possession of it in the name of God, and forthwith returned again unto St Francis, who rejoiced greatly at what they told him, and, thanking and praising God, spoke with a joyful countenance to these friars, saying, "My children, we draw near to our Lent of St Michael the Archangel. I firmly believe it to be the will of God that we spend this Lent upon Mount Alvernia, which, by divine dispensation has been prepared for us, that we by penance may merit from our Lord the consolation of consecrating this blessed mount to the honour and glory of God, of His glorious Mother the Virgin Mary, and of the holy angels."

FLOWERS OF SAINT FRANCIS

And having said this, St Francis took with him Brother Masseo of Marignano of Assisi; and Brother Angelo Tancredi of Rieti, who, in the world, had been a noble knight, and was still noted for his gentle courtesy; and Brother Leo, who was a man of the greatest simplicity and purity, for which cause St Francis greatly loved him.

And with these three brethren St Francis betook himself to prayer, and then, having also recommended himself and his companions to prayers of the brethren who were left behind, he set forth with these three, in the name of Jesus Christ crucified, to go to Mount Alvernia. And on the way he called Brother Masseo to him, and said, "Brother Masseo, thou shalt be our guardian and our superior on this journey, both on our way and while we sojourn together on the mount; and we will observe our wonted custom, which is, that one while we will say Office, one while we will speak of God, one while we will keep silence; and we take no thought beforehand of eating, or drinking, or sleeping, but when the evening comes we will beg a little bread, and stay and rest ourselves in that place which God shall prepare for us."

Then these three comrades bowed their heads, and making the sign of the cross went on their way: and the first evening they came to a house of the brethren, and there abode. The second evening, because the weather was bad and they were weary, they could not reach any house of friars, neither any town nor castle; wherefore, when the night came on, they took shelter in a ruined and deserted church, and there lay down to rest. Now, while his companions slept, St Francis betook himself to prayer; and, behold, in the first watch of the night there came to him a multitude of furious demons with great noise and frenzy, and began to attack him on all sides, in order to disturb him in his prayer; but they could not, because God was with him. When St Francis, then, had endured that conflict a long time, he began to cry aloud, "O accursed spirits, you can do nothing but by the divine permission; and therefore I bid you, on the behalf of the omnipotent God, to do with my body whatsoever He shall permit you to do, and most willingly will I endure it; because I have no greater enemy than my body, and therefore if you will avenge me upon it you shall do me good service." Then did the devils begin to torment him worse than before. But he cried out, and said, "O my Lord Jesus Christ, I thank Thee for this Thy great love and charity towards me; for it is a token of great love when the Lord punishes His servant well in this life, that so he may not be punished in the other. And I am ready gladly to endure every pain and suffering which Thou, my God, art pleased to send me for my sins." Then the devils dispersed and left him, being vanquished and confounded by his patience and constancy. And St Francis left the church in great fervour of spirit, and went into a wood

159

hard by, and there, beating his breast, with sighs and tears, sought after Jesus, the Beloved of his soul. And having found Him at last, in the secret of his heart, now he spoke reverently to Him as his Lord, now he made answer to Him as his judge, now he besought Him as his father, now he conversed with Him as his friend. On that night and in that wood, his companions, being awake and listening to him, heard him with many tears and cries implore the divine mercy on behalf of sinners. He was heard to weep aloud for the Passion of Christ, as if he had beheld it with his bodily eyes. On that same night he was seen praying with his arms outstretched, in the form of a cross, and thus lifted up and suspended for a long time in the air surrounded with a dazzling glory. And so, in these holy exercises, he passed all that night without sleeping.

And the next morning, his companions, knowing he was too weak to walk, went to a poor labourer of the country, and prayed him, for the love of God, to lend his ass to Brother Francis their father, for he was not able to travel on foot. When the poor man heard them speak of Brother Francis, he asked them, "Are you some of the brethren of that friar of Assisi of whom men speak so much good?" And the friars made answer, that it was even he for whom they would borrow the ass. Then that good man made ready the ass with great care and devotion, and brought it to St Francis, and with great reverence caused him to mount thereon. So the brethren set forth again, the poor man following behind his ass.

And when they had gone forward a little, the peasant said to St Francis, "Tell me, art thou Brother Francis of Assisi?" And St Francis answered, "Yes." "Take heed, then," said the peasant, "that thou be in truth as good as all men account thee; for many have great faith in thee, and therefore I admonish thee to be no other than what the people take thee for."

When St Francis heard these words, he was not angry at being thus admonished by a peasant, neither did he say within himself, as many a proud friar who in our days wears his cowl would say, "What right has such a creature as this to admonish me?" But instantly dismounting from the ass, he knelt down upon the ground before that poor man; and kissing his feet, humbly thanked him for that his charitable admonition. Then the peasant, together with the companions of St Francis, with great devotion raised him from the ground, and placed him again upon the ass, and so went on their way.

And when they were come to about the midst of the ascent of the mount, because the way was toilsome, and the heat exceeding great, the peasant was overcome with thirst, insomuch that he began to cry after St Francis, saying, "Alas! alas! I am dying of thirst; unless I have something to drink, I shall presently faint."

Then St Francis dismounted from the ass, and betook himself to prayer, and remained upon his knees, with his hands lifted up to heaven,

FLOWERS OF SAINT FRANCIS

until he knew by inspiration that his prayer was heard. Then he said to the peasant, "Run quickly to yonder rock, and there thou shalt find a living stream of water, which Jesus Christ of His mercy has caused to flow from the stone." So he went to the place which St Francis had shown to him, and found a beautiful fountain, issuing by virtue of the prayer of St Francis, from that hard rock; and he drank of it plentifully, and was refreshed. This done, St Francis, with his companions and the peasant, returned thanks to God for the miracle thus vouchsafed, and went on their way; and when they drew near to the rock Alvernia, it pleased St Francis to rest awhile under an oak, which was on the way, and is still to be seen there, and from thence he began to consider the position of the place and the country. And while he was thus considering, behold there came a great multitude of birds of divers regions, which, by singing and clapping their wings, testified great joy and gladness, and surrounded St Francis in such wise, that some perched upon his shoulders, some on his arms, some in his bosom, and others at his feet, which when his companions and the peasant saw, they marvelled greatly; but St Francis, being joyful of heart, said to them, "I believe, dearest brethren, that our Lord Jesus Christ is pleased that we should dwell on this solitary mount, inasmuch as our brothers and sisters, the birds, show such joy at our coming." And having said these words, he arose and proceeded to the place which had

been fixed upon by his companions; and so did
St Francis come to Mount Alvernia.

2. OF THE SECOND CONSIDERATION OF THE SACRED STIGMATA

The second consideration is of the conversation of St Francis and his companions upon
Mount Alvernia. Be it known, then, that when
Orlando heard that St Francis with three companions was come to dwell on Mount Alvernia,
he was filled with exceeding joy, and on the morrow he came with many others from his castle
to visit St Francis, bringing with him bread
and wine, and other things necessary for him
and his companions; and when he came thither,
he found them in prayer, and drew near and
saluted them. Then St Francis arose, and with
great joy and charity received Orlando and his
company; and so they began to converse together. And after they had spoken together for
some time, and St Francis had thanked him for
the devout solitude which he had bestowed upon them, and for his coming to visit them there,
he prayed Orlando to cause a little cell to be
made for him at the foot of a beautiful beech-
tree, which was about a stone's throw from the
place where they now were; and Orlando immediately caused it to be done. Then, because
evening was drawing on, and it was now time
for them to depart, St Francis preached to them
for a little space; and when he had finished
preaching, and had given them his blessing,
Orlando called St Francis and his companions
aside, and said to them, "Dearest brothers, it
163

never was my intention that you should be exposed on this savage mountain to any corporal necessity, which might hinder you from attending perfectly to spiritual things; and therefore it is my desire—and I say it to you now once for all—that you send freely to my house for every thing you want, and if you fail to do so I shall take it very ill at your hands." And so saying, he departed with his company and returned to his castle.

Then St Francis caused his companions to sit down, and taught them the manner of life they were to keep, that they might live religiously in this solitude; and, among other things, most earnestly did he enjoin on them the strict observance of holy poverty, saying, "Let not Orlando's charitable offer cause you in any way to offend against our lady and mistress, holy poverty. Hold it for certain, that the more we keep aloof from her, the more will the world keep aloof from us, and the greater want shall we endure; but if we closely embrace holy poverty, the world will come after us, and minister to us abundantly. God has called us into this holy religion for the salvation of the world, and has made this compact between the world and us,—that we should give it good example, and that it should provide for our necessities. Let us, then, persevere in holy poverty; for it is the way of perfection, and the pledge of eternal riches." And after many devout and holy words, he thus concluded: "This is the manner of life which I impose upon you and upon myself;

and because I behold my death approaching, I purpose to remain in solitude to recollect myself in God, and to weep over my sins in His sight. Therefore, when it shall so please him, let Brother Leo bring me a little bread and water, and on no account suffer any secular to come near me; but do you answer for me to them." And having thus said, he gave them his blessing, and went his way to his cell under the beech-tree; and his companions remained behind, fully purposed to obey his commands.

And a few days afterwards, as St Francis was considering the formation of the mountain, and marvelling at the great fissures and apertures in the solid rock, it was revealed to him by God in prayer that these strange caverns had been miraculously made at the hour of the Passion of Christ, when, according to the Evangelist's words, the rocks were rent; and this was by the will of God, who manifested Himself thus wonderfully upon Mount Alvernia, because there the Passion of our Lord Jesus Christ was to be renewed in the soul of His servant by love and compassion, and in his body by the impression of the sacred stigmata.

When St Francis had received this revelation, he forthwith shut himself up in his cell, and, in great recollection of soul, prepared himself for the mystery which was to be revealed in him; and from that time forth he began to taste more frequently the sweetness of divine contemplation, by which he was sometimes so absorbed in God, that he was seen by his companions to be raised corporally above the ground, and rapt in prayer; and in these raptures were revealed to St Francis not only things present and future, but even the secret thoughts and desires of the brethren, as was experienced by Brother Leo, at that time his companion.

For this same Brother Leo, being beset by a most grievous spiritual temptation, felt a longing desire to have some devout thing written by the hand of St Francis, feeling assured that if he had it the temptation would leave him, either wholly or in part. But, either out of shame or reverence, he dared not speak of his desire to St Francis, to whom nevertheless it was revealed by the Holy Ghost; whereupon he called the brother to him, and bade him bring him wherewithal to write, and with his own hand he wrote a verse in honour of Christ, according to Brother Leo's desire, and gave it to him, saying, "Take this, dearest brother, and keep it most diligently till the day of thy death. May God bless thee, and guard thee from all temptation! But if temptation come upon thee, be not afraid, for I hold thee to be most truly the servant of God, and most worthy of love when thou art pressed the hardest by temptation. And I tell thee in all sincerity, that on man should account himself to be a perfect friend of God until he has passed through manifold temptations and tribulations."

Now when Brother Leo had received this writing with great faith and devotion, all the temptation departed from him; and returning to his companions, he told them with great joy of the grace which he had received from God through that writing of St Francis; and the brothers laid it up and kept it diligently, and by it they were enabled to work many miracles.

And from that day forward Brother Leo set himself with a good and pure intention to scrutinise and attentively consider the life of St Francis; and in reward of his purity he was permitted many times to behold him rapt in God and suspended above the earth, sometimes at the height of three feet above the ground, sometimes four, sometimes raised as high as the top of the beech-trees, and sometimes so exalted in the air, and surrounded with so dazzling a glory, that he could scarce endure to look upon him.

And what did this simple friar when St Francis, in his raptures, was thus raised above his reach? He would go softly behind him, and, with tears, embrace and kiss his feet, saying, "My God, have mercy upon me, a sinner, and by the merits of this holy man let me find grace in Thy sight." And once when he was standing beneath the feet of St Francis, who was raised so high that he could not touch him, he saw a scroll descend from heaven and rest upon his head, whereon were these words, written in letters of gold: "*Here abideth the grace of God!*" And when he had read the scroll, he saw it return again to heaven.

By the gift of the grace of God which dwelt in him, St Francis was not only absorbed in God by ecstatical contemplations, but was often-

times comforted by angelical visitations. One
day when he was meditating upon his death,
and upon what might hereafter befall his Order,
he said, "O Lord God, when I am dead, what
will become of this Thy poor family, which in
Thy goodness Thou hast committed to me, a
sinner? Who will comfort, who will correct, who
will pray to Thee for it?"

Then did an angel of God appear to him,
and comforted him with these words: "I de-
clare to thee, on behalf of God, that thine Order
shall never fail until the day of judgment; and
no sinner, be he ever so great, who shall bear a
hearty love to this Order, but shall find mercy
with God; and no man shall live long who shall
maliciously persecute it. Nor shall any evil-
doer, who shall refuse to amend his life, long
persevere in thine Order. And be not thou
troubled if thou perceive some brethren who
are not good, and observe not the rule as they
ought to do, nor fear lest on that account this
religion will fail; for there will always be many
and many a one who will observe with great
perfection the life of Christ's Gospel, and the
purity of the rule; and all these, after their corporal life is ended, shall enter into life eternal,
without passing through Purgatory. Others will
observe it, but not perfectly; and these, before
they reach Paradise, shall remain for a while
in Purgatory; but the time of their purification
God will commit unto thee. 'But of those who
in no way observe the rule, take thou no care,'
saith the Lord; for neither doth he care for

them." And when the angel had said these words, he departed, leaving St Francis greatly strengthened and consoled.

And now the Feast of our Lady's Assumption drew near, and St Francis sought for a more secret and solitary place in which he might spend alone the Lent of St Michael the Archangel, which begins on the Feast of the Assumption. Therefore he called Brother Leo, and said thus to him: "Go and stand at the door of the brethren's oratory, and when I shall call thee, turn to me." And Brother Leo went and stood at the door, and St Francis went away a space, and called aloud, and Brother Leo heard and turned towards him. Then St Francis said, "My son, let us seek for some more secret place, where thou wilt not hear me when I call thus to thee." And when they had searched the mount, they found a place on the northern side most secret and well fitted for the purpose, but they could not reach it because of a frightful chasm in the rock; across this chasm they cast a tree to serve as a bridge, and so passed over. Then St Francis sent for the other friars, and told them that he purposed to spend the Lent of St Michael in that solitary place, and prayed them, therefore, to make for him a little cell, so that, though he should cry aloud, he might not be heard by them. And when the cell was made, he said to them, "Return now to your place, and leave me here alone; for, by the help of God, I intend to pass this Lent here, without any disturbance or perturbation of mind; therefore let none of you come to me, nor suffer any secular person to come near the cell. But thou only, Brother Leo, once a day shalt come to me with a little bread and water, and once at night at the hour of Matins, and thou shalt come in silence; and when thou art upon the bridge thou shalt say, *Domine labia mea aperies;* and if I answer thee, thou shalt come to the cell, and we will say Matins together; and if I do not answer thee, thou shalt forthwith depart." And this St Francis said because he was sometimes so absorbed in God that he heard nothing, nor felt any thing by his bodily senses. And having thus spoken, he gave them his blessing, and they returned to their place.

On the Feast of the Assumption, then, St Francis began the holy Lent, with great abstinence and austerity, macerating his body, and invigorating his soul by fervent prayers, vigils, and disciplines; and thus increasing more and more, and going on from virtue to virtue, he prepared his soul to receive divine mysteries and illuminations, and his body to sustain the cruel conflicts with the demons, who often attacked him sensibly. And among other times it befell one day in this Lent that St Francis went forth from his cell in great fervour of spirit, and went to pray in a cave hollowed out of a rock at the top of a steep and frightful precipice, when the devil suddenly appeared before him in a terrible form, and sought to hurl him to the bottom. St Francis, being unable to fly or to endure the horrible aspect of the devil, turned his face, hands, and whole body towards the rock, and recommended himself to God, groping with his hands, yet finding nothing to cling to. But, as it pleased God, who never suffers His servants to be tempted beyond what they are able to bear, the rock suddenly opened and received his body within it; and, as if he had placed his hands and face in liquid wax, the form of the hands and face of St Francis remained impressed upon the stone; and thus, by the help of God, he escaped out of the hands of the devil. But the injury which the devil could not then do to St Francis by casting him down the precipice, he inflicted long after his death upon one of his beloved and devoted brethren, who was standing in the same spot preparing some planks of wood for the safe passage of those who should come to the place out of devotion to St Francis and the miracle which had been wrought there. One day, when he had a heavy piece of wood on his shoulder, the devil cast him down thus laden to the bottom of the rock. But God, who had preserved St Francis from falling, delivered by his merits the devout friar from all injury in his fall; for as he fell, with a loud voice and great devotion he recommended himself to St Francis, who immediately appeared to him, and taking him in his arms, set him down at the bottom of the rock without his having sustained any injury whatsoever. The brethren, who had heard his cry when he fell, believing that he was assuredly dead, and that he had been dashed to pieces by his fall from so great a height upon those pointed rocks, took a bier and went round the mountain another way, with great weeping and lamentation, to collect his mangled remains and give them burial. Having, then, descended the mountain, behold, the brother who had fallen met them with the wood on his shoulder with which he fell, singing the *Te Deum* with a loud voice. And the brethren marvelling greatly thereat, he related to them in order the manner of his fall, and how St Francis had delivered him from all danger. Then all the brethren came with him to the place, devoutly chanting the *Te Deum*, and praising and thanking God and St Francis for the miracle that had been wrought in their brother.

St Francis, then, passing this Lent, as has been said, in the midst of these conflicts with the devil, received many consolations from God, not only by angelic visitations, but through the ministry of the wild mountain-birds. For, through all that Lent, a falcon, whose nest was hard by his cell, awakened him every night a little before the hour of Matins by her cry and the flapping of her wings, and would not leave him till he had risen to say Matins; and if at any time St Francis was more sick than ordinary, or weak, or weary, that falcon, like a discreet and charitable Christian, would call him somewhat later than was her wont. Now St Francis took great delight in this clock of his, because the great carefulness of the falcon drove away all slothfulness, and summoned him to prayer; and moreover during the daytime she would often abide familiarly with him.

To conclude this second consideration, St Francis, being much weakened in body both by his great abstinence and by his conflicts with the devil, and desiring to strengthen his body by the spiritual food of the soul, began to meditate upon the unbounded joy and glory of the blessed in heaven; and he besought of God to grant him some little foretaste of their bliss. Now while this thought was in his mind, an angel suddenly appeared to him in surpassing glory, having a viol in his left hand and a bow in his right. And as St Francis stood in amazement at the sight, the angel drew the bow once across the strings of the viol, when the soul of St Francis was instantly so ravished by the sweetness of the melody, that all his bodily senses were suspended, and he believed, as he afterwards told his companions, that, if the strain had been continued, the intolerable sweetness would have divided his soul from his body. And so much for the second consideration.

3. OF THE THIRD CONSIDERATION OF THE SACRED STIGMATA

We are come now to the third consideration, *i.e.* of the seraphical apparition, and the impression of the sacred stigmata.

As the Feast of the Holy Cross then drew nigh, in the month of September, Brother Leo went one night at his accustomed hour to say

Matins with St Francis. When he came to the bridge, he said, as he was wont to do, *Domine labia mea aperies;* but St Francis made no answer. Now Brother Leo turned not back as he had been commanded to do, but with a good and holy intention he passed the bridge and went straight into the cell; but there he found not St Francis. Thinking, therefore, that he was gone to pray in some solitary place, he went softly through the wood, seeking him in the moonlight. At last he heard his voice, and drawing near, he beheld him kneeling in prayer with his face and hands lifted up towards heaven, and crying, in fervour of spirit, "Who art Thou, my dearest Lord? and who am I, a most vile worm and Thy most unprofitable servant?" And these words he repeated over and over again, and added nothing more. At which Brother Leo, greatly marvelling, lifted up his eyes to heaven, and beheld a torch of most intense and glorious fire, which seemed to descend and light on the head of St Francis; and from the flame there seemed to issue forth a voice which spake with him, but Brother Leo knew not the words which were spoken. Hearing this, and accounting himself unworthy to stand in that holy place, and fearing also to offend St Francis and to disturb him by his presence, he went away silently, and stood afar off to behold what would follow; and looking earnestly upon St Francis, he saw him thrice spread forth his hands to the flame, and after a long time he beheld it mount again to heaven.

FLOWERS OF SAINT FRANCIS

Then he turned joyfully to go back to his cell, being greatly consoled by the vision. But, as he turned, St Francis heard the rustling of the leaves under his feet, and commanded him not to stir, but to await his coming. And Brother Leo in obedience stood still, and waited in so great fear that, as he afterwards told his companions, he would have wished that the earth might swallow him up rather than wait for St Francis, whose anger he exceedingly feared; for he took great heed always not to offend him, lest he should be deprived of his company.

When St Francis, then, came up to him, he said, "Who art thou?" and Brother Leo, in fear and trembling, answered, "Father, I am Brother Leo." And St Francis said to him, "Wherefore hast thou come hither, dear brother? did I not forbid thee to observe me? Tell me now, by holy obedience, whether thou hast seen or heard any thing?" And Brother Leo replied, "Father, I heard thee speak and say many times, 'Who art Thou, my dearest Lord? and who am I, a most vile worm and Thy most unprofitable servant?'" And then, kneeling before St Francis, Brother Leo accused himself of disobedience to his command, and besought his pardon with many tears. After which, he devoutly prayed him to expound to him the meaning of the words which he had heard, and to tell him also those which he had not heard. Then St Francis, seeing that, for his simplicity and purity, God had revealed so much to Brother Leo, condescended to reveal and expound also that which he desired further to know; and thus he spake to him: "Know, dearest brother, that when I said those words which thou didst hear, two great lights were before my soul, the one the knowledge of myself, the other the knowledge of the Creator. When I said, 'Who art Thou, my dearest Lord?' I was in a light of contemplation, in which I beheld the abyss of the infinite goodness and wisdom and power of God; and when I said, 'Who am I?' I was in a light of contemplation, wherein I saw the lamentable abyss of my own vileness and misery, and therefore I said, 'Who art Thou, the Lord of infinite wisdom and goodness, who dost vouchsafe to visit me, a vile and abominable worm?' And in that flame which thou didst behold was God, who under that appearance spake to me, as He spake of old to Moses. And among other things which He said to me, He asked of me three gifts; and I made answer: 'O Lord, I am all Thine; Thou knowest full well that I have nothing else but my cord and my tunic, and even these are Thine; what, then, can I offer or give to Thy Majesty?' Then He said to me, 'Search in thy bosom, and offer Me what thou shalt find there.' And I searched, and I found there a golden ball, and I offered it to God; and the like I did three times, even as God commanded me; and then I knelt down thrice, and blessed and gave thanks to God, who had thus given me something to offer Him. And immediately it was given me to understand that these three offerings signified holy obedi-

176

ence, most entire poverty, and most pure chastity, which God by His grace has enabled me so perfectly to observe that I have nothing to reproach myself thereupon. And whereas thou didst see me put my hand into my bosom and offer to God those three virtues, signified by these three golden balls which God had placed in my bosom, so God has infused such virtue into my soul, that for all the gifts and graces which of His sovereign bounty He has bestowed upon me, I should always with heart and voice praise and magnify Him. These are the words which thou didst hear when thou didst thrice see me lift up my hands. But take heed, dearest brother, that thou observe me no more, but return to thy cell with the blessing of God; and take heed to my words, for yet a few days, and God will work such strange and marvellous things upon this mountain as shall astonish the whole world; for He will do a new thing which He hath never done before to any creature upon this earth."

And when he had said these words, he bade him bring the book of the Gospels, because God had put it into his mind that, by thrice opening that book, he should learn what God would be pleased to do with him. And when the book was brought to him, St Francis went to prayer; and when he had prayed, he caused Brother Leo to open the book three times in the name of the most holy Trinity; and, by the divine disposal, it opened each time at the Passion of Christ. And by this it was given him

FLOWERS OF SAINT FRANCIS

to understand that, like as he had followed
Christ in the actions of his life, so he should
follow and be conformed to Him in the sufferings and afflictions of His Passion, before he
should pass out of this life. And from that day
forward St Francis began to taste more abundantly the sweetness of divine contemplation,
and of the divine visitations, among which he
had one, preparatory to the impression of the
sacred stigmata, after the following manner.
The day before the Feast of the most Holy
Cross, as St Francis was praying secretly in
his cell, an angel of God appeared to him, and
spake to him thus from God: "I am come to
admonish and encourage thee, that thou prepare thyself to receive in all patience and humility that which God will give and do to thee."

St Francis replied: "I am ready to bear patiently whatsoever my Lord shall be pleased to
do to me." And so the angel departed. On the
following day (being the Festival of the Holy
Cross), St Francis was praying before daybreak
at the entrance of his cell, and turning his face
towards the east, he prayed in these words:
"O Lord Jesus Christ, two graces do I ask of
Thee before I die; the first, that in my lifetime
I may feel, as far as possible, both in my soul
and body that pain which Thou, sweet Lord,
didst endure in the hour of Thy most bitter
Passion; the second, that I may feel in my heart
as much as possible of that excess of love by
which Thou, O Son of God, wast inflamed to suffer that cruel Passion for us sinners." And con-

tinuing a long time in that prayer, he understood that God had heard him, and that, as far as is possible for a mere creature, he should be permitted to feel these things.

Having then received this promise, St Francis began to contemplate most devoutly the Passion of Jesus Christ and His infinite charity; and so greatly did the fervour of devotion increase within him, that he was all transformed into Jesus by love and compassion.

And being thus inflamed in that contemplation, on that same morning he beheld a seraph descending from heaven with six fiery and resplendent wings; and this seraph in rapid flight drew near St Francis, so that he could plainly discern him, and perceive that he bore the image of one crucified; and the wings were so disposed, that two were spread over the head, two were outstretched in flight, and the other two covered the whole body. And when St Francis beheld it, he was much afraid, and filled at once with joy and grief and wonder. He felt great joy at the gracious presence of Christ, who appeared to him thus familiarly, and looked upon him thus lovingly; but, on the other hand, beholding Him thus crucified, he felt exceeding grief and compassion. He marvelled much at such a stupendous and unwonted vision, knowing well that the infirmity of the Passion accorded ill with the immortality of the seraphical spirit. And in that perplexity of mind it was revealed to him by him who thus appeared, that by Divine Providence this vision had been thus shown to him that he might understand that, not by the martyrdom of the body, but by the consuming fire of the soul, he was to be transformed into the express image of Christ crucified in that wonderful apparition. Then did all the Mount Alvernia appear wrapped in intense fire, which illuminated all the mountains and valleys around, as it were the sun shining in his strength upon the earth, whence the shepherds who were watching their flocks in that country were filled with fear, as they themselves afterwards told the brethren, affirming that this light had been visible on Mount Alvernia for upwards of an hour. And because of the brightness of that light, which shone through the windows of the inn where they were tarrying, some muleteers who were travelling in Romagna arose in haste, supposing that the sun had risen, and saddled and loaded their beasts; but as they journeyed on, they saw that light disappear, and the visible sun arise.

In this seraphical apparition, Christ, who appeared under that form to St Francis, spoke to him certain high and secret things, which in his lifetime he would never reveal to any person, but after his death he made them known to one of the brethren, and the words were these: "Knowest thou," said Christ, "what I have done to thee? I have given thee the stigmata which are the ensigns of My Passion, that thou mayst be My standard-bearer; and as on the day of My death I descended into limbo, and by virtue of My stigmata delivered thence all the souls whom I found there, so do I grant to thee that yearly on the anniversary of thy death thou mayst go to Purgatory, and take with thee to the glory of Paradise all the souls of thy three Orders, the Friars Minor, the Sisters, and the Penitents, and likewise all, others whom thou shalt find there, who have been especially devout to thee; that so thou mayst be conformed to Me in death, as thou hast been like to Me in life." Then, after long and secret conference together, that marvellous vision disappeared, leaving in the heart of St Francis an excessive fire and ardour of divine love, and on his flesh a wonderful trace and image of the Passion of Christ. For upon his hands and feet began immediately to appear the figures of the nails, as he had seen them on the Body of Christ crucified, who had appeared to him in the likeness of a seraph. And thus the hands and feet appeared pierced through the midst by the nails, the heads whereof were seen outside the palms of the hands and the soles of the feet. In like manner, on the right side appeared the image of an unhealed wound, as if made by a lance, and still red and bleeding, from which drops of blood often flowed and stained the tunic of St Francis.

Whence his companions, before they knew the truth from himself, perceiving that he would not uncover his hands and his feet, and that he could not set the soles of his feet upon the ground, and finding traces of blood upon his tunic when they washed it, understood certainly that he bore in his hands and feet and side the image and similitude of our Lord Jesus Christ crucified. And although he laboured hard to conceal these sacred stigmata, thus clearly impressed upon his flesh, yet finding that he could with difficulty hide them from his familiar companions, and fearing at the same time to reveal the secrets of God, he was in great doubt and trouble of mind whether or not he should make known the seraphical vision and the impression of the sacred stigmata. At last, being pricked in conscience, he called together certain of the brethren, in whom he placed the greatest confidence, and proposing to them his doubt in general terms, asked their counsel on the matter. Now among these friars there was one of great sanctity, called Brother Illuminatus; he, being truly *illuminated* by God, understood that St Francis must have seen something miraculous, and said thus to him: "Know, Brother Francis, that not for thyself alone, but for others, doth God reveal to thee His secrets, and therefore thou hast cause for fear lest thou be worthy of censure if thou conceal that which, for the good of others, has been made known to thee."

Then St Francis, being moved by these words, with great fear and reverence told them the manner of the aforesaid vision, adding that Christ, who had thus appeared to him, had said to him certain things which he would never make known so long as he should live.

Now although these sacred wounds, which had been impressed upon him by Christ, gave great joy to his heart, yet they caused unspeakable pain to his body; so that, being constrained by necessity, he made choice of Brother Leo, for his great purity and simplicity, to whom he revealed the whole matter, and suffered him to touch and dress his wounds on all days except during the time from Thursday evening till Saturday morning, for then he would not by any human remedy mitigate the pain of Christ's Passion, which he bore in his body, because at that time our Saviour Jesus Christ was taken and crucified and died for us. And it came to pass sometimes that when Brother Leo was removing the bandage from the wound in the side, St Francis, because of the pain caused thereby, would lay his hand upon his breast, and at the touch of that holy hand Brother Leo felt such sweetness of devotion as well nigh made him to fall fainting to the ground.

St Francis, having then completed the Lent of St Michael the Archangel, prepared himself by divine revelation to return with Brother Leo to St Mary of the Angels; and calling to him Brother Masseo and Brother Angelo, he commended that holy mount unto their care, and blessing them in the name of Jesus crucified, he suffered them, at their earnest prayer, to see, touch, and kiss his sacred hands adorned with those holy and glorious stigmata; and so leaving them in great joy and consolation, he came down from the holy mount.

4. OF THE FOURTH CONSIDERATION OF THE SACRED STIGMATA

As to the fourth consideration, be it known,

that after the true love of Christ had perfectly transformed St Francis into God, and into the true image of Christ crucified, that angelical man, having fulfilled the Lent of forty days in honour of St Michael the Archangel on the holy mountain of Alvernia, came down from the mount with Brother Leo and a devout peasant, on whose ass he rode, because, by reason of the nails in his feet, he could hardly go on foot. And the fame of his sanctity having been already spread abroad through the country by the shepherds who had seen Mount Alvernia all on fire, and who took it to be a token of some great miracle wrought by God in his person, no sooner had he descended from the mountain than all the people of the country through which he passed, men and women, great and small, pressed round him, eagerly desiring to touch and kiss his hands; and though he could not altogether repress their devotion, yet, in order to conceal the sacred stigmata, he wrapped bandages round his hands, and covered them with his sleeves, giving them only the fingers to kiss. But though he thus strove to conceal the secret of the sacred stigmata, in order to shun all occasion of worldly glory, it pleased God for His own glory to work many miracles by virtue of the same holy stigmata, and especially in this journey from Mount Alvernia to St Mary of the Angels. And the same hath He since renewed in many and divers parts of the world, both during the lifetime of St Francis and after his glorious death, that their mysterious and marvel-

FLOWERS OF SAINT FRANCIS

lous virtue, and the exceeding charity and mercy of Christ towards him, might be manifested to the world by clear and evident miracles, such as these which follow.

As St Francis drew near to a city on the confines of Arezzo, a woman came to him weeping bitterly, and carrying in her arms a boy of eight years old, most frightfully swollen with dropsy; and laying him down before St Francis, she besought him to pray to God for him. St Francis first betook himself to prayer, and then laying his holy hands upon the child, the swelling subsided at once, and he restored him to his mother, who received him with great joy, and took him home, thanking God and St Francis, and taking delight in showing her restored child to all her neighbours who came to her house to witness the cure.

On the same day St Francis passed on to St Sepolcro; and as soon as he approached Castello, a multitude of people poured forth from that city and the neighbouring towns to meet him, with olive-branches in their hands, crying aloud, "Behold the saint; behold the saint!" And in their devotion and eager desire to touch him, the people pressed mightily upon him; but he, being rapt in contemplation, and his mind wholly fixed on God, though thus pressed upon and dragged hither and thither by the multitude, was insensible of all that passed around, and knew nothing of all that was said or done, or even that he had passed by that city or through that country. When, therefore, the multitude had returned to their own houses, and he had reached a house of lepers about a mile on the other side of the town, coming to himself as if just returned from the other world, the heavenly contemplative asked his companion, "When shall we come to the town?" For his soul, fixed and rapt in the contemplation of heaven, had been unconscious of all things earthly, and perceived neither lapse of time, nor change of place, nor persons passing by. And the like befell him many different times, as his companions often experienced.

St Francis arrived that evening at the house of the brethren of Mount Casale, where was a friar so grieviously ill, and so cruelly afflicted by his sickness, that it seemed to be rather an infliction and torment of the devil than any natural infirmity; for sometimes he would cast himself down on the ground, trembling fearfully, and foaming at the mouth. At other times every nerve in his body seemed to be distended, or contracted, or distorted, and he would spring convulsively from the ground, and immediately fall prostrate again. St Francis, then, being seated at table, and hearing from the brethren the miserable condition of this friar, which seemed past remedy, took compassion on him, and taking a morsel of the bread which he was eating, he made the sign of the cross upon it with those holy hands which bore the stigmata of Christ, and sent it to the sick brother, who had no sooner eaten it than he was perfectly cured, and never more felt any return of his infirmity.   186

FLOWERS OF SAINT FRANCIS

On the following morning St Francis sent two of the brethren from that place to abide at Alvernia, and with them the peasant who had lent him the ass, desiring him to return to his house. And having remained a few days in that place, St Francis departed and went to the city of Castello. And behold many of the citizens came to meet him, bringing with them a woman who for a long time past had been possessed by a devil; and they humbly besought him to deliver her, because she troubled all the country round by howling fearfully, or shrieking piteously, or at times by barking like a dog. Then St Francis, having first prayed and made the sign of the most holy cross over her, commanded the devil to depart out of her; and forthwith he departed, leaving her whole both in mind and body. And as the news of the miracle spread among the people, another woman full of faith brought a child sick of a grievous ulcer, and devoutly besought him to bless it with his hand. Then St Francis, accepting her devotion, took the child, and removing the bandage, made the sign of the most holy cross thrice over the wound; and then, having bound it up again with his own hands, he delivered the child to his mother, who, as it was evening, laid him down immediately on his bed to sleep. In the morning, when she went to take him out of his bed, she found the wound unbandaged and perfectly healed, no trace remaining of it, save that in the place where it had been there was impressed the likeness of a red rose in testimony of the miracle, which remained until his death, and many a time excited him to devotion to St Francis, by whom he had been healed.

In that city, at the desire of the devout inhabitants, St Francis abode a month, during which time he wrought many miracles, and then departed to St Mary of the Angels with Brother Leo and a good man who had lent him the ass on which he rode. It so happened that, as they travelled night and day, finding no place where they could lodge for the night, they sought shelter from the cold and the snow, which was falling fast, in the cavity of a hollow rock. And as they remained under this miserable shelter, which scarcely protected them from the inclemency of the weather, the poor man to whom the ass belonged, not being able to sleep for the cold, and having no means of kindling a fire, began to complain bitterly, and to weep and almost to murmur at St Francis for having brought him into such a place. And St Francis, hearing him, had compassion on him, and in fervour of spirit stretched out his hand and touched him, when (wonderful to say) no sooner did the poor man feel the touch of that hand which had been pierced and enkindled by the seraph's fire than all sensation of cold departed from him, and such a glowing heat inflamed him within and without, as if he had been placed near the mouth of a fiery furnace, that, being instantly relieved and comforted both in body and soul, he fell asleep, and slept (as he said himself) all that night through, even till the morning, more sweetly amid the rocks and snow than he had ever slept in his own bed.

Now when they had journeyed on another day, they came to St Mary of the Angels, and as they drew nigh to it, Brother Leo lifted up his eyes and beheld a most beautiful cross, and upon it the image of the Crucified, going before St Francis, who followed after it; so that when he stood still, the cross stood still; and when he went forward, the cross went ever before him; and such was the splendour of that cross, that it not only illumined the face of St Francis, but made all the way around him bright, and so continued shining till he entered the convent of St Mary of the Angels. St Francis, then, coming with Brother Leo, was received by the brethren with great charity and joy, and from that day forward St Francis dwelt for the most of his time at St Mary of the Angels until the day of his death. And the fame of his sanctity and of his miracles went forth more and more through the Order and through the whole world, although out of the depth of his humility he concealed the gifts and graces of God as far as he could, and called himself the greatest of sinners.

St Francis finding that, by reason of the stigmata of Christ, his bodily strength was gradually wasting away, and that he could no longer rule over the Order, hastened to assemble a general chapter; and the brethren being all met together, he humbly laid before them his incapacity, by reason of his infirmities, any longer

FLOWERS OF SAINT FRANCIS

to fill the office of general, although he might not resign the generalate, to which he had been appointed by the Pope, nor name a successor without his express sanction; but he constituted Brother Peter of Catania his vicar, affectionately and with all his heart recommending the Order to him and to the provincial ministers. And having done this, St Francis, being strengthened in spirit, raised his eyes and hands to heaven, and said, "To Thee, O Lord my God, —to Thee do I commend Thy family, which till now Thou hast committed to me, and of which now, by reason of my infirmities, which Thou knowest, O my sweetest Lord, I can no longer take care. I commend it also to the provincial ministers, who shall render an account to Thee at the day of judgment if any brother perish by their negligence, or evil example, or over-sharp correction." And by these words, as it pleased God, all the brethren understood that he spoke of the sacred stigmata (which he called his infirmities), and none of them could refrain from weeping for devotion. And thenceforth he left all the care and government of the Order in the hands of his vicar and of the provincial ministers; and he said, "Now that for my infirmities I have given over the care of the Order, I have henceforth nothing to do but to pray to God for this one religion, and to give a good example to our brethren. And I know moreover that, even were I freed from my infirmities, the greatest good which I could do to the Order would be to pray for it continually to God, that He would be pleased to defend and rule and preserve it."

Now, as we have said before, St Francis did all in his power to conceal the sacred stigmata, and after he received them always covered his hands and his feet; yet could he not hinder that many times several of the brethren contrived to see and touch them, and especially the wound of the side, which with the greatest diligence he sought to conceal. Thus a brother who waited on him, having one day persuaded him to take off his tunic in his presence that he might shake the dust out of it, clearly saw the wound in the side; and thrusting his hand suddenly into the bosom of St Francis, he touched it with three fingers, and ascertained its length and breadth, and in like mannner it was discovered at another time by his vicar. But it was still more clearly attested by Brother Ruffino, a man of most sublime contemplation, of whom St Francis was wont to say that in all the world he knew not a holier man; and for his great sanctity he loved him most heartily and granted to him all that he desired. In three several ways did this Brother Ruffino certify both himself and others of the reality of the sacred stigmata, and especially of that in the side. The first was that, having obtained permission from St Francis to wash his clothes, he continually found the traces of blood on the right side of the tunic, whereupon St Francis reproved him for spreading out the garment in order to discover the mark of the wound. Another time the said Bro-

FLOWERS OF SAINT FRANCIS

ther Ruffino put his finger into the wound in the side; when St Francis, for the pain he felt, cried aloud, "God forgive thee, Brother Ruffino, for what thou hast done." A third time this brother besought St Francis with great urgency to exchange capes with him, to which the charitable father having unwillingly consensed, in the exchange of the garments, he clearly saw the wound in the right side. Brother Leo likewise, and many others of the brethren, saw the sacred stigmata during the lifetime of St Francis; and although for their sanctity these brethren were worthy of all faith upon their simple word, yet did they swear upon the sacred Scriptures that they had seen them plainly. Several Cardinals also, who enjoyed great familiarity with St Francis, composed devout and beautiful hymns, antiphons, and proses in honour of his sacred stigmata. The Sovereign Pontiff, Alexander, when preaching to the people in the presence of the Cardinals, among whom was the holy Brother Bonaventure, himself a Cardinal, affirmed that he had seen with his own eyes the sacred stigmata of St Francis during his lifetime. And the Lady Jacoba of Settesoli, who was the greatest lady in Rome of her time, and most devout to St Francis, before and after his death saw and kissed them with great reverence; for she came from Rome to Assisi by divine revelation, at the death of St Francis; and thus it came to pass. A few days before his death, St Francis lay sick with certain of his companions in the Bishop's palace, and notwithstanding his infirmity he oftentimes sang canticles in honour of Jesus Christ. One of his companions, therefore, said to him one day: "Father, thou knowest that the citizens of this place have great faith in thee and account thee to be a holy man, and therefore they may perhaps think that if thou be what they take thee for, being so grievously sick, thou shouldst in this thine infirmity think upon death, and rather weep than sing. And know that this singing of thine, and of ours whom thou wilt have to sing with thee, is heard by many in the palace and without, for as much as this palace is guarded by many armed men on thine account, who may perhaps take scandal thereat. Therefore I think," said this friar, "that thou wilt do well to depart hence, and to return to St Mary of the Angels; for we are not well here among seculars." Then St Francis answered him: "Thou knowest, dearest brother, that two years ago, when we were at Foligno, God revealed the end of my life to thee, and He revealed it also to me—that in this sickness, and in a few days, this my life shall come to an end. And in this revelation God assured me of the remission of all my sins, and of the bliss of Paradise. Until I received that revelation, I wept over my sins and at the thought of death; but since I have received it, I have been so full of joy that I can no longer weep; and therefore I sing, and will sing to God, who hath bestowed on me the gift of His grace, and hath certainly promised me the gift of heavenly glory. For our departure hence, it pleaseth me well, and I willingly consent thereto; but find you a way to carry me, for because of my infirmity I cannot walk." Then the brethren took him up and bore him on their shoulders, and many of the citizens went with them. And coming to a hostel which was on the way, St Francis said to those who bore him: "Set me down upon the ground, and turn my face towards the city"; and when he was thus turned towards Assisi, he blessed the city with many blessings, saying: "Blessed be thou of God, O holy city, forasmuch as by means of thee many souls shall be saved, and in thee many servants of God shall dwell, and of thy children many shall be elected to eternal life." And when he had said these words, he caused himself to be borne onwards to St Mary of the Angels; and then they carried him to the infirmary, and laid him down to rest. Then St Francis called to him one of his companions, and said to him: "Dearest brother, God has revealed to me that by this sickness, a few days hence, I am to pass from this life; and thou knowest that the devout Lady Jacoba di Settesoli, who is so dear to our Order, would be deeply grieved, should she hear of my death, not to have been present at it; therefore signify to her that if she desires to see me again in life, she must come hither with all speed." And the brother made answer: "Too true, father; for indeed, because of the great devotion she bears thee, most unmeet were it that she should not be present at thy death." "Go, then," said St Francis; "bring pen and paper, and write as I shall bid thee." And when he had brought them, St Francis dictated the letter in the following form: "To the Lady Jacoba, the handmaid of the Lord, Brother Francis, the poor little one of Christ, wisheth health and the fellowship of the Holy Ghost in our Lord Jesus Christ. Be it known to thee, most beloved, that Christ our Lord hath revealed to me the day of my death, which is near at hand. And therefore, if thou wouldst find me alive, as soon as thou shalt receive this letter, do thou set forth immediately, and come to St Mary of the Angels; for if thou come not forthwith, thou shalt not find me alive. And bring with thee the hair-cloth wherein to wrap my body, and the cerecloth which shall be needed for my burial. I pray thee also that thou wouldst bring me some of the food which thou didst prepare for me when I was sick at Rome." Now, while this letter was being written, it was revealed to St Francis that the Lady Jacoba was coming to him, and was already near at hand, and that she had brought with her all the things which were asked for in the letter. Having, then, received this revelation, St Francis bade the brother who was writing to write no more, for it was not needed, but to lay aside the letter; whereupon the brethren greatly marvelled why he would not have it finished nor sent. And in a short space afterwards, there came a loud knocking at the door, and St Francis bade the porter open it; which, when he had done, he saw the Lady Jacoba, the most noble of all the ladies of Rome, with two of her sons, who were senators of Rome, and a great company of horsemen, and they entered the house; and the Lady Jacoba went straight to the infirmary to St Francis. And St Francis felt great consolation at her coming, and she also rejoiced exceedingly to find him alive, and to speak with him. Then she declared to him how, being at Rome in prayer, God had revealed to her that his life would shortly be at an end, and that he would send for her and ask those things of her which she had now brought with her. And she brought them to St Francis and gave him to eat; and when he had eaten, and was now much strengthened thereby, the Lady Jacoba knelt at the feet of St Francis, and with such exceeding devotion kissed and bathed with her tears those feet, marked and adorned with the wounds of Christ, that the brethren who were standing round thought they beheld the Magdalen at the feet of Jesus Christ, and could in no way remove her from him. And after a long space of time they raised her up, and, taking her aside, they asked her how it was she had come thus opportunely, and thus well provided with all the things that were needful for St Francis, both in his life and for his burial. And the Lady Jacoba answered, that as she was praying one night in Rome she heard a voice from heaven, which said, "If thou would find St Francis alive, go without delay to Assisi, and take with thee those things which thou hast been accustomed to prepare for him in sickness, and those which shall be needed for his burial." And the lady continued, "As the voice bade me do, so I have done." So the Lady Jacoba abode at Assisi until St Francis passed from this life and was buried; and she and all her company paid great honour to his burial, and all the cost of it. And then returning to Rome, that noble lady soon afterwards died a holy death, desiring, out of devotion to St Francis, to be carried to St Mary of the Angels, and there to be buried; which was done according to her will.

5. HOW JEROME, WHO AT FIRST BELIEVED NOT, SAW AND TOUCHED THE SACRED STIGMATA OF ST FRANCIS

On the death of St Francis his glorious stigmata were seen and kissed, not only by the said Lady Jacoba and her company, but by many citizens of Assisi; among others by a knight of great renown, named Jerome, who had doubted much, and disbelieved them; as St Thomas disbelieved the wounds of Christ. And to assure himself and others, he boldly, in the presence both of the brethren and of seculars, moved the nails in the hands and feet, and strongly pressed the wound in the side. By which means he was enabled to bear constant witness to the truth of the miracle, swearing on the Gospels that he had seen and touched the glorious stigmata of St Francis, which were seen and touched also by St Clare and her religious, who were present at his burial.

6. OF THE DAY AND HOUR OF THE DEATH OF ST FRANCIS

St Francis, the glorious confessor of Christ,

197

passed from this life in the year of our Lord
1226, on Saturday the 4th of October, and was
buried on the Sunday following. He died in the
twentieth year of his conversion (that is, from
the time when he began to do penance), the
second year after the impression of the sacred
stigmata, and the forty-fifth of his age.

7. OF THE CANONISATION OF ST FRANCIS

St Francis was canonised in the year 1228
by Pope Gregory IX., who came in person to
Assisi for his canonisation.

And this shall suffice for the fourth consideration.

8. OF THE FIFTH AND LAST CONSIDERATION OF THE SACRED STIGMATA

The fifth and last consideration is of certain
apparitions, revelations, and miracles, which
God vouchsafed after the death of St Francis,
in confirmation of the truth of his sacred stigmata, and to certify the day and hour on which
he received them. In the year of our Lord, then,
1282, in the month of October, Brother Philip,
the minister of Tuscany, by the command of
Brother John Buonagrazia, the minister general, required under holy obedience Brother Matthew of Castiglione, a man of great devotion
and sanctity, to tell him what he knew of the
day and hour in which the sacred stigmata were
impressed by Christ on the body of St Francis,
because he had heard that it had been revealed
to him. And Brother Matthew, being constrained by holy obedience, made answer thus: "Be-

ing of the community of Alvernia, last May I was praying in my cell, which is on the spot where the seraph is believed to have appeared. And in my prayer I besought God most devoutly that He would be pleased to make known to some person the day, the hour, and the place in which the sacred stigmata were impressed on the body of St Francis. And persevering thus for a long time in this prayer, St Francis appeared to me in great glory, and said to me, 'My son, what prayer art thou making to God?' And I said to him, 'Father, I am praying such and such things.' And he said to me, 'I am thy Father Francis. Dost thou know me?' 'Yes, father,' said I. Then he showed me the sacred stigmata in his hands and feet and side, saying, 'The time is now come when God wills that to be manifested for His glory, which the brethren have not hitherto sought to know. Know, then, that He who appeared to me was no angel, but Jesus Christ Himself under the appearance of a seraph, who, with His own hands, impressed those wounds upon my body, as He Himself received them in His body on the cross. And thus it was that on the day before the Exaltation of the Holy Cross, an angel came to me, and bade me, on the part of God, to prepare to receive with patience whatsoever He should be pleased to send me. And I made answer that I was prepared to receive and endure whatever God should be pleased to appoint for me. And on the following morning, being the morning of Holy Cross day, which in that year fell on a Friday, I left

199

FLOWERS OF SAINT FRANCIS

my cell at daybreak in great fervour of spirit, and went to pray in that very spot where thou now dwellest, and where I was often accustomed to pray. And as I was praying, there descended through the air with great rapidity the figure of a young man crucified, in the guise of a seraph with six wings. At which marvellous sight I knelt down humbly, and began devoutly to contemplate the unbounded love of Jesus Christ crucified, and the unbounded anguish of His Passion. And such compassion did this spectacle excite within me, that it seemed to me as if I felt that Passion in my own body, and the whole mountain shone like the sun in His presence; and, thus descending, He came close to me. And standing before me, He spoke to me certain secret words, which I have never yet revealed to any one, but the time is now at hand when they shall be revealed. Then, after a little space, Christ departed and returned to heaven, and I found myself thus signed with these wounds. Go then,' said St Francis, 'and assure thy minister of these things; for this is the work of God and not of man.' Having said these words, St Francis blessed me and returned to heaven, accompanied by a great multitude of glorious spirits." All these things the said Brother Matthew declared that he had seen, not sleeping, but waking. And he made oath that he had thus related them to the said minister in his cell at Florence, when so enjoined by him to do under holy obedience.

CHAPTER FIFTY-FOUR

It happened as a devout and holy friar was
reading in the legend of St Francis the chapter
concerning the sacred stigmata, he began in
great anxiety of mind to ponder what those
most secret words could be, spoken by the seraph to St Francis, which he would never reveal
to any one in his lifetime. And he said thus to
himself: "St Francis would never tell these
words to any one while he was alive; but now
since his corporal death he would perhaps reveal them, were he devoutly besought to do so."
And from that day forth the fervent friar betook himself to prayer, beseeching God and St
Francis to reveal these words to him; and after
persevering for eight years in this prayer, it was
at last granted in the following manner. One
day after dinner he was making his thanksgiv-
ing in the church, and remained there praying
with greater devotion than usual, and with many
tears; he was presently summoned by another
friar, by order of the Father Guardian, to go
with him to the city on the business of the convent. Not doubting, therefore, that obedience
is more meritorious than prayer, he no sooner
heard the command of his Superior than he left
the church, and went humbly with the brother
who called him. And this act of obedience was
so pleasing to God, that by it he merited what
by all these long years of prayer he had not

obtained; for as soon as they had passed through the gate, they met two foreign friars, who seemed as if they had come from far, one of whom appeared young, and the other lean and old; and by reason of the bad weather they were both wet and muddy. On which the obedient friar spoke thus to his companion: "Oh, dearest brother, if the business on which we are going may brook some little delay, seeing that these stranger brethren have great need of a charitable reception, I pray thee let me first go and wash their feet, —and specially those of this ancient brother, and thou mayst wash the feet of the younger, —and then we will go upon the business of the convent." Then the other friar yielding to the charity of his companion, they returned to the house, and most charitably received those stranger brethren, bringing them into the kitchen to warm and dry themselves at the fire, at which eight other brethren of the place were already warming themselves. And after they had been awhile at the fire, they took them aside to wash their feet, as they had agreed together to do. Now as the obedient brother was washing the feet of the ancient friar, he beheld on them the marks of the sacred stigmata, and immediately embracing them in joy and wonder, he began to cry: "Either thou art Christ, or thou art St Francis!" At that cry, and at these words, the brethren who were at the fire rose up, and drawing near, beheld with great fear and reverence those glorious stigmata. Then the ancient friar suffered them at their earnest desire to behold them near, to touch and kiss them. And as they wondered more and more, and scarce believed for joy, he said to them, "Doubt not and fear not, beloved brethren and children; I am your father, Brother Francis, who by the will of God founded three Orders. And inasmuch as this brother, who but now has washed my feet, has been beseeching me for these eight years past, and to-day more fervently than ever, to reveal to him the secret words spoken to me by the seraph when he gave me the stigmata, which words I would never reveal during my lifetime, now by the command of God, for his perseverance and for his prompt obedience, by which he left the sweetness of contemplation, I am sent to reveal to him, before you, that which he has asked to know."

Then St Francis, turning to the friar, said thus: "Know, dearest brother, that when I was on Mount Alvernia, wholly absorbed in the remembrance of the Passion of Christ in that seraphical apparition, I was thus stigmatised by Christ in my body, and then He spoke thus to me: 'Knowest thou what I have done to thee? I have given thee the signs of My Passion that thou mayest be My standard-bearer. And as on the day of My death I descended into Limbo, and by virtue of My stigmata drew forth and took with me to Paradise all the souls whom I found there, so do I now grant to thee, in order that thou mayest be conformed to Me in death as thou hast been in life, that when thou shalt have passed out of this life, thou shalt descend into

Purgatory every year on the anniversary of thy death, and by the virtue of the stigmata which I have given thee shalt deliver thence and take with thee to Paradise all the souls which thou shalt find there of thy three Orders—Minors, Sisters, and Penitents,*—of those moreover who shall have been devout to thee.' And these words I never told to any one while I was in life." Having said these words, St Francis and his companion immediately disappeared. Many brethren heard this related by the eight friars who witnessed the vision, and heard the words of St Francis.

CHAPTER   FIFTY-FIVE

HOW ST FRANCIS APPEARED, AFTER HIS DEATH, ON MOUNT ALVERNIA TO BROTHER JOHN, WHILE HE WAS IN PRAYER

St Francis once appeared on Mount Alvernia to Brother John, a man of great sanctity, while he was in prayer, and spoke with him for a long space of time; and before he departed he said to him, "Ask of me what thou wilt." And Brother John made answer, "Father, I pray thee, tell me that which I have long desired to know, —what thou wast doing, and where thou wast, when the seraph appeared to thee." And St Francis replied, "I was praying in that place whereon the chapel of Count Simon da Battifolle now stands, and I asked two favours of my Lord Jesus Christ. The first was that He

* Members of the Third Order.

would grant to me in my lifetime to feel, as far as might be possible, both in my soul and body, all that He had suffered in His most bitter Passion. The second favour which I asked was, that I might feel in my heart that exceeding love which enkindled His, and moved Him to endure that Passion for us sinners. And then God put it into my heart that it was granted to me to feel both, as far as is possible for a mere creature; and this promise was well fulfilled to me by the impression of the stigmata." Then Brother John asked him whether those secret words spoken to him by the seraph had been truly related by the brother who affirmed that he had heard them from the mouth of St Francis, in the presence of eight friars. And St Francis made answer, that they were even so as that brother had said. Then Brother John, emboldened to ask by the saint's liberality in granting his requests, said thus: "O father, I beseech thee most earnestly that thou wilt suffer me to see and kiss thy most sacred stigmata; not that I have any doubt upon the matter, but because such has always been my most earnest desire." And St Francis graciously showing them to him, Brother John plainly saw and kissed them. And lastly he said to him, "Father, grant me, if it be the will of God, to feel in some small measure the consolation which thou didst experience when thou didst behold our dear Lord come down to thee to give thee the stigmata of His Passion." And St Francis replied, "Dost thou see these nails?" "Yes, father," said Brother

FLOWERS OF SAINT FRANCIS

John. "Touch once more," said St Francis, "this nail which is in my hand." Then Brother John, with great fear and reverence, touched that nail, and as he touched it there issued forth from it as it were a cloud of incense in the form of a little rod, which, entering the nostrils of Brother John, filled both his soul and body with such over powering sweetness that he was immediately rapt in God, and he remained insensible in that ecstasy from that hour, which was the hour of Tierce, until Vespers. And of that vision and familiar converse with St Francis Brother John never spoke to any but his confessor till the day of his death; but on his death-bed he revealed it to several of the brethren.

CHAPTER FIFTY-SIX
OF A HOLY FRIAR WHO SAW A WONDERFUL VISION OF A COMPANION WHO WAS DEAD

In the province of Rome a very devout and holy friar saw this wonderful vision. A brother, who was exceedingly beloved by him, died one night, and was buried in the morning at the entrance of the chapter-room. On the same day the friar withdrew after dinner into a corner of the chapter-room, and there prayed most fervently to God and St Francis for the soul of this his beloved companion. And persevering in prayer with many tears till midday, when all the rest lay down to sleep, he suddenly heard a loud noise in the cloister. Being seized with great terror, he cast his eyes on the grave of his companion, and beheld St Francis standing at the entrance of the chapter-room, and behind him a great multitude of friars surrounding the grave. And looking farther, he saw in the midst of the cloister a great and intense fire burning, and in it the soul of his deceased companion; and looking round the cloister, he beheld our Lord Jesus Christ going round it, with a great company of angels and saints. And as he beheld these things in great amazement, he saw that when Christ passed by the chapter-room, St Francis with all those friars knelt down, and said thus to Him: "I beseech Thee, my dearest Lord and Father, by that inestimable charity which Thou didst show to the human race in Thine Incarnation, to have mercy upon the soul of this my brother, which is burning in that fire." And Christ answered nothing, but passed on. And returning again the second time, and passing by the chapter-room, St Francis knelt down again with his friars, and besought Him in these words: "I beseech Thee, most pitiful Father and Lord, by the unbounded charity which Thou didst show to the human race when Thou didst die for it on the wood of the cross, to have mercy on the soul of this my brother." And Christ again passed by, and heeded him not. And going again round the cloister, He passed the third time by the chapter-room, and then St Francis, kneeling down as before, showed Him his hands and his feet and his side, saying, "I pray Thee, merciful Lord and Father, by that great anguish and that great consolation which I experienced when Thou didst impress these stigmata upon my flesh, to have mercy on the soul of this my brother which is in the flames of Purgatory." Wonderful to tell, Christ being thus besought for the third time by St Francis, in the name of his stigmata, immediately stood still, and, looking upon them, He granted his prayer, saying, "I grant to thee, Francis, the soul of thy brother." And hereby He assuredly intended to honour and confirm the glorious stigmata of St Francis, and openly to testify that the souls of his brethren which go to Purgatory have no easier way of deliverance than by virtue of his stigmata, by which they are freed from pain, and brought to the glory of Paradise, according to the words which Christ said to St Francis when He imprinted them upon his body.

No sooner had our Lord spoken these words than the fire in the cloister vanished, and the dead friar came to St Francis, and, together with him and with Christ, all that blessed company, with their glorious King, ascended into Heaven. For which cause the friar his companion, who had prayed for him, seeing him delivered from suffering and received into Paradise, was filled with exceeding joy. And then he related the whole vision in order to the other friars, and they all together praised and gave thanks to God.

CHAPTER   FIFTY-SEVEN

A noble knight of Massa di San Pietro, named
Landulph, who was most devout to St Francis,
and had received the habit of the Third Order
from his hand, was thus certified of his death
and of the truth of his most sacred and glorious stigmata. When St Francis lay on his death-
bed, the devil entered into a woman of that
place, and cruelly tormented her, and withal
made her to speak so learnedly and so subtile-
ly, that she overcame all the clerks and learned men who came to dispute with her. It came
to pass that the devil, departing from her, left
her free for the space of two days, after which
he returned again, and afflicted her more cruelly than before. Which when Landulph heard,
he went to the woman, and asked the devil
which dwelt within her wherefore he had departed from her for those days, and why he had
since returned to torment her worse than before. And the devil answered thus: "When I left
her, I went with all my companions in these
parts, being gathered together in great force, to
the deathbed of the beggar Francis, to dispute
with him, and carry away his soul; but, because
it was surrounded and defended by a multitude of angels, far more numerous than we, who
carried it straight to Heaven, we were forced to
retire discomfited; and therefore have I returned to make up to this wretched woman for the
peace in which I left her for those days."

FLOWERS OF SAINT FRANCIS

And then Landulph conjured him in the name of God to tell him what was the truth regarding the holiness of St Francis, whom he affirmed to be dead, and of St Clare, who was still alive. And the devil answered him: "I must tell thee the truth whether I will or not. The anger of God the Father was so enkindled against the sins of the world, that He was ready to pass sentence upon it, and to destroy all men and women from the face of the earth, unless they would repent. But Christ His Son, praying for sinners, promised to renew His life and Passion in the person of a man, namely, in Francis, a poor mendicant: by his life and doctrine many throughout the world should be brought back into the way of truth, and many also to penance. And now, to show to the world what He had wrought in St Francis, He has been pleased that the stigmata of His Passion, which He had imprinted on his body during life, should be seen and touched by many since his death. In like manner did the Mother of Christ promise to renew her virginal purity and her humility in the person of a woman, even St Clare, that by her example many women might be delivered out of His hands. And the Eternal Father, being appeased by these promises, deferred His final sentence." Then Landulph, wishing to know for certain whether the devil, who is the abode and father of lies, spoke truth in these matters, and especially with regard to the death of St Francis, sent a faithful servant of his to Assisi, to inquire at St Mary of the Angels whether St Francis were alive or dead; whither, when the messenger had arrived, he found that he was indeed dead, and bought certain information to his lord that St Francis had passed from this life on the very day and hour of which the devil had spoken.

CHAPTER   FIFTY-EIGHT

HOW POPE GREGORY IX., WHO HAD DOUBTED OF THE STIGMATA OF ST FRANCIS, WAS ASSURED OF THEIR TRUTH

Passing over all the miracles of the sacred stigmata of St Francis, it shall suffice in conclusion of this fifth consideration, to relate the following: Pope Gregory IX. having some little doubt, as he afterwards related, concerning the wound in the side of St Francis, the Saint one night appeared to him, and raising his right arm a little, discovered to him the wound in his side. He then bade him bring a flask and place it beneath the wound, and when the Pope had done so, he saw it filled to the brim with blood mingled with water, which flowed from the wound; when all doubt immediately departed from Him. After this, with the concurrence of all the Cardinals, he approved the sacred stigmata of St Francis by a special bull granted to the friars at Viterbo in the eleventh year of his papacy; and in the following year he issued another, with still more copious privileges. Pope Nicholas III. and Pope Alexander confirmed the same, with fuller privileges, decreeing that whosoever should

211

FLOWERS OF SAINT FRANCIS

deny the sacred stigmata might be proceeded a-
gainst as a heretic. And this shall suffice concerning the fifth consideration of the glorious
and sacred stigmata of our father St Francis,
whose life may God give us grace to follow in
this world, that by virtue of his glorious stigmata we may deserve to be saved with him in
Paradise! To the praise of Jesus Christ and His
poor servant St Francis!

Amen.

LIFE OF BROTHER JUNIPER

CHAPTER   ONE

ONE OF THE MOST CHOSEN disciples and first companions of St Francis was Brother Juniper, a man of profound humility and of great fervour and charity, of whom St Francis once said, when speaking of him to some of his companions, "He would be a good Friar Minor who had overcome the world as perfectly as Brother Juniper." Once when he was visiting a sick brother at St Mary of the Angels, as if all on fire with the char ity of God, he said to him, "Can I do thee any service?" And the sick man answered, "Thou wouldst do me a great pleasure if thou couldst get me a pig's foot to eat." Brother Juniper answered immediately, "Leave it to me; thou shalt have one at once." So he went and took a knife from the kitchen, and in fervour of spirit went into the forest, where were many swine feeding, and he caught one and cut off one of its feet, and ran off with it, leaving the swine with its foot cut off; and he came back to the convent, and carefully washed the foot, and diligently prepared and cooked it. Then he brought it with great charity to the sick man, who ate it with avidity; and Brother Juniper was filled with joy and consolation, and related the history of his assault upon the swine for his diversion. Meanwhile the swineherd, who had seen the brother cut off the foot, went and told the tale in order, and with great bitterness, to his lord, who, being informed of the fact, came to the convent and abused the friars, calling them hypocrites, deceivers, robbers, and evil men. "Why," said he, "have you cut off the foot of my swine?" At the noise which he made, St Francis and all the friars came together, and with all humility made excuses for their brother, and, as ignorant of the fact, promised, in order to appease the angry man, to make amends for the wrong which had been done to him. But he was not to be appeased, and left St Francis with many threats and reproaches, repeating over and over again that they had maliciously cut the foot off his swine, refusing to accept any excuse or promise of repayment; and so he departed in great wrath. And as all the other friars wondered, St Francis, being full of prudence, thought within himself, "Can Brother Juniper indeed have done this through indiscreet zeal?" So he sent for him, and asked him privately, "Hast thou cut off the foot of a swine in the forest?" To which Friar Juniper answered quite joyfully, not as one who had committed a fault, but believing he had done a great act of charity, "It is true, sweet father, that I did cut off that swine's foot; and if thou wilt listen compassionately, I will tell thee the reason. I went out of charity to visit the brother who is sick." And so he related the matter in order, adding, "I tell thee, dear father, that this foot did the sick brother so much good, that if I had cut off the feet of a hundred swine instead of one, I verily believe that God would have been pleased therewith." To whom St Francis, in great zeal for justice, and in much bitterness of heart, thus answered: "O Brother Juniper, wherefore hast thou given this great scandal? Not without reason doth this man complain, and thus rage against us; perhaps he is even now going about the city spreading this evil report of us, and with good cause. Therefore I command thee by holy obedience, that thou go after him until thou find him, and cast thyself prostrate before him, confessing thy fault, and promising to make such full satisfaction that he shall have no more reason to complain of us, for this is indeed a most grievous offence." Brother Juniper was much amazed at these words, wondering that any one should have been angered at so charitable an action; for all temporal things appeared to him of no value, except so far as they can be charitably applied to the service of our neighbour. So he made answer, "Doubt not, father, but that I shall soon content and satisfy him. And why should there be all this disturbance, seeing that the swine was rather God's than his, and that it furnished the means for an act of charity?" And so he went his way, and came to the man, who was still chafing and past all patience, and told him for what reason he had cut off the pig's foot, and all with such fervour, exultation, and joy, as if he were telling him of some great benefit he had done him which deserved to be highly rewarded. The man grew more and more furious at his discourse, and loaded him with much abuse, calling him a fantastical fool and a wicked thief. Brother Juniper, who delighted in insults

FLOWERS OF SAINT FRANCIS

cared nothing for all this abuse; but marvelling
that any one should be angry at what seemed
to him only a matter of rejoicing, he thought
he had not made himself well understood, and
so repeated the story all over again, and then
flung himself on the man's neck and embraced
him, telling him that it had all been done out
of charity, and inciting and begging him to give
the remainder also for the same motive; and all
this with so much charity, simplicity, and humility, that the man's heart was changed within
him, and he threw himself at Brother Juniper's
feet, acknowledging with many tears the injuries which by word and deed he had done to him
and his brethren. Then he went and killed the
swine, and having cut it up, he brought it, with
many tears and great devotion, to St Mary of
the Angels, and gave it to those holy friars in
compensation for the injury he had done them.
And St Francis, considering the simplicity and
patience under adversity of this good Brother
Juniper, said to his companions and those who
stood by, "Would God, my brethren, that I had
a forest of such Junipers!"

CHAPTER   TWO
INSTANCE OF BROTHER JUNIPER'S GREAT POWER
AGAINST THE DEVIL

The devils could not endure the purity of Brother Juniper's innocence and his profound
humility, as appears in the following example.
A demoniac one day fled in an unaccustom-

ed manner, and through devious paths, seven miles from his home. When his parents, who had followed him in great distress of mind, at last overtook him, they asked him why he had fled in this strange way. The demoniac answered, "Because that fool Juniper was coming this way. I could not endure his presence, and therefore, rather than wait his coming, I fled away through these woods." And on inquiring into the truth of these words, they found that Brother Juniper had arrived at the time the devil had said. Therefore, when demoniacs were brought to St Francis to be healed, if the evil spirit did not immediately depart at his command, he was wont to say, "Unless thou dost instantly leave this creature, I will bring Brother Juniper to thee." Then the devil, fearing the presence of Brother Juniper, and being unable to endure the virtue and humility of St. Francis, would forthwith depart.

CHAPTER   THREE
HOW, BY THE CONTRIVANCE OF THE DEVIL, BROTHER JUNIPER WAS CONDEMNED TO THE GALLOWS

Once upon a time, the devil, desiring to terrify Brother Juniper, and to raise up scandal and tribulation against him, betook himself to a most cruel tyrant, named Nicholas, who was then at war with the city of Viterbo, and said to him, "My lord, take heed to watch your castle well, for a vile traitor will come here shortly from Viterbo to kill you and set fire to your castle. And by this sign you shall know him: he will come in the guise of a poor beggar, with his clothes all tattered and patched, and with a torn hood falling on his shoulders; and he will carry with him an awl, wherewith to kill you, and a flint and steel, wherewith to set fire to the castle; and if you find not my words to be true, punish me as you will." At these words Nicholas was seized with great terror, believing the speaker to be a person worthy of credit; and he commanded that a strict watch should be kept, and that if such a person should present himself he should be forthwith brought before him. Presently Brother Juniper arrived alone; for, because of his great perfection, he was allowed to travel without a companion as he pleased.

Now there met him certain wild young men, who began to mock him, and treat him with great contempt and indignity. And Brother Juniper was no way troubled thereat, but rather incited them to ill-treat him more and more. And as they came to the castle-gate, the guards seeing him thus disfigured, with his scanty habit torn in two (for he had given half of it on the way to a beggar, for the love of God, so that he had no longer the appearance of a Friar Minor), recognised the signs given of the expected murderer, and dragged him with great fury before the tyrant Nicholas. They searched him to find whether he had any offensive weapons, and found in his sleeve an awl, which he used to mend his sandals, and also a flint and steel, which he carried with him to strike a light when he abode, as he often did, in the woods or in desert places. Nicholas, seeing the signs given by the devil, commanded that a cord should be fastened round his neck, which was done with so great cruelty that it entered into the flesh. He was then most cruelly scourged; and being asked who he was, he replied, "I am a great sinner." When asked whether he wanted to betray the castle to the men of Viterbo, he answered, "I am a great traitor and unworthy of any mercy." Being questioned whether he intended to kill the tyrant Nicholas with that awl, and to burn the castle, he replied that he should do greater things than these, should God permit him. This Nicholas then, being wholly mastered by his fury, would examine no farther, but without delay condemned Brother Juniper, as a traitor and murderer, to be fastened to a horse's tail, and so dragged on the ground to the gallows, there to be forthwith hanged by the neck. And Brother Juniper made no excuse for himself, but, as one who joys to suffer for the love of God, he was full of contentment and rejoicing. So the command of the tyrant was carried into effect. Brother Juniper was tied by the feet to the horse's tail, and dragged along the ground, making no complaint, but, like a meek lamb led to the slaughter, he submitted with all humility. At this spectacle of prompt justice, all the people ran together to behold the execution of so hasty and cruel a judgment, but no one knew the culprit. Nevertheless it befell, by the will of God, that a good man who had seen Brother Juniper taken, and forthwith judged, ran to the house of the Friars Minor, and said, "I pray you, for the love of God, to come with me at once, for a poor man has been seized and immediately condemned, and led to death. Come, that he may at least place his soul in your hands, for he seems to me a good man, and he has had no time to make his confession; they are even now leading him to the gallows, and he seems to have no fear of death nor care of his soul. Oh, be pleased to come quickly!" Then the guardian, who was a compassionate man, went at once to provide for the salvation of this soul; and when he came to the place of execution, he could not get near for the crowd; but, as he stood watching for an opening, he heard a voice say, "Do not so, do not so, cruel men; you are hurting my legs!" And as he recognised the voice of Brother Juniper, the guardian, in fervour of spirit, forced his way through the crowd, and tearing the bandage from the face of the condemned, he saw that it was indeed Brother Juniper, who looked upon him with a cheerful and smiling countenance. Then the guardian, with many tears, besought the executioners and all the people for pity to wait a little space, till he should go and beseech the tyrant to have mercy on Brother Juniper. The executioners promised to wait a few moments, believing, no doubt, that he was some kinsman of the prisoner. So the devout and pious guardian went to the tyrant

Nicholas, weeping bitterly, and said, "My lord, I am so filled with grief and amazement that my tongue can scarcely utter it, for it seems to me that in this our land has been committed to-day the greatest sin and the greatest evil which has been wrought from the days of our fathers even until now, and I believe that it has been done through ignorance." Nicholas heard the guardian patiently, and inquired, "What is this great sin and evil which has been committed to-day in this land?" And the guardian answered, "It is this, my lord, that you have condemned (and, as I assuredly believe, unjustly) to a most cruel punishment one of the holiest friars at this time in the Order of St Francis, to whom you profess a singular devotion." Then said Nicholas, "Now tell me, father guardian, who is he; for perhaps, knowing him not, I have committed a great fault?" "He," said the guardian, "whom you have condemned to death is Brother Juniper, the companion of St Francis." Then was the tyrant amazed, for he had heard the fame of Brother Juniper's sanctity; and, pale with fear, he hastened together with the guardian to Brother Juniper, and loosed him from the horse's tail and set him free, and in the presence of all the people he prostrated himself on the ground before Brother Juniper, and with many tears confessed his fault, and the cruelty of which he had been guilty towards that holy friar; adding, "I believe indeed that the end of my wicked life is at hand, since I have thus without reason

223

cruelly tortured so holy a man. For, in punishment of my evil life, God will send me in a few days an evil death, though this thing I did ignorantly." Brother Juniper freely forgave the tyrant Nicholas: but a few days afterwards God permitted a most cruel death to overtake him. And so Brother Juniper departed, leaving all the people greatly edified.

CHAPTER FOUR
HOW BROTHER JUNIPER GAVE ALL THAT HE HAD TO THE POOR FOR THE LOVE OF GOD

Brother Juniper was so full of pity and compassion for the poor, that when he saw any one poor or naked he immediately took off his tunic, or the hood of his cloak, and gave it to him. The guardian therefore laid an obedience upon him not to give away his tunic or any part of his habit. A few days afterwards, a poor half-naked man asked an alms of Brother Juniper for the love of God, who answered him with great compassion, "I have nothing which I could give thee but my tunic, and my superior has laid me under obedience not to give it, nor any part of my habit, to any one. But if thou wilt take it off my back I will not resist thee." He did not speak to a deaf man; for the beggar forthwith stripped him of his tunic, and went off with it. When Brother Juniper returned home, and was asked what had become of the tunic, he replied, "A good man took it off my back, and went away with it." And as the virtue of compassion increased in him, he was not contented with giving his tunic, but would give books, or cloaks, or whatever he could lay his hands on, to the poor. For this reason the brethren took care to leave nothing in the common rooms of the convent, because Brother Juniper gave away every thing for the love of God and to the glory of His name.

CHAPTER   FIVE
HOW BROTHER JUNIPER TOOK CERTAIN LITTLE BELLS FROM THE ALTAR AND GAVE THEM AWAY FOR THE LOVE OF GOD

Brother Juniper was one Christmas-day in deep meditation before the altar at Scesi. Now this altar was very fairly and richly adorned, and, at the desire of the sacristan, Brother Juniper remained to keep guard over it while he went to his dinner. And as he was absorbed in devout meditation, a poor woman came and asked alms of him for the love of God. To whom Brother Juniper made answer, "Wait a while, and I will see if I can find any thing for thee on this grand altar." Now there was upon the altar an exceedingly rich and costly hanging of gold, with silver bells of great value. "These bells," said Brother Juniper, "are a superfluity"; so he took a knife and cut them off the hanging, and gave them to the poor woman out of compassion. The sacristan, after he had eaten three or four mouthfuls, bethought him of the ways of Brother Juniper, whom he had left in charge; and began exceedingly to doubt whether, in his charitable zeal, he might not do some damage to the costly altar. As soon as the suspicion entered his head, he rose from the table, and went into the church, to see if any of the ornaments of the altar had been removed or taken away; and when he saw that the hanging had been cut, and the bells carried off, he was beyond measure troubled and scandalised. Brother Juniper, seeing that he was very angry, said to him, "Be not disturbed about those little bells, for I have given them to a poor woman who had great need of them, and here they were good for nothing but to make a pompous display of worldly vanity." When the sacristan had heard this, he went with all speed to seek the woman in the church, and throughout the city; but he could neither find her nor meet with any one who had seen her. So he returned, and in great wrath took the fringe, and carried it to the general, who was at Assisi, saying, "Father general, I demand justice on Brother Juniper, who has spoilt this hanging for me, the very best I had in the sacristy. See how he has destroyed it by cutting away all the silver bells, which he says he has given to a poor woman!" And the guardian answered him, "It is not Brother Juniper who has done this, but thine own folly; for thou oughtest by this time to have known his ways: and I tell thee, I only marvel that he did not give away the whole hanging. Nevertheless I will give him a sound correction for this fault." And, having called the brethren together in chapter, he sent for Brother Juniper, and, in the presence of the whole community, reproved him most severely concerning the said bells; and, waxing wrathful as he spoke, he raised his voice till it became hoarse. Brother Juniper cared little or nothing for these words, for he delighted in reproaches, and rejoiced when he received a good humiliation; but his one thought in return was to find a remedy for the general's hoarseness. So when he had received his reproof, he went straight to the town for flour and butter, to make a good hasty-pudding; with which he returned when the night was far spent, lighted a candle, and went with his hasty-pudding to the door of the general's cell and knocked. The general came to open it, and seeing him with a lighted candle and a pipkin in his hand, asked, "Who is there?" And Brother Juniper answered, "Father, when you reproved me to-day for my faults, I perceived that your voice grew hoarse. I thought it was from over-fatigue. I considered what would be the best remedy, and have had this hasty-pudding made for you; therefore I pray you eat of it, for I tell you that it will ease your throat and your chest." "What an hour of the night is this," said the general, "to come and disturb other people!" And Brother Juniper made answer, "See, it has been made for you; I pray you eat of it without more ado, for it will do you good." But the general, being angry because of the lateness of the hour, and Brother Juniper's pertinacity, answered him roughly, bidding him go his way, for at such an hour he would not eat. Then

Brother Juniper, seeing that neither persuasions nor prayers were of any avail, said, "Father, since you will not eat the pudding which was made for you, at least do this for me: hold the candle for me, and I will eat it." And the general, being a devout and kindly man, seeing the piety and simplicity of Brother Juniper, and that he had done all this out of devotion, answered, "Well, since thou wilt have it so, thou and I will eat together." And so the two ate this hasty-pudding together, out of an importunate charity, and were more refreshed by their devotion than by the food.

CHAPTER SIX

HOW BROTHER JUNIPER KEPT SILENCE FOR SIX MONTHS TOGETHER

Brother Juniper once determined with himself to keep silence for six months together, in this manner. The first week for love of the Eternal Father. The second for love of Jesus Christ His Son. The third for love of the Holy Ghost. The fourth in reverence to the most holy Virgin.

CHAPTER SEVEN

A READY REMEDY FOR TEMPTATIONS OF THE FLESH

As Brother Giles, Brother Simon of Assisi, Brother Ruffino, and Brother Juniper, were one day discoursing together concerning God and the salvation of the soul, Brother Giles said to the other brethren, "How do you deal with temptations to impurity?" Brother Simon said, "I consider the vileness and turpitude of the sin till I conceive an exceeding horror of it, and so escape from the temptation." And Brother Ruffino said, "I cast myself on the ground, and with fervent prayer implore the mercy of God and of the Mother of Jesus Christ till I am freed from the temptation." And Brother Juniper answered, "When I feel the approach of a diabolical suggestion, I run at once and shut the door of my heart, and, to secure its safety, I occupy myself in holy desires and devout meditations; so that when the suggestion comes and knocks at the door of my heart, I may answer from within, 'Begone; for the room is already taken, and there is no space for another guest;' and so I never suffer the thought to enter my heart; and the devil, seeing himself baffled, retires discomfited, not from me alone, but from the whole neighbourhood." Then Brother Giles made answer and said, "Brother Juniper, I hold with thee; for there is no surer way of overcoming this enemy than flight; inasmuch as he attacks us within by means of the traitor appetite, and without through our bodily senses; and so by flight alone can this masterful foe be overcome. And he who resists it in any other way, after all the toil of the conflict, rarely comes off victorious. Fly, then, from this vice, and thou shalt gain the victory."

CHAPTER EIGHT

Brother Juniper, desiring to make himself de-
spicable in the sight of men, stripped himself
one day of all but his inner garment; and, making a bundle of his habit and other clothes, he
entered the city of Viterbo, and went into the
market-place, in order to make himself a laugh-
ing-stock. When he got there, the boys and
young men of the place, thinking him to be
out of his senses, ill-treated him in many ways,
throwing stones and mud at him, and pushing
him hither and thither, with many words of derision; and thus insulted and evil entreated,
he abode there the greater part of the day, and
then went his way to the convent. And when
the friars saw him they were full of indignation.
And chiefly because he had gone thus through
the city with his bundle on his head, they reproved and threatened him sharply. One said,
"Let us put him in prison." Another, "He de-
serves to be hanged." And others, "He cannot be too severely punished for the scandal
he has given to-day in his own person, to the
injury of the whole Order." And Brother Juniper, being full of joy, answered with all humility, "You say well indeed; for I deserve all these
punishments, and far worse than these."

CHAPTER NINE

As Brother Juniper was once entering Rome,
the fame of his sanctity led many of the devout
Romans to go out to meet him. As soon as he
saw this number of people coming, he took it
into his head to turn their devotion into sport
and ridicule. So, catching sight of two children
who were playing at see-saw upon two pieces
of wood, he moved one of them from his place,
and mounting on the plank in his stead, he began to see-saw with the other. Meanwhile the
people came up and marvelled much at Brother Juniper's see-sawing. Nevertheless they
saluted him with great devotion, and waited
till he should have finished his play to accompany him honourably to the convent. Brother
Juniper took little heed of their salutation, reverence, or patient waiting, but gave his whole
attention to his see-saw. And when they had
waited thus for a long time, they began to grow
tired, and to say, "What folly is this?" Some
few, who knew his ways, were moved to still
greater devotion; but at last they all departed,
leaving Brother Juniper on the see-saw. When
they were gone, Brother Juniper remained full
of consolation, because he knew what sport had
been made of him. So he came down from his
see-saw, and entering Rome with all meekness
and humility, came to the convent of the Friars
Minor.

CHAPTER TEN

It happened once, when Brother Juniper was
in a house of the brethren that, for some reas-
onable cause, all the friars were obliged to go
out, and Brother Juniper alone remained at
home. Then the guardian said to him, "Brother
Juniper, we are all going out, and therefore, by
the time we come back, I wish thee to prepare
a little food for the refreshment of the brethren."
"Most willingly," replied Brother Juniper;
"leave it to me." When all the brethren, as has
been said, were gone out, Brother Juniper said
to himself, "What superfluous carefulness is
this, that a brother should be lost in the kitchen,
and deprived of all opportunity of prayer! Of a
surety, as I am now left in this charge, I will cook
enough to serve the brethren, were they as many
more, for a fortnight to come." So he went to the
town and borrowed some large pots for cooking;
then he got fresh meat and salt, chickens, eggs,
and vegetables; he begged wood also, and made
a great fire, upon which he set everything together to boil: the fowls in their feathers, the eggs
in their shells. Meanwhile one of the friars, to
whom Brother Juniper's simplicity was well
known, returned to the house; and seeing these
great caldrons on such an enormous fire, he sat
down in amazement to watch the care and diligence with which Brother Juniper was proceeding in his cookery. And having observed him
for some time to his great recreation, this friar
went out of the kitchen, and told the other bre-

thren that Brother Juniper was certainly preparing a wedding banquet. The brethren took it for a jest; but presently Brother Juniper took his caldrons off the fire, and bade them ring the bell for dinner. Then the brethren took their places at the table, and he came into the refectory, all rubicund with his labours and with the heat of the fire, and said to the brethren, "Eat a good dinner now, and then we will go to prayer: and no one need think of cooking for a long time to come, for I have cooked more than enough to last us all for more than a fortnight." And so saying, he set down his hotch-potch before them; but there was never hog in the Campagna of Rome so hungry that he could have eaten it. Brother Juniper praised his way of cooking because it was so great a saving of time; and seeing that the other friars ate none of it, he said, "These fowls are good for the head; and this food will keep the body in health, so wholesome is it." And the brethren were all in admiration at the devotion and simplicity of Brother Juniper. But the guardian, being angry at such folly, and grieved at the waste of so much good food, severely reproved Brother Juniper. Then Brother Juniper fell on his knees before the guardian, and humbly confessed his fault to him and all the brethren, saying, "I am a very wicked man. Such a one committed such a sin, for which he was condemned to lose his eyes. Such another was hanged for his crimes. But I deserve far worse for my evil deeds. And now I have wasted so much of the gifts of God

FLOWERS OF SAINT FRANCIS

and the substance of the Order." And thus lamenting he departed; nor would he come into the presence of any one of the brethren for the rest of that day. Then said the father guardian, "My dearest brethren, I would that this brother might spoil as much of our substance, if we had it, daily as he has done to-day, were it only for the edification he has given us by the simplicity and charity with which he has done it."

CHAPTER   ELEVEN
HOW BROTHER JUNIPER WENT ONE DAY TO ASSISI FOR HIS OWN CONFUSION

Once when Brother Juniper was dwelling in the valley of Spoleto, knowing that there was to be a great solemnity at Assisi, and that many were resorting thither with great devotion, it came into his head to go there also; and you shall hear in what guise he went. He stripped himself of all but his inner garment, and thus, passing through the midst of the city of Spoleto, he came to the convent. The brethren, much displeased and scandalised, rebuked him sharply, calling him a fool and a madman, and a disgrace to the Order of St Francis, and declared that he ought to be put in chains as a madman. And the general, who was then on the spot, called all the friars together, and gave Brother Juniper a very sharp correction in the presence of them all. And, after many words, he ended with this severe sentence: "So great and grievous is thy

fault, that I know not what sufficient penance
to give thee." And Brother Juniper answered,
as one who delighted in his own confusion,
"Father, I will tell you: send me back from this
solemnity in the same garb in which I came to
it."

CHAPTER   TWELVE

HOW BROTHER JUNIPER FELL INTO AN ECSTASY
DURING THE CELEBRATION OF MASS

As Brother Juniper was one day hearing Mass
with great devotion, he fell into an ecstasy, and
so continued for a long space of time. And when
he came to himself, he said with great fervour
of spirit to the other frairs, "Oh, my brethren,
who is there in this world so noble that he would
disdain to carry a basket of mud all the world
over, in the hope of obtaining a house full of
gold?" Then he added, "Alas, why will we not
endure a little shame to obtain eternal life?"

CHAPTER   THIRTEEN

OF THE SORROW WHICH BROTHER JUNIPER FELT
AT THE LOSS OF HIS COMPANION BROTHER AMAZIAL-
BENE

Brother Juniper had a companion named Amazialbene, whom he loved most tenderly, and
who possessed the virtues of patience and o-
bedience in the utmost perfection; for, when

235

beaten and ill-treated on all sides, he never complained or uttered a word of remonstrance. He was often sent to places where he met with persons who treated him most cruelly, and he bore it all patiently and without the least resentment. At the command of Brother Juniper, he would laugh or weep. At last, as it pleased God to ordain, this Brother Amazialbene died, in high reputation for sanctity; and when Brother Juniper heard of his death, he felt greater sorrow thereat than he had ever experienced in this life for any earthly thing. And thus did he express in words the great bitterness of his heart, saying, "Alas, woe is me; for there is no good left me now, and all the world is darkened to me by the death of my sweet and most loving brother Amazialbene!"

CHAPTER   FOURTEEN
OF THE HAND WHICH BROTHER JUNIPER SAW IN THE AIR

Brother Juniper being one day in prayer, and, it may be, proposing to himself to do great things for God, he saw a hand in the air, and heard with his bodily ears a voice which said thus to him, "O brother Juniper, with that hand thou canst do nothing." Then he arose immediately, and with his eyes raised to Heaven, he went many times round and round the convent, repeating aloud, "True indeed, most true indeed!"

CHAPTER FIFTEEN

When St Francis was speaking with Brother Leo on Mount Alvernia, he said to him, "Brother *Lamb*, wash this stone with water." Then Brother Leo went forth and washed it with water. Then said St Francis, with great joy and gladness, "Wash it with wine"; and it was done. "Wash it," said St Francis again, "with oil"; and Brother Leo did so. Then said St Francis, "Brother Lamb, wash this stone with balm." And Brother Leo answered, "O sweet father, how am I to get balm in this wilderness?" Then St Francis replied, "Know, Brother Lamb, that this is the stone on which Christ was seated when He once appeared to me in this place, and therefore did I bid thee wash it four times, and no more, because Jesus Christ then promised me four singular graces or my Order. The first, and all those who shall cordially love our Order, and all the friars who shall presevere therein, shall die a good death. The second, that those who persecute this holy religion shall be notably punished. The third, that no evil-doer, continuing in his perversity shall be able to persevere long in this Order. The fourth, that this religion shall endure until the day of judgment."

LIFE OF THE BLESSED BRO-
THER GILES (OR EGIDIUS)

THE COMPANION OF ST FRANCIS

CHAPTER ONE

INASMUCH AS THE EXAMPLE OF holy men serves to detach the minds of devout hearers from transitory pleasures, and to excite them to the desire of eternal salvation, to the honour of God and of His most holy Mother, our Blessed Lady St Mary, we will say a word concerning the graces wrought by the Holy Ghost in the soul of our holy brother Giles, who, even while he wore the secular habit, being touched by the spirit of God, began to endeavour in all his actions to please God alone.

At that time St Francis appeared as a new herald of Christ to give an example of holy living, of humility, and penance. And two years after his conversion a man named Bernard, endowed with marvellous prudence and rich in temporal goods, and Peter of Catania, were drawn by his example to the observance of evangelical poverty. By the counsel of St Francis they distributed all their temporal possessions, for the love of God, among the poor, arraying themselves, in the glory of patience and evangelical perfection, with the habit of the Friars Minor; and all their life long did they keep the promise then made with the greatest fervour and perfection. About a week after this conversion and distribution, Brother Giles, being still in the secular habit, and seeing the contempt of earthly things manifested by these noble knights of Assisi, to the great admiration of the whole world, on the Feast of St George in the year 1209, very early in the morning, as one in earnest about his salvation, went in great fervour of spirit to the church of St Gregory, where was the monastery of St Clare. Being greatly desirous to see St Francis, he went, as soon as he had finished his prayers, towards the hospital for lepers, where St Francis dwelt apart in profound humility, with Brother Bernard and Brother Peter of Catania.

Being come to a crossway, and not knowing which road to take, he prayed to Christ, our precious guide, who led him straight to the hut. And as he pondered upon the cause of his coming, he met St Francis returning from the forest, where he had been praying.

Then Brother Giles threw himself at his feet, and besought him to receive him into his company for the love of God. And St Francis, beholding the devout countenance of Brother Giles, answered and said, "Dearest brother, God hath conferred a great grace upon thee. If the emperor were to come to Assisi, and propose to make one of its citizens his knight or secret chamberlain, would not such an offer be joyfully accepted as a great mark of honour and distinction? How much more shouldst thou rejoice that God has called thee to be His knight and chosen servant, to observe the perfection of His holy gospel! Therefore, do thou stand firm in the vocation to which God hath called thee." And he took him by the hand and raised him up, and bringing him into the hut,

he called Brother Bernard, and said to him,
"Almighty God has sent us a good brother; let
us, therefore, rejoice in the Lord, and eat together in charity." When they had eaten, Brother Francis and this Giles went to Assisi for
cloth to make him a habit; and by the way they
met a poor woman, who asked an alms for the
love of God. St Francis, not knowing where to
find any thing for the poor woman, turned to
Brother Giles with an angelic countenance, and
said, "For the love of God, dearest brother, let
us give her this mantle." And Brother Giles
obeyed with so willing a heart, that the holy
father thought he saw him and his alms received forthwith into heaven, whereat he experienced an exceeding interior joy. St Francis having procured the cloth, and caused the habit to
be made, received Brother Giles into the Order,
and he became one of the most glorious religious whom the world has ever seen in the contemplative life. Immediately after his reception,
St Francis went with him into the March of Ancona, singing and praising with him the Lord
of heaven and earth. And he said to Brother
Giles, "My son, our religion shall be like unto
the fisherman, who cast his nets into the water
and took a great multitude of fishes, whereof he
kept the larger and cast the smaller back into
the sea." Brother Giles marvelled at this prophecy, for the Order at that time numbered only
three friars besides St Francis himself. Moreover, St Francis had not yet begun to preach
publicly to the people, but only admonished

men and women as he met with them by the
way, saying, with loving simplicity, "Love God,
and fear Him, and do worthy penance for your
sins." And Brother Giles would say, in his turn,
"Do this which my spiritual father says to you,
for he speaks excellently well."

CHAPTER   TWO

HOW BROTHER GILES WENT TO ST JAMES'S, IN GALICIA

By the permission of St Francis, Brother Giles
went once, in the process of time, to St James's,
in Galicia, and in that whole journey he only
once broke his fast, because of the great poverty
of the country. And as he went asking alms, and
finding none who would give to him, he came
one evening by chance to a barn, where a few
beans lay scattered on the ground. These he
gathered up, and supped on them; and in this
barn he passed the night, for he loved to abide
in solitary places remote from the haunts of
men, the better to give himself to watching and
prayer. And God so strengthened him by this
supper, that if he had eaten of ever so rich a banquet he could not have been so well refreshed.
Proceeding then upon his way, he met with a
poor man, who asked an alms of him for the
love of God. And Brother Giles, charitable as
he was, had nothing to give but the habit he
wore. So he cut the cowl from his cloak, and gave
it to that poor man for the love of God, and so
journeyed on without his cowl for twenty days

together. And as he was returning through Lombardy, a man called to him, to whom he went willingly, expecting to receive an alms; but when he stretched out his hand, the man put a pair of dice into it, inviting him to play. Brother Giles replied very humbly, "God forgive thee, my son." And as he passed through the world he met with much mockery and insult, and endured it all in peace.

CHAPTER THREE
OF BROTHER GILES'S MANNER OF LIFE WHEN HE WENT TO THE HOLY SEPULCHRE

Brother Giles, by the permission of St Francis, went to visit the Holy Sepulchre of Christ; and being come to the port of Brundisium, he was obliged to tarry there many days, because there was no ship ready to sail. Brother Giles, desiring to live by his labour, got a vessel and filled it with water, and went round the city, crying, "Who wants water?" And for his labour he received bread, and all things necessary for the bodily support of himself and his companion. Then he passed over the sea, and with great devotion visited the Sepulchre of Christ and the other Holy places. And as he returned, he abode for some days in the city of Ancona; and because he was accustomed to live by his labour, he made baskets of rushes, and sold them, not for money, but for bread for himself and his companion; and he carried the dead to their burial for the same wages. And when even this

245

FLOWERS OF SAINT FRANCIS

failed him, he begged at the table of Jesus
Christ, asking alms from door to door. And so
with much labour, and in much poverty, he returned to St Mary of the Angels.

CHAPTER   FOUR

HOW BROTHER GILES PRAISED OBEDIENCE MORE
THAN PRAYER

As a brother was one day praying in his cell,
his superior sent him an obedience to leave his
prayer and go to ask alms. The friar went forthwith to Brother Giles, and said to him, "Father, I was in prayer, and the guardian has sent
me to beg; now it seems to me far better that
I should continue praying." Brother Giles answered, "My son, have you never yet known
or understood what prayer is? True prayer is to
do the will of our superior; and it is great pride
in him who has submitted his neck to the yoke
of holy obedience to desire to follow his own
will in any thing, in order, as he thinks, to perform a work of greater perfection. The perfectly obedient religious is like a horseman mounted on a mettled steed, which carries him swift-
ly and fearlessly on his way; and the disobed-
ient religious, on the contrary, is like a man seated on a meagre, weak, or vicious horse, who is
in danger of perishing by the way, or falling into the hands of his enemies. I tell thee that
though a man were raised to so high a degree of
contemplation as to hold converse with angels,
yet were he interrupted in that colloquy by the

voice of obedience, he ought immediately to leave communing with the angels, and obey the command of his superior."

CHAPTER FIVE
HOW BROTHER GILES LIVED BY THE LABOUR OF HIS HANDS

When Brother Giles was once living in a convent of the Friars Minor at Rome, he desired, as he had done ever since his entrance into the Order, to employ himself in manual labour, and thus did he spend his day. Early in the morning he heard Mass with great devotion; then he went into a forest about eight miles from Rome, and brought home a great bundle of wood on his back, which he sold for bread and other provisions. One day as he was bringing home a load of wood, a lady met him and offered to buy it; so, having agreed with her as to the price, he carried it to her house. The lady, notwithstanding the agreement, seeing that he was a religious, gave him much more than she had promised. Then said Brother Giles, "Good lady, I would not have the vice of avarice to gain the mastery of me, and therefore I will not take from thee more than we agreed upon." And, instead of taking more than the stipulated sum, he took but half of it, and went his way, leaving the lady in great admiration. Brother Giles always showed the like scrupulous integrity in all his dealings. He helped the labourers to gather the olives and pluck the grapes.

247

Being one day in the market-place, he heard a man asking another to help him to beat walnuts, offering him a reward for so doing; but the other excused himself because the place was far off and difficult of access. Then Brother Giles said to him, "My friend, if thou wilt give me a part of the walnuts, I will come with thee to beat them." So the agreement having been made, he went with the man; and first making the sign of the cross, he climbed the old walnut-tree, and in great fear began to beat. When he had finished beating, he gathered up more for his share than he knew how to carry; so he took off his habit, and having tied the sleeves and the hood, he made a sack of it, and filling it with walnuts, he took it upon his back and carried it to Rome, and with great joy gave the walnuts to the poor for the love of God. When the corn was reaped, Brother Giles went with other poor persons to gather the ears of corn; and if any one offered him a handful of grain, he would say, "Brother, I have no granary wherein to store it, and what I gather I give for the most part to the poor for the love of God." Brother Giles had little leisure to help others at such times, for he had to fulfil his appointed task, and also to say the canonical hours, and make his accustomed mental prayer. When he once went to the fountain of St Sixtus to fetch water for the monks of that place, a man asked him to give him some water to drink. Brother Giles answered, "How can I take the vessel half filled to the monks?" The man, being angry, spoke many injurious and reproachful words to Brother Giles, who returned very sorrowful to the monks. Then he borrowed a large vessel, and came back forth with to the fountain for water, and finding the man there, he said, "Take, my friend, and drink as much as thy soul desireth, and be not angry that it seemed to me unjust to take a scant measure of water to those holy monks." Then he, being constrained and conscience-stricken by the charity and humility of Brother Giles, acknowledged his fault, and from that day forth held him in great reverence.

CHAPTER   SIX
HOW BROTHER GILES WAS MIRACULOUSLY ASSISTED IN A GREAT NECESSITY WHEN, BY REASON OF A HEAVY FALL OF SNOW, HE WAS HINDERED FROM GOING OUT TO QUEST

Brother Giles was once staying in Rome, at the house of a Cardinal, when Lent was drawing near; and being unable there to enjoy the quiet of mind which he desired, he said to the Cardinal, "Father, I pray you give me permission to go with my companion to spend this Lent in some solitary place"; and the Cardinal answered him, "Alas! dearest brother, whither wouldst thou go? This is a time of great scarcity; you are not well accustomed to these desert places; therefore I beseech thee remain with me, for I account it a singular grace to be permitted to provide for your wants for the love of God." But Brother Giles was determined to go; so he went out of Rome to a high mountain, where there had been formerly a castle, and where there was now a forsaken church dedicated to St Lawrence; and he entered therein with his companion, and remained there in prayer and meditation. They were not known in the place, and therefore little reverence or consideration was shown to them, so that they were in great poverty, added to which a heavy fall of snow came on, which lasted many days. They could not leave the church; they had no food with them, neither was any thing brought them from without; and thus they remained shut up for three days and three nights. Brother Giles, seeing that he could earn nothing for his livelihood, nor go out to beg alms, said to his companion, "My dearest brother, let us cry aloud to the Lord, that of His loving pity He would provide for this our extreme necessity; for we have heard of many holy monks who, being in great straits, have called upon God to provide for them in their need." So, after their example, these two holy men betook themselves to prayer, beseeching God with all their hearts to provide a remedy for their distress; and God, who is all-compassionate, had regard to their faith and devotion and simplicity in the following manner. A certain man, casting his eyes upon the church where Brother Giles and his companion were shut up, said to himself by an inspiration from God, "It may be that some devout person is

doing penance in that church, and by reason
of the snow he can obtain no supply for his
wants, and may perhaps die of hunger." And
by the inspiration of the Holy Ghost he said,
"Of a surety I will go and see whether my imag-
ination is true or not." So he took bread and
a flask of wine, and went his way, and with great
difficulty arrived at the church, where he found
Brother Giles and his companion most devoutly absorbed in prayer; and they were so
wasted with famine that they looked rather like
dead than living men; and he had great compassion for them, and having warmed and comforted them he returned and told his neighbours
of the extremity and necessity of these friars,
and prayed and exhorted them, for the love of
God, to provide for their wants. Many, therefore, after his example, brought them bread
and wine and other things necessary for food,
for the love of God, and so arranged among
themselves that, during that whole Lent, all
things needful were provided for them. And
Brother Giles, reflecting on the great mercy of
God and the charity of these people, said to
his companion, "Dearest brother, hitherto we
have prayed to God to provide for our necessities, and He has heard us; now it behoves us
to give thanks to Him, and to pray for those
who have fed us by their alms, and for all Christian people." And such grace did God grant to
the fervour and devotion of Brother Giles, that
many, after his example, forsook this blind
world, and many who had no vocation to relig-

ion did most austere penance in their own homes.

CHAPTER SEVEN
OF THE DAY OF THE HOLY BROTHER GILES'S DEATH

On the vigil of St George, at the hour of Matins, fifty-two years having now elapsed since he received the habit of St Francis, the soul of Brother Giles was received by God into the glory of Paradise.

CHAPTER EIGHT
HOW A HOLY MAN BEING IN PRAYER SAW THE SOUL OF BROTHER GILES PASS TO ETERNAL LIFE

A holy man who was praying when Brother Giles passed from this life, saw his soul, with a multitude of others just freed from Purgatory, ascend into heaven; and he beheld Jesus Christ, with a multitude of angels, meeting the soul of Brother Giles, and so ascending again with all those angels and blessed souls, and with the sound of a most ravishing melody, to heaven.

CHAPTER NINE
HOW, BY THE MERITS OF BROTHER GILES, THE SOUL OF THE FRIEND OF A FRIAR PREACHER WAS DELIVERED FROM THE PAINS OF PURGATORY

While Brother Giles was lying sick, a few days before his death, a friar of St Dominic became sick unto death. Another friar, who was a friend of his, said to the sick brother, "My brother, I desire, if God permit, that after thy death thou return to me and tell me in what state thou art"; and the sick man promised to return if it should be possible. He died on the same day with Brother Giles, and after his death he appeared to the living Friar Preacher, and said, "It is the will of God that I should fulfil my promise." Then said the living man to the dead, "How is it with thee?" and the dead answered, "Well; for I died on the same day that a holy Friar Minor, named Giles, passed from this life; for whose great sanctity Christ granted to him that he should carry with him to holy Paradise all the souls that were in Purgatory, among whom I was suffering great torments; and now, by the merits of the holy Brother Giles, I am delivered from them"; and having said this, he forthwith disappeared: and that friar revealed the vision to no man. But after a time this same friar fell sick, and immediately suspecting that God had struck him because he had not revealed the virtues and the glory of Brother Giles, he sent for the Friar Minor; and there came to him ten, two by two; and they being gathered together with the Friars Preacher, he declared to them with great devotion the aforesaid vision; and, diligent inquiry having been made, it was found that the two had indeed passed from this life on one and the same day.

CHAPTER TEN

Brother Bonaventura of Bagnioreggio said of
Brother Giles, that God had given him especial graces, not only for himself, but for all those
also who should recommend themselves to him
with a devout intention in any spiritual necessity. He wrought many miracles, both during his lifetime and after his death, as appears
by his legend, and passed from this life on the
Feast of St George in the year 1252. He is buried in the convent of the Friars Minor
at Perugia.

CHAPTERS CONTAINING CERTAIN INSTRUCTIONS AND NOTABLE SAYINGS OF BROTHER GILES

CHAPTER ONE

THE GRACE OF GOD, AND THE virtues which flow therefrom, are a way and a ladder that leads to heaven; but vices and sins are a ladder and a way leading to the depths of hell. Vices and sins are a venomous and mortal poison, but virtues and good works are a salutary medicine. One grace draws and leads another after it; one vice drags another in its train. Grace desires not to be praised, and vice cannot endure to be despised. The mind reposes tranquilly in humility, whose daughter is patience.

Holy purity of heart sees God, and true devotion enjoys Him.

If thou lovest, thou shalt be loved.

If thou servest, thou shalt be served.

If thou fearest, thou shalt be feared.

If thou dost good to others, fitting it is that others should do good to thee.

But blessed is he who truly loves, and desires not to be loved again.

Blessed is he who serves, and desires not to be served.

Blessed is he who fears, and desires not to be feared.

Blessed is he who does good to others, and desires not that others should do good to him.

But because these things are very sublime and of high perfection, therefore they that are foolish can neither understand nor attain unto them.

R

FLOWERS OF SAINT FRANCIS

There are three things that are very sublime and very profitable, which he who has once acquired shall never fall.

The first is, that thou bear willingly and gladly, for the love of Jesus Christ, every affliction that shall befall thee.

The second is, that thou daily humble thyself in every thing thou doest, and in every thing thou seest.

The third is, that thou love faithfully with all thy heart that invisible and supreme Good which thou canst not behold with thy bodily eyes.

Those things which are most despised and decried by worldly men are most truly pleasing and acceptable to God and His saints; and those things which are most loved and esteemed, and are most pleasing in the eyes of worldly men, are most despised, contemned, and hated by God and His saints.

This frightful disorder proceeds from human ignorance and malice; for wretched man loves most those things which he ought to hate, and hates those which he ought to love.

Brother Giles said one day to another friar, "Tell me, dearest brother, is thine a good soul?" and the brother answered, "I know not." Then said Brother Giles, "My brother, I would have thee to know that the things which make a soul good and blessed are holy contrition, holy humility, holy charity, holy devotion, and holy joy."

CHAPTER TWO

All those things which we can think with our heart, or speak with our tongue, or see with our eyes, or feel with our hands, are as nothing in comparison with those which we can neither think, nor see, nor touch. All the saints and wise men who have passed away, and all those who are now in this present life, and all those who shall come after us,—all those who have spoken or written, or shall speak or write, of God,—shall never be able to say so much of Him as a grain of millet in comparison with the whole extent of heaven and earth; nay, a thousand million times less. For all that holy Scripture tells us of God is but as the lisping prattle of a mother to her babe, who could not understand her words did she speak after any other manner. Brother Giles said once to a secular judge, "Dost thou believe that the gifts of God are great?" And the judge said, "I believe it." To which Brother Giles replied, "I will show thee that thou dost not truly believe it." And then he said to him, "What is the value of thy worldly possessions?" The judge answered, "Perhaps about ten thousand pounds." Then Brother Giles said, "Wouldst thou give this property of thine for ten thousand pounds?" The judge answered, without hesitation, "Assuredly, I would do so willingly." Then Brother Giles said, "It is a thing most certain that all the possessions of this world are nothing worth in comparison with heavenly things; wherefore, then, givest thou not these possessions of thine to Christ, to pur-

259

chase these celestial and eternal riches?" And the judge, being wise with the foolish wisdom of this world, made answer to that pure and simple Brother Giles, "Dost thou believe, Brother Giles, that there is any man whose external actions accord perfectly with the measure of his internal belief?" And Brother Giles replied, "Listen, my beloved: it is most certain that all the saints have striven actually to carry into effect, to the utmost extent of their power, all that they knew and understood to be the will of God; and those things which they were unable to carry into execution in external act, they fulfilled by the holy desires of their will, which supplied their defect of power to perform the action." Brother Giles said again, "If any man had perfect faith, he would soon arrive at perfection, and attain to a full assurance of his salvation. What harm, or what injury, could any temporal adversity in this present life do to the man who, with firm faith, looks forward to that eternal and supreme and most perfect blessedness? And what can any prosperity or temporal good in this world avail the wretched man who looks forward to eternal perdition? Nevertheless, let no man, however sinful he be, despair, so long as he lives, of the infinite mercy of God; inasmuch as there is not a tree in the world so twisted and knotted and gnarled but may be fashioned and polished and beautified by the hand of man; so likewise there is no man in this world so wicked and so sinful but God can convert him, and adorn him with singular graces and many virtuous gifts."   269

No man can attain to any knowledge or understanding of God but by the virtue of holy humility; for the direct way to ascend is first to descend. All the perils and grievous falls which have happened in this world have arisen from nothing else but the exaltation of the head, *i.e.* of the mind, by pride. This is proved by the fall of the devil, who was driven out of Heaven; and by that of Adam, our first parent, who was banished from Paradise by the exaltation of his head, *i.e.* by disobedience, We see it also in the example of the Pharisee spoken of by Christ in the Gospel, and in many others also.

And so also the contrary truth, *i.e.* that all the great blessings which have ever been bestowed upon the world have proceeded from abasement of the head, *i.e.* from the humiliation of the mind, as is proved by example of the blessed and most humble Virgin Mary, the publican, the good thief on the cross, and many others in holy Scripture. And, therefore, good it were if we could find some great and heavy weight, which, being tied round our neck, would draw us down to the earth, and force us to humble ourselves.

A friar once said to Brother Giles, "Father, tell me, how can we avoid this pride?" To whom Brother Giles made this reply: "Rest assured, my brother, that thou canst never hope to be free from pride until thou hast first placed thy mouth where thou dost set thy feet; but if thou wilt well consider the gifts of God, thou wilt clearly see that thou hast reason to bow thy head. And again, if thou wilt meditate on thy defects and thy manifold offences against God, in all and by all thou wilt find reasons for humbling thyself. But woe to those who desire to be honoured in their unworthiness! He hath one degree of humility, who knows himself to be opposed to his own true good. He hath a second, who restores the goods of another to their proper owner, and does not appropriate them to himself. For every virtue and every good thing which a man finds in himself, instead of appropriating it to himself, he is bound to refer to God, from whom all graces, and all virtues, and all good things proceed. And on the other hand, every sinful passion of the soul, and every vice which a man finds within himself, he should attribute to himself considering that they all proceed from himself and his own malice, and from no other source.

"Blessed is the man who knows and accounts himself to be vile in the eyes of God, and also in the sight of men.

"Blessed is he who always judges himself and condemns himself, and none but himself; for he shall not be condemned in that last and terrible eternal judgment.

"Blessed is he who shall submit himself wholly to the yoke of obedience and the judgment of others, as the holy Apostles before and after they received the Holy Spirit."

Brother Giles said also: "Let him who would acquire and possess perfect peace and quiet of mind account every man his superior, and himself the inferior and subject of all.

"Blessed is the man who, in his works and in his words, desires neither to be seen nor known for anything else but for what God made him.

"Blessed is the man who knows how to keep and hide within his heart divine revelations and consolations; for there is nothing so secret but God can reveal it when it pleases Him. If the most holy and perfect man in the world were to esteem and account himself to be the vilest and most miserable sinner in the world, this would be true humility.

"Holy humility loves not to talk, nor the holy fear of God to use many words."

Brother Giles said again: "It seems to me that holy humility is like the thunderbolt; for, even as the thunderbolt makes a fearful noise, crushing, breaking, and burning that whereon it lights, and yet we can never find that thunderbolt itself, so does humility strike, and disperse, and burn up, and consume every evil and vice and sin, and yet itself can nowhere be seen.

"He who possesses humility, by that humility finds grace with God, and perfect peace with his neighbour."

CHAPTER   FOUR

He who fears nothing, shows that he has nothing to lose. The holy fear of God orders, gov-
erns, and rules the soul, and prepares it to receive His grace.

If a man possesses any grace or any divine
virtue, it is holy fear which preserves it in him.

And he who has not acquired grace or virtue,
acquires it by means of holy fear.

The holy fear of God is a channel of divine
grace, inasmuch as it quickly leads the soul in
which it dwells to the attainment of holiness and
all divine graces. No creature that ever fell into
sin would have so fallen if it had possessed the
holy fear of God. But this holy gift of fear is given
only to the perfect, because the more perfect
any man is, the more timorous and humble he is.

Blessed is the man who looks upon this
world as his prison-house, and continually
bears in mind how grievously he has offended
his Lord.

Greatly ought a man to fear, lest pride should
give him a sudden thrust, and cause him to fall
from the state of grace in which he is; for no
man is ever secure from falling, so beset are we
by foes; and these foes are the flatteries of this
wretched world and of our own flesh, which,
together with the devil, is the unrelenting enemy of our soul.

A man has greater reason to fear being de-
luded and overcome by his own malice than
by any other enemy.

SAYINGS OF BROTHER GILES

It is impossible for a man to attain to any divine grace or virtue, or to persevere in it, without holy fear.

He who has not the fear of God within him is in great danger of eternal perdition.

The fear of God makes a man obey humbly, and bow his head beneath the yoke of obedience; and the more a man fears God, the more fervently he adores Him.

The gift of prayer is no small gift, to whomsoever it is given.

The virtuous actions of men, howsoever great they may seem to us, are not to be reckoned or rewarded according to our estimation, but according to the estimation and good pleasure of God; for God does not look to the amount of the labour, but to the amount of humility and love. Our surest way, then, is always to love, and to keep ourselves in humility; and never to trust to ourselves to do any good, but always to distrust the thoughts which spring up in our own mind under the appearance of good.

CHAPTER   FIVE

BROTHER GILES ON THE VIRTUE OF HOLY PATIENCE AT ALL TIMES

He who with steadfast humility and patience endures tribulations for the fervent love of God, shall soon attain to great graces and virtues; he shall be lord of this world, and shall receive the earnest of that glorious world which is to come.

265

FLOWERS OF SAINT FRANCIS

Every thing which a man does, be it good or evil, he does it unto himself. Therefore, be not thou offended with him who injures thee, but rather, in humble patience, sorrow only for his sin, having compassion on him, and praying fervently to God for him. For, in as far as a man is strong to suffer and endure injuries and tribulations patiently for the love of God, so great, and no greater, is he before God; and the weaker a man is to endure sufferings and adversities for the love of God, the less is he in the sight of God.

If any man praise thee and speak well of thee, render thou that praise unto God alone; and if any man reproach thee or speak evil of thee, do thou help him by speaking still worse of thyself.

If thou wouldst make thine own cause good, strive to make it appear evil, and to make that of thy companion good, ever accusing thyself and excusing thy neighbour. When any one strives and contends with thee, if thou wouldst conquer, lose, and thou shalt conquer; for if thou wilt strive to obtain the victory, when thou shalt believe thou hast obtained it, thou shalt find thyself shamefully defeated. And therefore, my brother, believe me assuredly that the certain way to gain is to lose. But if we endure not tribulation well, we shall never attain to eternal consolation. It is a far more blessed and meritorious thing to endure injuries and rerpoaches patiently, and without murmuring, for the love of God, than to feed a hundred poor, or to keep a perpetual fast. But what profits it a man, or how does it benefit him, to afflict his body with many

266

fasts, vigils, and disciplines, if he cannot endure the lightest insult from his neighbour? And yet from this he might derive greater reward and higher merit than from all the sufferings he could inflict of his own will upon himself; for to endure reproaches and injuries from our neighbour with humble and uncomplaining patience, will purge away our sins faster than they could be cleansed by a fountain of many tears.

Blessed is the man who has ever before the eyes of his mind the remembrance of his sins, and of the favours of God; for he will endure with patience all tribulations and adversities for which he expects so great consolation. The man who is truly humble looks for no reward from God, but endeavours only to satisfy Him in all things, knowing himself to be His debtor; every good thing which he has he acknowledges to come from the free bounty of God, and every evil that befalls him to proceed from his sins alone.

A friar once said to Brother Giles, "Father, what shall we do if some great adversity or tribu lation befall us in these times?" to whom Brother Giles replied, "My brother, I would have thee to know, that if we be such men as we ought to be, though the Lord should rain down stones and javelins from heaven, they could not harm or injure us; because, if a man be in truth such as he ought to be, every evil and tribulation would be turned to his good; for we know what the Apostle saith, that all things shall be turned into good for those who love God; and in like manner all things shall turn to the condemnation and punishment of the man whose will is evil.

"If thou wouldst be saved and attain to eternal glory, desire not revenge, nor the punishment of any creature; for the inheritance of the saints is ever to do good and to receive evil. If thou didst but know, indeed, how much and how grievously thou hast offended thy Creator, thou wouldst know that it is meet and right that all creatures should persecute thee, and inflict pain and sorrow on thee, to avenge the offences which thou hast offered to their Creator.

"It is a great and high virtue in a man to overcome himself; for he who overcomes himself shall overcome all his enemies, and persevere in all good. But still greater virtue would it be in a man to suffer himself to be overcome by all other men, for thus would he become victor over all his enemies, *i.e.* sin, the devil, the world, and his own flesh. If thou wilt be saved, renounce and despise every consolation which thou canst receive from all the things of this world, and from all mortal creatures, because greater and more frequent are the falls which arise from prosperity and consolation than those which come from adversity and tribulation."

A religious once complained of his superior in the presence of Brother Giles, because of a severe obedience which he had received from him; to whom Brother Giles made answer, "Dearest brother, the more thou dost complain, the heavier dost thou make thy burden, and the harder it will be to carry it; and the more humbly and devoutly thou dost submit thy neck to the yoke of holy obedience, the sweeter and the lighter will that yoke be to bear. But it seems to me that thou art not willing to bear reproach in this world for the love of Christ, and yet desirest in the next to be with Christ thou art not willing in this world to be persecuted and evil spoken of for Christ, and in the other world thou wouldst fain be blessed and welcomed by Christ; thou willest not to labour in this world, and thou wouldst repose and take thy rest in the other. I tell thee, brother, brother! that thou dost grievously deceive thyself, for it is by the way of shame and humiliation and reproach that a man attains to true celestial glory; and by patiently enduring derision and contumely for the love of Christ, doth a man attain to the glory of Christ. For the worldly proverb says well, *He who gives not what costs him something, shall not receive that which he desires.*

"The horse is a noble and useful creature; for in his swiftest course he suffers himself to be ruled, guided, and turned hither and thither, backwards and forwards, according to the will of the rider; and so should it be with the servant of God, who should suffer himself to be ruled, guided, twisted, and bent, according to the will of his superior; nay, of all others, for the love of Christ. If thou wilt be perfect, strive earnestly to be virtuous and gracious, and fight valiantly

269

against all vices, bearing patiently all adversities, for the love of thy Lord, who was troubled, afflicted, reproached, beaten, crucified, and slain for thy love, and not for His own fault, nor for His own glory, nor for His own profit, but only for thy salvation. And to do this which I say, it is absolutely needful that thou overcome thyself; for little will it profit thee to lead and draw other souls to God, if thou be not first drawn and led to Him thyself."

CHAPTER   SIX
BROTHER GILES ON SLOTH AND THE RESULTS THEREOF

The slothful man loses both this world and the next, because he bears no fruit in himself, and is of no profit to others.

It is impossible for a man to acquire any virtue without diligence and great labour. When thou mightest stand in a place of safety, stand not in a place of danger.

He abides in a place of security who painfully and diligently labours and toils in God, and for the Lord his God, not for fear of punishment or hope of reward, but for the love of God. The man who refuses to labour and suffer for the love of Christ, truly refuses to share the glory of Christ; and thus, inasmuch as diligence is useful and profitable to us, is negligence hurtful and dangerous.

As sloth is the way to hell, so holy diligence is the way to heaven.

SAYINGS OF BROTHER GILES

Most solicitous and diligent ought a man to
be in acquiring and preserving virtue and the
grace of God by a continual faithful co-oper-
ation with the grace vouchsafed to him; for it
often happens that he loses the fruit among
the leaves, and the grain amid the straw. On
some our good God graciously bestows fruit
with but few leaves; to others He gives fruit
and leaves together; there are others, again,
who have neither fruit nor leaves. It seems to
me a greater thing to know how well to guard
and secretly to preserve the gifts and graces
vouchsafed us by God, than to know how to
gain them; for though a man know well to acquire and gather up wealth, yet, if he know not
well how to store it up and to preserve it, he
will never be rich; while another, who carefully
treasures up what by little and little he has acquired, becomes a man of great wealth.

Oh, what a quantity of water would the Ti-
ber contain, did none of it flow away in other
channels!

Man asks of God an infinite gift, a gift which
has no measure and no bound, and yet he will
but love God by measure and within bounds.
He who desires to be loved by God, and to receive from Him an infinite, immense, and su-
perabundant reward, ought to love God su-
premely and immensely, and to serve Him
without limit or cessation. Blessed is he who
loves God with all his heart and all his mind,
and labours and suffers with both mind and
body for the love of God, and yet seeks no re-
271

ward under heaven, but accounts it only to be his bounden duty.

If one man were exceedingly poor and needy, and another were to say to him, "I will lend thee something very precious for the space of three days; and know, that if thou turn this thing to good account within the space of these three days, thou shalt gain infinite treasure, and become rich for evermore"; certain it is that this poor man would be most diligent in turning that precious thing to the best possible account. And so I say to thee, that the thing which God hath lent to us is our body, which in His goodness He hath lent us for three days; inasmuch as our whole life here below may be compared to three days.

If, then, thou wouldst be rich, and eternally enjoy the sweetness of His divine presence, strive to make the best profit thou canst of this loan from the hand of God for the space of these three days, *i.e.* of this thy body, which He hath lent thee for the brief space of thy mortal life; for if thou art not diligent to labour and traffic in this present life, whilst yet thou hast time, thou shalt never enjoy the everlasting riches, nor repose eternally in the calm rest of heaven.

But if all the wealth of the world were in the hands of a man who made no use of it, either for himself or others, what would it profit either him or them? Assuredly it would be of no use or benefit whatever.

On the other hand, a man who possesses little may, by turning that little to good account, bring forth abundant fruit, both for himself and for the benefit of others.

There is a proverb of this world which says, "Never set an empty pot to boil on the fire, expecting thy neighbour to come and fill it." And in like manner the good God will not have thee to leave any grace empty and unused; because He never gives a single grace to any man that it should remain unused, but He gives it, on the contrary, that it should be filled and used by the performance of good works; for a good will is not sufficient unless it be fulfilled and carried into effect by holy actions.

A wandering man said once to Brother Giles, "Father, I pray thee, give me some little consolation"; to whom Brother Giles made answer, "My brother, strive to be well with God, and then shalt thou have the consolation thou needest; for unless a man prepare within his soul a fair dwelling, in which God may abide and rest, he will never find peace, or home, or consolation amongst creatures."

When any man wishes to do evil, he asks not much counsel how to do it; but to do well he takes much counsel, and makes long delay. Brother Giles said once to his companions, "My brethren, it seems to me that there is no one nowadays who wishes to do those things which he sees to be most profitable to him both in soul and body. Believe me, my brethren, for I can attest it in all truth, that the more a man shuns and avoids the yoke of Christ, the more grievous he makes it to himself, and the more heav-

ily it weighs upon him; and the more gener-
ously a man takes it up, lending himself volunt-
arily to its weight, the lighter and the sweeter
he will find it to bear. Now it is the will of God
that man should labour in this world for the
good of the body, provided he neglect not that
of the soul; for the soul and the body, without
any manner of doubt, shall be united together
to suffer or to enjoy for all eternity; *i.e.* either
to suffer eternally in hell inconceivable pains
and torments, or to enjoy with the saints and
angels in Paradise perpetual joys and unspeakable consolations, as the reward of their good
works. But if a man do good without humility,
it shall be turned into evil; for there are many
who have done many works which appeared
good and praiseworthy, but because they wanted humility the works have become corrupt, and
have thus shown that they sprang from pride;
for those which have their root in humility
never decay."

A friar once said to Brother Giles, "Father,
it seems to me that we have not yet learned to
know our true good." And Brother Giles replied, "My brother, it is certain that every one
practises the art which he has learned, for no
man can do well what he has not learned to do;
wouldst thou know then, my brother, that the
most noble art in the world is that of well-
doing; and who can know it except he first
learn it?"

Blessed is the man whom no created thing
can disedify; but more blessed is he who re-

ceives edification from every thing which he
sees and hears.

CHAPTER SEVEN

BROTHER GILES ON THE CONTEMPT OF TEMPORAL
THINGS

Many shall be the sorrows and troubles of the
miserable man who sets his heart and desires
upon earthly things, for which he forsakes and
loses the things of heaven, and at last those of
earth also. The eagle flies very high; but if a
weight be laid upon his wings, he can no longer soar aloft: and so by the weight of earthly
things man is hindered from soaring on high, *i.e.*
from attaining to perfection; but the wise man,
who lays the weight of the remembrance of
death and judgment on the wings of his heart,
cannot fly and range freely amid the vanities
and riches of this world, lest they should prove
to him an occasion of damnation. We daily see
men of the world toil and labour hard, and place
themselves in many bodily dangers, to acquire
its false riches; and then, after they have thus
laboured and acquired, in a moment they die,
and leave behind them all that they had gathered together in their lifetime. Therefore there is
no dependence to be placed on this deceitful
world, which deceives every man who trusts to
it, for it is a liar. But he who desires to be truly great and rich indeed, let him love and seek
the true and eternal riches, which never sati-
ate, or weary, or fail.

FLOWERS OF SAINT FRANCIS

Let us take example from the beasts and birds, who, when they receive their food are content, and seek only what they need from hour to hour; and so also ought man to be content with what is just sufficient temperately to supply his necessities, and ask no more. Brother Giles said that St Francis loved the ants less than any other animal, because of the great care they take in the summer to gather and lay up a store of grain against the winter; and that he said he loved the birds far better, because they gather nothing one day for another.

But this gives us an example that we should not remain idle in the summer-time of this present life, lest we should be found empty and without fruit in the winter of the last and final judgment.

CHAPTER   EIGHT

BROTHER GILES ON THE VIRTUE OF HOLY CHASTITY

Our frail and miserable human flesh is like to the swine, which loves to wallow in the mire, and finds its delight therein. Our flesh is the devil's soldier; for it resists and fights against all those things which are pleasing to God and profitable for our salvation. A friar said to Brother Giles, "Father, teach me how to preserve myself from sins of the flesh." And Brother Giles answered him, "My brother, he who wishes to move a large stone, or any other great weight, and carry it to any other place, must try to move it rather by ingenuity than force. And so, if we desire to overcome the vice of impurity, and to acquire the virtue of chastity, we must set to work rather by the way of humility, and by a good and discreet method of spiritual discipline, than by a rash and presumptuous use of penitential austerities. Every vice troubles and obscures the fair glory of holy chastity; for it is like a bright mirror which is clouded and darkened, not only by contact with impure and defiling things, but by the mere breath of man. It is impossible for a man to attain to any spiritual grace, so long as he is inclined to carnal concupis cence; and therefore, whithersoever thou turn thyself, thou shalt never be able to attain to spiritual grace until thou canst master all the vices of the flesh. Wherefore, fight valiantly against thy frail and sensual flesh, thine own worst enemy, which wages war against thee day and night. And know that he who shall overcome this mortal enemy of ours has most certainly defeated and discomfited all his other enemies, and shall attain to spiritual grace, and every degree of virtue and perfection."

Brother Giles said, "Amongst all other virtues, I would set the virtue of chastity first, because sweet chastity contains all perfection in itself; but there is no other virtue which can be perfect without chastity."

A friar asked Brother Giles, saying, "Father, is not the virtue of charity greater and more excellent than that of chastity?" And Brother

277

Giles said, "Tell me, brother, what is there in this world more chaste than holy charity?"

Brother Giles often sang this sonnet:

"O holy chastity, how good art thou!
How precious and so sweet!
They who have tasted thee know;
But fools understand thee not."

A friar said once to Brother Giles, "Father, thou dost so often commend the virtue of chastity, that I would fain ask of thee what it is?" And Brother Giles answered, "My Brother, chastity is, in strict truth, the careful and continual custody of our corporal and spiritual senses, in order to preserve them pure and immaculate for God alone."

CHAPTER NINE

BROTHER GILES ON THE TEMPTATIONS OF THIS WORLD

MAN is unable to possess in tranquillity the great graces which he receives from God, because many contrarieties and perturbations and oppositions arise against those graces; for the more acceptable any man is to God, and more vehemently is he assailed and buffeted by the devil. In order, therefore, to correspond with the grace which he has received from God, he must maintain an unceasing warfare; for the fiercer conflict, the more glorious shall be the victor's crown. But we have not many conflicts, nor many impediments, nor many temptations,

278

because we have advanced but a little way in the spiritual life.

True it is, however, that if a man walk warily and well in the way of God, he shall feel neither fatigue nor weariness in his journey; but the man who travels by the world's broad way shall never be free from labour, weariness, anguish, tribulation, and pain, even to the day of his death.

Then said one of the friars to Brother Giles, "Father, it seems to me that thou teachest us two things, the one contrary to the other; for thou sayest first, the more virtuous a man is, and the more acceptable to God, the greater conflicts has he to endure in the spiritual life; and next thou sayest the contrary, *i.e.* that the man who walks well and warily in the way of God, shall feel neither weariness nor fatigue in his journey." To whom Brother Giles thus explained the contrariety of these two sayings: "It is most certain, my brother, that the devils bring a more fearful array of temptations against those who have a good will than against those who have not. But what harm can the devils and all the evils of this world do to the man who walks on discreetly and fervently in the way of God, and labours and toils faithfully therein, knowing and seeing as he does that his reward shall a thousand times over-pay his labour? And further, I tell thee, of a truth, that he who is enkindled with the fire of divine love, the more fiercely he is assailed by temptations to sin, the more deeply will he hold it in ab-

279

horrence and detestation. The malignant demons ever hasten to tempt a man when he is
under some bodily weakness or infirmity, or
when he is in some great sorrow or anguish, or
in a state of tepidity, or when he is hungry or
thirsty, or has received some insult or affront,
or some spiritual or temporal injury; for those
wicked spirits know well that it is at such times,
and in such circumstances, that he is most open
to temptation. But I say to thee, of a truth, that
for every temptation and for every vice which
thou shalt overcome, thou shalt acquire a virtue;
and for each vice, in the conquest of which thou
shalt overcome thyself, thou shalt obtain a larger grace and a brighter crown."

A friar once asked counsel of Brother Giles,
saying, "Father, I am frequently assailed by an
evil temptation, and I have oftentimes besought the Lord to deliver me from it, and yet
He takes it not from me ; counsel me, father;
what ought I to do?" To whom Brother Giles
made the following reply: "My brother, when a
king arrays one of his knights in strong armour
of proof, it is a token that he requires him to
fight valiantly for the love of him against his
enemies."

Another friar said to him, "Father, what can
I do to attain to greater fervour and love of
prayer? for when I go to pray I am hard, cold,
dry, and indevout." Brother Giles answered
him thus : "A king has two servants : one of
them has armour of proof, and the other has
none; both desire to go forth and fight against

the enemies of the king. He who is well armed
enters into the battle and fights valiantly; but
the other, who is unarmed, says thus to his lord:
'My liege, you see that I am unarmed and de-
fenceless; but for your love I will gladly enter
into the battle, and fight there all unarmed as
I am.' Then the good king, seeing the love of
his faithful soldier, says to his servants, 'Go
with this my true follower, and provide him
with all the armour necessary for his defence,
that he may securely enter into the conflict;
and emblazon his shield with my royal bearings,
that he may be known as my loyal knight.'
And thus it oftentimes comes to pass, when a
man goes to prayer, that he feels himself to be
naked, indevout, cold, and hard of heart; but
when he puts a force upon himself, and for the
love of our Lord enters boldly into the battle-
field of prayer, our loving Lord and King, beholding the gallant bearing of His faithful
knight, gives him, by the hands of His minis-
tering angels, fervent devotion and good will.
When a man has begun some great and labor-
ious work, such as clearing the ground and cul-
tivating the vine that it may bring forth its fruit
in due season, he is often tempted by the great
toil and manifold hindrances he meets with to
weary of his work, and even to repent that he
ever began it. But if notwithstanding he perseveres until the harvest-time, he will forget all
that he has endured in his joy at the fruit of his
labours. And so the man who is strong to resist temptations shall attain to great consol-

281

ations; for after tribulation, as St Paul tells us, shall be given the consolations and the crowns of eternal life. And not only shall they who resist temptation obtain the rewards of heaven, but they shall be recompensed even in this life; as says the Psalmist, 'Lord, according to the multitude of my temptations and sorrows, Thy consolations shall rejoice my soul.' So that the greater the conflict and the temptation, the more glorious shall be the crown."

A friar, asking counsel of Brother Giles concerning a temptation, said, "O father, I am beset by two evil temptations: the one, that when I do any thing good, I am immediately tempted to vain-glory; the other, that when I do any thing evil, I forthwith fall into such sadness and despondency, that I am almost in despair." To whom Brother Giles replied, "My brother, thou dost well and wisely to mourn for thy sins; but I counsel thee to do so discreetly and temperately, and always to remember that the mercy of God is greater than thy sins. And if the infinite mercy of God receives to penance a man who is a great sinner, and who sins wilfully, when he repents, thinkest thou that the good God will forsake the man who sins not wilfully, he being also contrite and penitent? I counsel thee likewise not to refrain from doing well, for fear of vain-glory; for if the husbandmen were to say in the seed-time, 'I will not sow my seed, lest perhaps the birds come and eat it up,' assuredly he would reap no fruit that year. But if he sow his seed, although the birds may consume a portion of it, he will gather in the greater part when the harvest-time comes. And so with the man who is tempted to vain-glory, but continually resists the temptation, I say that he does not by reason of it lose the merit of his good works."

A friar said to Brother Giles, "Father, I have read that St Bernard once said the seven Penitential Psalms with such devotion and tranquillity of mind, that he thought of nothing else the whole time but of the words of the psalms he was saying." And Brother Giles answered him thus: "My brother, I think more of the prowess of the knight who holds and valiantly defends a castle which is assailed and compassed round by enemies, so that he suffers none of them to effect an entrance, than if he were dwelling therein in peace, and undisturbed by any hostile assault."

CHAPTER TEN
BROTHER GILES ON THE NECESSITY OF HOLY PENANCE

A man ought continually to afflict and macerate his body, and willingly endure every injury, tribulation, anguish, shame, contempt, reproach, adversity, and persecution, for the love of our good Master and Lord Jesus Christ, who gave us an example of all this in His own Person; for, from the moment of His glorious Nativity until that of His most holy Passion, He continually endured anguish, tribulation,

283

pain, contempt, sorrow, and persecution, only
for our salvation. And therefore, if we would
attain to a state of grace, it is above all things
necessary that, as far as possible, we walk in
the footsteps of our good Master Jesus Christ.
A secular once said to Brother Giles, "Father,
how can we seculars attain to a state of grace?"
And Brother Giles replied, "My brother, a man
must first repent of his sins with great contrition of heart; next, he must confess them to
the priest with bitter and heartfelt sorrow, accusing himself of them sincerely, without excuse or concealment; next, he must perfectly
perform the penance enjoined him by the confessor; also he must guard himself from every
vice, from all sin, and from all occasions of sin;
he must likewise exercise himself in good works
towards God and his neighbour; and by so doing, a man shall attain to a state of grace and
virtue."

Blessed is the man who feels a continual sorrow for his sins, weeping over them day and
night in bitterness of heart, only because of the
offence he has thereby offered to God.

Blessed is the man who shall always have
before his eyes the sorrows, pains, and afflictions of Jesus Christ, and who for his love shall
neither desire nor receive any temporal consolation in this bitter and tempestuous world,
until he shall attain to the celestial consolations of eternal life, wherein all his desires
shall be fulfilled in a plenitude of joy.

CHAPTER ELEVEN

Prayer is the beginning, the middle, and the
end of all good; prayer illuminates the soul,
and enables it to discern between good and evil.
Every sinner ought to pray daily with fervour
of heart, *i.e.* he should pray to God humbly to
give him a perfect knowledge of his own miser-
ies and sins, and of the benefits which he has
received and still receives from the good God.
But how can that man know God who knows
not how to pray? And for all those who shall
be saved, it is above all things needful that,
sooner or later, they be converted to the use of
holy prayer. Brother Giles said thus: "If a man
had a son who had been condemned for his
evil deeds to death or banishment, most certainly he would use every means in his power,
and labour day and night, to obtain from the
emperor the pardon of his son, and his release
from banishment or death; he would make
many prayers and supplications, and give presents or pay fines to the utmost of his power,
either in his own person or by the hands of his
kindred and friends. Now, if a man do all this
for the mortal life of his son, how much more
careful and diligent ought he to be in praying to
God, and in beseeching good men in this world
and the saints in heaven to pray for his own
immortal soul, when it is banished from the
heavenly city, or when it lies under sentence
of eternal death for its many sins!"

A friar said to Brother Giles, "Father, it

seems to me that a man ought to feel great sorrow and grief of heart when he experiences not the grace of devotion in his prayer." Brother Giles answered him, "My brother, my counsel to thee is to proceed calmly and gently; for if thou hast a little good wine in a bottle, and if in that same bottle there were dregs below the good wine, thou would assuredly take care not to shake or move it, for fear of mixing the good wine with the dregs. Now, until thy prayer be freed from all vicious and carnel concupiscence, thou shalt receive no divine consolation because that prayer is not pure in the sight of God which is mingled with the dregs of carnality. And therefore a man should strive as much as possible to free himself from all the dregs of worldly concupiscence, that his prayer may be pure before God, and that he may derive devotion and divine consolation from it."

A friar asked Brother Giles this question: "Father, why is it that a man is more disturbed by temptations during prayer than at any other time?" To which Brother Giles made the following answer: "When a man has to bring any question for the determination of the judge, and he goes to him for aid or counsel, his adversary no sooner hears of it than he straightway appears to oppose and resist his appeal, and to throw every impediment in the way of his cause. And so it is when a man goes to prayer, for he goes to seek help from God in the cause of his soul: and immediately appears his adversary the devil, with his temptations, to make great opposition and resistence, and to use every effort, artifice, and labour to hinder his prayer, lest it should prove acceptable in the sight of God, and to take from it all merit and all consolation. And this we may plainly see; for when we are speaking of worldly things we perhaps feel no temptation, nor experience any distraction of mind; but when we go to prayer to delight and console ourselves, we are suddenly pierced with many arrows, *i.e.* by divers temptations, which the devil puts in our way in order to distract our mind, that the soul may have no delight or consolation in its converse with God." Brother Giles said, furthermore, that a man in prayer ought to be like a good knight in battle, who, however hard pressed by his enemy, scorns to leave the field, but resists manfully, striving to overcome his foe, that he may rejoice and triumph in the glory of victory. But if he should leave the battle for fear of wounds or death, he would assuredly meet with nothing but shame, confusion, and dishonour. And so ought we to do, *i.e.* we ought not to intermit our prayer for every temptation which may present itself, but resist courageously; for, as the Apostle says, "Blessed is the man that endureth temptation; for, when he hath overcome, he shall receive the crown of eternal life." But if, because of temptations, a man abandons prayer, he will certainly be defeated, dishonoured, and overcome by his adversary the devil.

Another friar said to Brother Giles, "Father, I see some men who have received from God

287

the gift of tears, which they shed abundantly and devoutly in their prayer; and I can experience none of these graces when I pray to God." To whom Brother Giles made answer: "My brother, I counsel thee to labour humbly and faithfully in this thy prayer, for the fruits of the earth cannot be gathered in without labour and fatigue having been used beforehand; and even after this labour and toil the desired fruit follows not immediately, nor until its appointed season; so also God gives not these graces in prayer immediately nor until the fitting time is come, and the mind is wholly purified from all carnal vices and affections. Therefore, my brother, do thou labour humbly in prayer; for God, who is all good and all gracious, knows all things, and discerns what is best for thee; and when the fit time and season comes, He will, in His loving mercy, give thee abundant fruit of consolation."

Another friar said to Brother Giles, "What art thou doing, Brother Giles? What art thou doing, Brother Giles?" And he answered, "I am doing evil." And that friar said to him, "What evil doest thou?" Then Brother Giles turned to another friar, and said to him, "Tell me, my brother, which, thinkest thou, is readiest, our Lord God to give us His grace, or we to receive it?" And that friar made answer, "Most assuredly God is readier to give us grace than we to receive it." Then said Brother Giles, "Do we well in this?" And that friar said, "Nay; but we do evil." Then Brother Giles turned to the friar who spoke first, and said, "See, brother, this shows us clearly that we do evil, and that I spoke truly when I answered thee that I was doing evil." Brother Giles said also, "Many works are praised and commended in holy Scripture, such as the works of mercy and other holy operations; but when the Lord speaks of prayer, He saith thus: 'Our heavenly Father seeketh men to adore Him on earth in spirit and in truth.'" Brother Giles said again, that true religious are like wolves; because they never come into public and frequented places but upon great necessity, and seek immediately to return to their secret haunts rather than remain long among men.

Good works adorn the soul; but prayer adorns and illuminates it beyond all others. A friar who was a very familiar companion of Brother Giles said to him, "Father, why goest thou not sometimes to speak of the things of God, to teach and to labour for the salvation of souls?" To whom Brother Giles replied, "My brother, I desire to fulfil my duty to my neighbour with humility, and without injury to my own soul; and that is by prayer." "At least," said the friar, "go sometimes to visit thy parents." And Brother Giles answered: "Knowest thou not what our Lord says in the Gospel, 'He who shall leave father, or mother, or brethren, or sisters, for My sake, shall receive an hundredfold'?" And he added, moreover, "A gentleman entered the Order of Friars Minor whose possessions valued, perhaps, sixty thousand pounds; great, then, shall be the reward of those who leave much for the love of God, since it is to be returned to them an hundredfold. But we who are blind, when we see any man virtuous and pleasing to God, do not understand his perfection, because of our own blindness and imperfection. Were we truly spiritual, we should seldom desire to see or speak with any one, except upon great necessity; for the truly spiritual man desires to dwell apart from creatures, and to be united to God in contemplation."

Then Brother Giles said to another friar, "Father, I would fain know what is contemplation?" And the friar answered, "Father, truly I know not." Then Brother Giles said, "To me it seems that contemplation is a divine fire, a sweet devotion infused by the Holy Ghost, a rapture and suspension of the mind inebriated by the ineffable taste of the divine sweetness, and a sweet and tranquil enjoyment of the soul which is rapt and suspended in loving admiration of the glories of heaven, and an inward and burning consciousness of that celestial and unspeakable glory."

CHAPTER   TWELVE

OF BROTHER GILES ON HOLY SPIRITUAL PRUDENCE

O servant of the heavenly King, who wouldst learn the mysteries and profitable and virtuous lessons of holy spiritual doctrine, open wide the ears of thine understanding, receive with earnest desire of heart, and carefully lay up in the treasure-house of thy memory, the precious store of these spiritual doctrines, warnings, and

SAYINGS OF BROTHER GILES

admonitions, which I now unfold to thee; by
the which thou shalt be illuminated and directed in thy journey on the way of the spiritual
life, and shalt be defended from the malignant
and subtle assaults of thy material and immat-
erial enemies; and so, with humble boldness,
shalt steer thy course safely through the stormy
sea of this present life, until thou shalt attain
to the desired haven of salvation. Listen, then,
my son, and note well what I say to thee.

If thou wouldst see well, pluck out thine
eyes and become blind; if thou wouldst hear
well, become deaf; if thou wouldst speak well,
become dumb; if thou wouldst walk well, stand
still, and travel only with thy mind; if thou
wouldst work well, cut off thy hands, and labour with thy heart; if thou wouldst love well,
hate thyself; if thou wouldst live well, mortify
thyself; if thou wouldst gain much, and become
rich, lose, and become poor; if thou wouldst
enjoy thyself and take thine ease, afflict thyself, and continually fear and distrust thyself;
if thou wouldst be exalted and had in honour,
humble and reproach thyself; if thou wouldst
be reverenced, despise thyself, and do reverence to those who despise and reproach thee;
if thou wouldst always receive good, continually endure evil; if thou wouldst be blessed, desire that all men should curse thee and speak
evil of thee; if thou wouldst enjoy true and
eternal repose, labour and afflict thyself, and
desire every kind of temporal suffering. Oh,
what great wisdom is it to know and do all

these things! but, because it is so high and so
sublime, it is granted by God to few. But I say,
of a truth, that if any man will study these
things and carry them into effect, he will have
no need to go to Paris or Bologna to study any
other theology. For, if a man were to live a
thousand years, and have no external action to
perform, nor any word to speak with his tongue,
I say that he would have enough to do within
his own heart, in labouring internally at the
purification and government and justification
of his heart and mind.

A man should not desire either to see, to
hear, or to speak any thing but for the profit
of his soul. The man who knows not himself is
not known. Woe to us, then, when we receive
the gifts and graces of the Lord, and know not
how to acknowledge them! Woe still greater to
those who neither receive nor acknowledge
them, nor care to receive or possess them!
Man was made to the image of God, and changes as he will; but the good God never changes.

CHAPTER   THIRTEEN
BROTHER GILES: USEFUL USELESS KNOWLEDGE

The man who would know much, must labour
much and humble himself much, abasing himself and bowing his head until his mouth be in
the dust; and then will the Lord bestow on him
great wisdom and knowledge. The highest wisdom is to do always that which is good; acting

virtuously, and guarding carefully against every sin and every occasion of sin, and ever keeping in mind the judgments of God. Brother Giles said once to a man who desired to go to a school to learn secular knowledge, "My brother, wherefore wouldst thou go to this school? I would have thee to learn that the sum of all knowledge is to fear and to love, and these two things are sufficient for thee; for so much knowledge as he can use, and no more, is sufficient for a man. Busy not thyself in learning those things which may be useful to others, but study always and seek and use those which are profitable to thyself. For we often greatly desire knowledge by which we may aid others, and think little of that by which we may profit ourselves; and I say to thee, that the word of God dwells not with the speaker, nor with the hearer, but with the faithful doer thereof. Some men who cannot swim cast themselves in the water to save others from drowning, and so are lost together with them. If thou dost not work out thine own salvation, how shalt thou work out that of thy neighbour? And if thou dost not thine own work well, how shalt thou do the work of another man? for it is not credible that thou shouldst love the soul of another better than thine own.

"The preachers of God's word ought to be standard-bearers, lights and mirrors to the people.

"Blessed is the man who so guides others in the way of salvation, that he ceases not to walk therein himself.

FLOWERS OF SAINT FRANCIS

"Blessed is the man who so teaches others to run therein, that he ceases not to run himself. More blessed is he who so helps others to become rich, that he fails not also to enrich himself.

"I believe that a good preacher admonishes and preaches to himself far more than to other men.

"It seems to me that he who would convert and draw the souls of sinners into the way of God, ought to stand in continual fear lest he should be perverted by them, and drawn by the way of sin and the devil's road to hell."

CHAPTER   FOURTEEN
BROTHER GILES: SPEAKING WELL & SPEAKING ILL

The man who speaks good words and such as are profitable to the soul is truly the mouth of the Holy Ghost; and the man who speaks evil and useless words is certainly the mouth of the devil.

When good spiritual men meet at times to converse together, they should always discourse concerning the beauty of virtue, that they may increase in the love of it, and that virtue may increase in them; that so delighting in it more and more, they may exercise themselves the more diligently in all virtues, and by this continual exercise may attain to a greater love of them; and by this love and this continual exercise and delight in virtue, they may ascend to an ever-increasing and more fervent love of God, and to a higher degree in the spiritual life, and obtain from the Lord greater gifts and a larger measure of divine grace.

The more strongly a man is tempted, the more needful it is that he speak continually of holiness and virtue; for as by means of unholy talk of evil things a man is easily led to do evil, so oftentimes by speaking of virtue a man is led and disposed to virtuous actions. But what shall we say of the good which proceeds from virtue? It is such and so great that we cannot worthily express its sublime, admirable, and infinite excellence.

And again, what shall we say of evil, and of the eternal penalty which follows sin? For it is an abyss so fearful and so deep, that it is beyond the power of our mind to think, or our mouth to speak. I do not think there is less virtue in keeping silence well, than in speaking well; and therefore it seems to me that a man ought to have a neck as long as a crane's, that, when he has to speak, his words may have a long way to travel before they reach his mouth; *i.e.* when a man would speak, let him think and think again, and examine and re-examine very diligently, the how and the why, the time and the manner, the state and condition of his hearers, and his own motive and intention.

CHAPTER   FIFTEEN

What will it profit a man to fast much, and pray, and give alms, and afflict his body, and to have his soul filled with heavenly thoughts, if, after all, he come short of the desired and blessed haven of salvation, holy and steadfast perseverance? We may sometimes behold a fair and tall ship upon the waters, strong and newly built, and laden with a rich and regal freight; and suddenly, by the rising of a tempest, or by the unskilfulness of the helmsman, that proud vessel sinks and miserably perishes, and never reaches the desired haven. What avails it then all its riches and strength and beauty, now wofully lost in the depths of the sea?

Again, we may sometimes see a small and battered vessel, carrying but little wealth on board, but steered by a good and wary pilot, pass safely through all the perils of the waves, and anchor safely in the long-looked-for harbour; and so it is with voyagers on this world's tempestuous sea. " And therefore," said Brother Giles, "a man should always fear; and though he be in great prosperity, or in high dignity, or in a state of great perfection, or of great perfection in his state, yet if he have not a good pilot, *i.e.* holy discretion, he may perish miserably in the deep abyss of sin: therefore we see plainly that perseverance is of all things the most needful for us; for, as the Apostle says, 'Not he who begins is crowned, but he who perseveres unto the end.' When a tree has been planted, it does not immediately grow; and af-

296

ter it is grown, it does not immediately bear fruit ; and when it has borne fruit, not all its fruit is tasted by its master, but some falls to the ground and is spoilt, some is eaten by worms; yet if it abide until the due season, the greater part will be gathered by the owner of the tree. And what would it profit me," continued Brother Giles, "though I had enjoyed the delights of the kingdom of heaven for a hundred years, if thereafter I should not persevere and make a good end?"

He said also, "I account these to be the two greatest gifts and graces which God can bestow on us in this life, *i.e.* lovingly to persevere in His service, and ever to preserve ourselves from falling into sin."

CHAPTER   SIXTEEN
BROTHER GILES ON THE VIRTUE OF TRUE RELIGION

BROTHER Giles said of himself, "I would rather have a small measure of the grace of God in religion, than I would have many graces from God as a secular and living in the world; for in the world are many more perils and hindrances, and far fewer remedies, than in religion." He said also, "It seems to me that a sinful man fears his good far more than he fears his evil or injury; for he fears to enter religion and to do penance, and he does not fear to offend God and lose his own soul by remaining hard and obstinate in the world, awaiting his eternal damnation in the mire and misery of his sins."

A secular asked Brother Giles, "Father, what wouldst thou advise me to do—to enter religion, or to remain and do good works in the world?" To whom Brother Giles thus replied: "My brother, it is certain that if a man knew of a great treasure hidden in an open field, he would not ask counsel of any one to ascertain whether or not he should take possession of it and carry it to his own house: how much more ought a man to strive and hasten with all care and diligence to possess himself of that heavenly treasure which is to be found in holy religious orders and spiritual congregations, without stopping to ask counsel of so many!" The secular, on receiving this answer, immediately distributed all that he possessed to the poor; and having thus stripped himself of all things, entered forthwith into religion.

Brother Giles said, "Many men enter religion, and do not carry into effect and operation those things which belong to the perfection of that holy state; but these are like the ploughman who arrayed himself in the armour of Orlando, and knew not how to manage it, or how to fight under its weight. It is not every man who can ride a restive and vicious horse; and if he attempt to mount it, he will perhaps be thrown when the animal rears or runs away."

Brother Giles added, moreover, "I account it no great matter for a man to enter into the king's court; nor do I think it any great thing for a man to retain certain graces or favours from the king; but it is a very great thing for him to be able to dwell and converse discreetly in the king's court, persevering wisely and prudently in his service.

"Now the court of the great King of Heaven is holy religion, and there is no great labour in entering it, and receiving therein certain graces and favours from God; but the great thing is, that a man should know how to live well therein, and to persevere in it discreetly until the day of his death."

Brother Giles said also, "I would choose rather to be in the secular state, continually and devoutly desiring to enter into holy religion, than to be clothed in the religious habit without the exercise of goods works, but persevering in sloth and negligence. And therefore ought the religious ever to strive to live well and virtuously, knowing that he can be saved in no other state but that of his profession."

On another occasion Brother Giles said, "It seems to me that the Order of the Friars Minor was instituted by God for the utility and great edification of the people; but woe to us friars if we be not such men as we ought to be! Certain it is that there can be found in this life no man more blessed than we; for he is holy who followeth the holy, and he is truly good who walketh in the way of the good, and he is rich who goeth in the path of the rich; and the religion of the Friars Minor is that which follows more closely than any other the footsteps and

the ways of the Best, the Richest, and the Most
Holy who ever was or ever will be, even our
Lord Jesus Christ."

CHAPTER   SEVENTEEN

BROTHER GILES ON THE VALUE OF HOLY OBEDIENCE

The more strictly the religious holds himself
bound by the yoke of holy obedience for the
love of God, the more abundantly will he bear
fruit unto God; the more entirely subject he is
to his superior, to the glory of God, the freer
and the purer shall he be from his sins. The
truly obedient religious is like a knight well
mounted and well armed, who fearlessly and
securely makes his way through the ranks of
the enemy, because no one dares to oppose
him. But he who obeys with murmuring and
unwillingness is like a soldier who, entering the
battle unarmed and ill mounted, is soon thrown
to the ground and wounded by his enemies,
and, it may be, made captive or slain.

The religious who wishes to live according
to his own will, shows that he desires to build
his eternal abode in the lowest depths of hell.
When the ox bows his head beneath the yoke,
he ploughs the ground well, so that it will bring
forth good fruit in due season ; but when the
ox strays about at his own pleasure, the land
remains wild and uncultivated, and brings forth
no fruit at the harvest-time. And so the religious who bows his head beneath the yoke of

holy obedience, bears much fruit in due season to the Lord his God; but he who obeys not his superior from his heart, remains barren and wild and fruitless in his profession. Wise and magnanimous men bow their heads promptly, fearlessly, and without hesitation, beneath the yoke of holy obedience; but foolish and pusill-animous men struggle to withdraw their neck from the yoke, and refuse to obey any creature. I hold it to be greater perfection in a servant of God simply to obey his superior for the reverence and love of God, than it would be to obey God Himself were He to command him in His own Person; for he who is obedient to a vicar of the Lord would assuredly be still more obedient to the Lord Himself, were He to lay His commands upon him.

And so it seems to me that in the case of a man who has promised obedience to another, were he vouchsafed the grace of conversing with angels, and were he, whilst thus conversing, to be called by him to whom he has promised obedience, it would be his duty immediately to leave his communing with angels, and go to perform the obedience given him for the glory of God.

He who having placed his neck under the yoke of holy obedience desires to withdraw it, in order to follow a life of greater perfection, in that man, I say, if he be not already well established in the virtue of obedience, such a desire is but a sign of great pride and presumption lurking secretly within his soul. Obedience

is the way to attain every good and every virtue, and disobedience is the way to every evil
and to every vice.

CHAPTER   EIGHTEEN

BROTHER GILES ON THE REMEMBRANCE OF DEATH

If a man had ever before the eyes of his mind
the remembrance of death, and of the final
eternal judgment, and of the pains and torments of the lost souls, certain it is that he
would never have a will to sin or to offend God.
And if it were possible for a man to have lived
from the beginning of the world until now, and
in all that time to have endured every kind of
adversity, tribulation, grief, sorrow, and affliction, and so to die, and then his soul go to receive the eternal bliss of heaven, what harm
would he have received from all the evil which
he had endured during all that past time?

Again, if for the same space of time a man
had enjoyed every kind of earthly pleasure and
consolation, and then, if when he came to die,
his soul were to fall into the eternal torments
of hell, what would all the good things which
he had enjoyed in the time past avail him?

A stranger said once to Brother Giles, " I
tell thee, I would fain live a long time in this
world, and have great riches and abundance
of all things, and be held in great honour." To
whom Brother Giles made answer, "My brother, wert thou to be lord of the whole world,

302

and wert thou to live therein a thousand years
in every kind of temporal enjoyment, pleasure,
delight, and consolation, tell me, what guerdon
or what reward couldst thou look for from this
miserable flesh of thine, which thou wouldst
so diligently serve and cherish? But I say to
thee, that he who lives according to the will of
God, and carefully keeps from offending God,
shall receive from God, the Supreme Good, an
infinite eternal reward, great and abundant
riches, and great honour, and long eternal life
in that perpetual celestial glory; to which may
our good God, Lord, and King, Jesus Christ,
bring us all, to the honour of the same Lord
Jesus Christ, and of His poor servant Francis."